Greek
Phrase Book & Dictionary

Other languages in the *Collins Phrase Book & Dictionary* series:

FRENCH

GERMAN

ITALIAN

JAPANESE

PORTUGUESE

SPANISH

These titles are also published in a Language pack containing
60-minute CD and phrase book

HarperCollins*Publishers*
Westerhill Road,
Bishopbriggs, Glasgow G64 2QT

www.collins.co.uk

First published 2005

Reprint 10 9 8 7 6 5 4 3 2 1 0

ISBN 0 00-717980-4

Typeset by Davidson Pre-Press Graphics Ltd, Glasgow

Printed in Italy by Amadeus Srl

Introduction

Your *Collins Phrase Book & Dictionary* is a handy, quick-reference guide that will help you make the most of your stay abroad. Its clear layout will save you valuable time when you need that crucial word or phrase. There are four main sections in this book:

Everyday Greece – photoguide

Packed full of photos, this section allows you to see all the practical visual information that will help with using cash machines, driving on motorways, reading signs, etc.

Phrases

Practical topics are arranged thematically with an opening section Key talk containing vital phrases that should stand you in good stead in most situations.

Phrases are short, useful and each one has a pronunciation guide so that there is no problem saying them.

Eating out

This section contains phrases for ordering food and drink (and special requirements) plus a photoguide showing different eating places, menus and practical information to help choose the best options. The menu reader allows you to work out what to choose.

Dictionary

The practical 5000-word English-Greek and Greek-English Dictionary means that you won't be stuck for words.

And finally, there is a short Grammar section explaining how the language works.

So, just flick through the pages to find the information you need. Why not start with a look at Pronouncing Greek on page 6. From there on the going is easy with your *Collins Phrase Book & Dictionary*.

Useful websites

Currency Converters
www.x-rates.com

Foreign Office Advice
www.fco.gov.uk/travel/
countryadvice.asp

Passport Office
www.ukpa.gov.uk

Health Advice
www.thetraveldoctor.com
www.doh.gov.uk/traveladvice

Driving Abroad
www.drivingabroad.co.uk/
driving_tips_countries/greece
/driving_in_greece.htm

Pets
www.defra.gov.uk/animalh/
quarantine/qindex.shtml

Weather
www.bbc.co.uk/weather

Facts
www.cia.gov/cia/publications/
factbook/geos/gr.html

Internet Cafes
www.cybercafes.com

Transport
www.greekferries.gr
www.ferries.gr

www.dolphins.gr *(hydrofoil service to Greek islands)*
www.osenet.gr/eng.htm *(Hellenic Railways Organisation)*
www.travelinfo.gr/train.htm *(schedules)*

Tourism
www.greektourism.gr *(Greek National Tourism Organisation)*
www.visiteurope.com/greece
www.travelinfo.gr
www.greektravel.com
www.travelgreece.com

Accommodation
www.greekhotels.gr
www.greecetravel.com/
campsites *(camping)*
www.europeanhostels.com/
fall/listings/greece *(hostels)*

Food & Wine
www.gourmed.gr

Other
www.xo.gr/en/index.jsp
(Greek Yellow Pages in English)

Contents

Pronouncing Greek

In the pronunciation system in this book, Greek sounds are represented by spellings of the nearest possible sounds in English. When you read the pronunciation, sound the letters as if you were reading English (but make sure you also pronounce vowels at the end of a word). The vowels in **heavy type** show where the stress falls (in the Greek script it is usually marked with an accent). The following notes should help:

	REMARKS	EXAMPLE	PRONOUNCED
gh	like **r** at back of throat	γάλα	**gh**ala
dh	like **th** in this	δάχτυλο	**dh**akhteelo
th	like **th** in thin	θέατρο	**th**eatro
ks	like **x** in fox	ξένος	**ks**enos
r	slightly trilled **r**	ρόδα	**r**odha
kh	like **ch** in loch or a rough **h**	χάνω	**kh**ano

Here are a few tricky letter combinations:

αι	m**e**t	**e**	γυναίκα	ghee**ne**ka
αυ	c**a**fé	**af**	αυτό	**af**to
	or h**a**ve	**av**	αύριο	**av**reeo
ει	m**ee**t	**ee**	είκοσι	**ee**kosee
ευ	**ef**fect	**ef**	Δευτέρα	dh**ef**t**e**ra
	every	**ev**	Ευρώπη	**ev**ropee
γγ	ha**ng**	**ng**	Αγγλία	a**ng**l**ee**a
γκ	**g**et	**g**	γκάζι	**g**azee
	ha**ng**	**ng**	άγκυρα	**a**ngeera
ντ	ha**nd**	**nd**	αντίο	and**ee**o
	dog	**d**	ντομάτα	**d**omata
μπ	**b**ag	**b**	μπλούζα	**b**looza
οι	m**ee**t	**ee**	πλοίο	pl**ee**o
ου	m**oo**n	**oo**	ούζο	**oo**zo

The letters η, ι, υ, οι, and ει have the same sound (**ee**) and αι and ε have the same sound (**e** as in m**e**t). You should also note that the Greek question mark is a semi-colon, i.e. **;**.

ανοικτο OPEN *aneekto*

κλειστο CLOSED *kleesto*

ENTRANCE *eesodhos* **Είσοδος**

EXIT *eksodhos* **ΕΞΟΔΟΣ**

OPENING HOURS

Mon   Wed   Sat

Δευτ   Τεταρ   Σαββατο
8ºº - 16ºº

Τριτη   Πεμπτη - Παρασκευη
8ºº - 14ºº   17ºº - 20ºº

Tues   Thurs   Fri

Shops generally open in the morning (8 am until 2 pm) and again in the evening (approx 5–8 pm). They close in the afternoon and all day Sun. However, in busy tourist areas they usually open all day every day.

ROOMS *dhomateea*

ΔΩΜΑΤΙΑ

δωμάτια

The Greek alphabet can seem daunting. Capital letters are written differently from lower case letters. Here are some examples.

δ Δ = d
η Η = e
λ Λ = l
μ Μ = m
ν Ν = n
ξ Ξ = x
π Π = p
ρ Ρ = r

Ελλάδα Greece

The word for Greece is *eladha*. Many national organisations begin with **E (EOT)**, the national tourist office. Greek language is *eleneeka*.

PUSH *otheesate*

ΩΘΗΣΑΤΕ

PULL *elksate*

ΕΛΞΑΤΕ

A kiosk (*pereeptero*). These kiosks sell all kinds of things including maps, postcards, stamps, cigarettes, snacks and drinks. They often have a payphone and will give directions.

Everyday Greece

 Greece is in the eurozone and the euro has replaced the *drachma*.

PAY HERE tam**ee**o

ΤΑΜΕΙΟ

Decimals are generally written with a comma or full stop. This is 3 euro 50 cents per kilo. Greece is metric so weights are in kilos.

PRICE

ΤΙΜΗ: 13, 60 ΕΥΡΩ

price (teem**ee**)   euro (evr**o**)

OPENING TIMES
Banking hours are usually 8am-2pm Mon-Thurs, and 8am-1pm on Fridays.

EXCHANGE
MONEY
SERVICE

CHANGE
Travel agents as well as banks offer exchange services.

The Greek word for bank is
τράπεζα *trapeza*.

Greece's currency is the euro, ευρώ (evr**o**), which breaks down into 100 euro cents. Notes: 5, 10, 20, 50, 100, 200, 500. Coins: 2 euro, 1 euro, 50 cent, 20 cent, 10 cent, 5 cent, 2 cent, 1 cent.

Greek people refer to cents as λεπτά (*lepta*) The reverse of the coins carry different designs in each European member country. Euro notes are the same throughout Europe. The backs of coins carry different designs from each of the member European countries.

Everyday Greece

Cash machines operate as at home. You find 24-hour cashpoints at many banks and in tourist areas, with instructions in English, French, German and Italian.

Service is usually included in a restaurant bill so tipping is discretionary. Some Greeks tip, some don't, so there is no obligation.

OUT OF ORDER *dhen leetoryee*

ΔΕΝ ΛΕΙΤΟΥΡΓΕΙ

NO SMOKING ZONE

Smoking is banned on public transport and in cinemas, theatres etc.

PHARMACY
Look out for a red cross for the pharmacy (*farmakeeo*). For minor ailments, ask advice from the pharmacist.

WELCOME *kalos eelthate*

DANGER *keendheenos*

HOSPITAL You can recognise the sign for hospitals or health centres by the red cross. The word for hospital is νοσοκομείο *nosokomeeo*.

Everyday Greece

INFORMATION
The Greek tourist office is **EOT**.

ACCOMMODATION

The Greek for hotel is *ksenodhokheeo*. A guesthouse is *panseeon*. The Tourist Office can advise about hotels and other accommodation.

RUBBISH

You have to take all household rubbish to the nearest roadside skip.

ROOMS *dhomateea*

English newspapers are widely available in Summer. *Athinorama* is a listings magazine published in English in Athens.

SEASONS AND WEATHER

Wild flowers abound in Spring – particularly on Crete.

You can ski in Greece from December to April.

Greek post boxes are yellow and it is usually quite easy to find one. Red boxes are for express post around Athens. Times of collections are on the box in larger towns.

Closed for holidays
14–25 August

TOILETS

ΤΟΥΑΛΕΤΕΣ

WC

ГYNAIKΩN WOMEN

ΑΝΔΡΩΝ MEN

LADIES

A word about Greek plumbing: because of the sewerage system, all (yes, all) toilet paper must be deposited in the bin beside the toilet, not thrown into the toilet bowl. This applies wherever you are in Greece. It may seem strange, but please abide by this rule, otherwise the drains get blocked and some unfortunate person has the task of removing all the toilet paper from the pipes.

GENTS

κρύο

COLD
kreeo

ζεστό

HOT
zesto

AIR CONDITIONING

ΚΛΙΜΑΤΙΖΟΜΕΝΕΣ

Timetables

DAYS

Δευτέρα *dheftera*	Monday
Τρίτη *treetee*	Tuesday
Τετάρτη *tetartee*	Wednesday
Πέμπτη *pemptee*	Thursday
Παρασκευή *paraskevee*	Friday
Σάββατο *savato*	Saturday
Κυριακή *keereeakee*	Sunday

MONTHS

Ιανουάριος *eeanooareeos*	January
Φεβρουάριος *fevrooareeos*	February
Μάρτιος *marteeos*	March
Απρίλιος *apreeleeos*	April
Μάιος *maeeos*	May
Ιούνιος *eeooneeos*	June
Ιούλιος *eeooleeos*	July
Αύγουστος *avghoostos*	August
Σεπτέμβριος *septemvreeos*	September
Οκτώβριος *oktovreeos*	October
Νοέμβριος *noemvreeos*	November
Δεκέμβριος *dhekemvreeos*	December

TODAY *seemera*

ΟΡΧΗΣΤΡΑ ΠΑΡΓΑΣ
Τηλ: 0684 - 31.176 & 0944-28.27.42
ΣΗΜΕΡΑ

HOUR *ora*　　　**HOURS** *ores*

ΩΡΑ　　ΩΡΕΣ

09.00 π.μ.

am = *pro meseemvreeas*

13.00 μ.μ.

pm = *meta meseemvreeas*

ΕΙΣΙΤΗΡΙΑ

TICKETS
eeseeteereea

You can buy from a range of tickets,
single tickets to all-day tickets.
A single ticket is
ena aplo eeseeteereeo
A return ticket is
ena eeseeteereeo me epeestrofee.
An all-day ticket is
ena eemereeseeo eeseeteereeo.

DEPARTURES
anakhoreesees

ΑΝΑΧΩΡΗΣΕΙΣ

ARRIVALS
afeeksees

ΑΦΙΞΕΙΣ

You have to validate any
ticket you buy for public
transport in a validating
machine. These are
found at the entrance
of buses, train platforms
and metro stations.
Simply insert your ticket
in the slot for punching.

BUS STATION TIMETABLE

Timetables in tourist areas often have English translation.

katheemereenas
= weekdays

dhromologheea
= services

savatoo = Saturdays

keereeakee = Sundays

Getting around

CENTRE *kendro*

ΚΕΝΤΡΟ

ΔΗΜΟΣ ΑΘΗΝΑΙΩΝ
ΠΛΑΤΕΙΑ ΣΥΝΤΑΓΜΑΤΟΣ

plateea = square

LEFT *areestera*

αριστερά

INFORMATION *pleeroforeeyes*

(i) **ΠΛΗΡΟΦΟΡΙΕΣ**

RIGHT *dhekseea*

δεξιά

TAXI

You can ring for a taxi, wait at a stand or flag one down in the street.

Μοναστηράκι
Monastiraki
Πλάκα
Plaka

Brown signs show the way to local places of interest. Plaka is the area beneath the Acropolis which is full of lively bars, shops and restaurants.

Taxis are quite cheap, but you should still ask the price beforehand. The grey taxis are for long-distance journeys, i.e. town to town.

The word for beach is *paraleea*.

Παραλία Βάλτου
Valtos Beach
Κάστρο
Kastle

odhos = road, street

ΟΔΟΣ
ΗΠΙΤΟΥ
ΙΡΙΤΟΥ

apo = from from (8–2)

ΑΠΟ 8 → 2

BUS

There are good bus services within cities and regular long-distance coaches for people in towns and rural areas.

BUS STOP *stasee*

The bus company

Trolley buses operate in Athens. You must validate tickets when you get on the bus. Machines are usually near the entrance.

City bus stops have the route and time-table posted.

FERRY

There are many ferries to the islands and the high-speed 'flying dolphins' (ιπτάμενο δελφίνι *eeptameno dhelfeenee*) provide a fast service. Visit their website *www.dolphins.gr*. You can buy ferry tickets from travel agents or at the quayside. Prices are listed for various ticket types to different destinations. There are many day-trips available.

METRO

There is no eating, drinking or smoking on the Athens metro. It opens at 5.30am and closes at midnight. Signs are in Greek and English and lines are colour-coded.

Προς Δάφνη To Dafni

Driving

The red diagonal line shows you are leaving a town or village.

Speed limits in Greece are in kilometres.

No motor-bikes allowed from midnight to 7am.
Note that it's compulsory to wear a crash helmet.

Από 00:00 π.μ.
Εως 07:00 π.μ.

Ακρόπολη
Akropoli

Many signs will have the Greek spelling and a transcription in the Western alphabet.

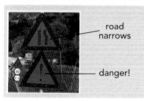

road narrows

danger!

ΠΡΟΣΟΧΗ
ΕΚΤΕΛΟΥΝΤΑΙ
ΕΡΓΑ
ΤΑΧΥΤΗΣ 10 ΧΛΜ.

caution road works

speed limit

10 ΧΛΜ.

10 km per hour

P

ME ΚΑΡΤΑ

ME = WITH

Parking with a ticket

me karta

No parking on odd months (Jan, March, May, etc)

No parking on even months (Feb, April, June, etc)

ΜΗ ΠΑΡΚΑΡΕΤΕ   **MH** = NO

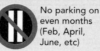

NO PARKING
mee parkarete

MOTORWAY
aftokeeneetodhromos
Signs are green in Greece.

European routes are marked green, as are motorways in Greece

Watch out at toll stations. Stay in the blue cash or card paying lane. The orange lane is Teletoll, i.e. for cars with an electronic device for prepaying.

Blue signs for main roads where no toll required.

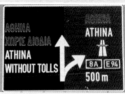

Green signs for motorway – tolls payable.

TYRES *elasteeka*

ΕΛΑΣΤΙΚΑ

Some petrol stations change tyres.

Petrol pumps are colour-coded, as in the rest of Europe, to show which is leaded (still available), unleaded and diesel.
An attendant fills your tank as there is no self-service.

Λιπαντήριο	
Unleaded	0.78 9
	0.82 9
Super Unleaded	0.86 7
Diesel	0.65 9

Breakdown service – tel 154

north (*voras*) abbrev. **B**

βορράς

δύση		ανατολή
west (*dheesee*) abbrev. **Δ** | νότος | east (*anatolee*) abbrev. **A** |

south (*notos*) abbrev. **N**

AIR *aeeras*

Αερας

WATER *nero*

Νερο

Shopping

In Greece, especially in big towns and cities, you find well-stocked supermarkets and hypermarkets. Some open all day, others open in the morning and evening only, depending on the size of the supermarket, time of year, etc.

BAKERY

For a big loaf, ask for ένα κιλό *ena keelo* (a kilo loaf). For a small loaf ask for μισόκιλο *meesokeelo* (a half-kilo loaf). For a round sandwich bun ask for ένα ψωμάκι *ena psomakee*. Many bakers sell sandwiches.

The word for shoes is παπούτσια (*papootseea*) and for sandals σανδάλια (*sandaleea*).

PAY HERE *tameeo*

ΤΑΜΕΙΟ

The rural answer to the department store! In the country areas and smaller villages you sometimes find vans like this selling clothes, food, linen, chairs and tables, even live chicks. They have a megaphone to advertise their wares.

4TH FLOOR

4ος ΟΡΟΦΟΣ

Δώρο! — *dhoro* free gift

Μόνο — *mono* only

1.230 € το άτομο — *to atomo* per person

Many towns have a weekly market with fresh, local produce. It's best to go early. As well as food, markets sell clothes, shoes and all kinds of household items.

Quantities are expressed in kilos and grams. If you want to ask for ham, cheese, salami, etc in slices, ask for *fetes*. 10 slices is *dheka fetes*.

PASTA *makaroneea*

MAKAPONIA

NUTRITION LABELS

energy	**ENEΡΓEIA**
proteins	**ΠPΩTEΪNEΣ**
carbs	**YΔATANΘPAKEΣ**
fats	**ΛIΠAPA:**

PRICE *teemee*

TIMH

MILK
The colour-coding of milk *γάλα (ghala)* cartons varies from one company to another.

milk

pleeres = full-cream

eemeepakho = semi-skimmed

apakho = skimmed

Keeping in touch

Red postboxes are for express mail in the Athens area. Yellow boxes are for general post, and often detail collection times.

POST OFFICE *takheedhromeeo*

Post Offices open from about 8am to 2pm. They're not open in the afternoon or Saturday. Stamps can also be bought at kiosks and at shops selling postcards.

Payphones abound in Greece – just look for the blue sign. Instructions are easy to follow. Cards are easier to use than coins – ask for *meea teelekarta*.

TEL:

τηλ:

Some kiosks have a small payphone on the counter – the card goes in at the side. The telephone offices (OTE) have cardphones too, and it may be possible to have someone call you back on a phone in the OTE office.

PHONECARD

International dialling codes

UK 00 44	Australia 00 61
USA 00 1	Greece 00 30

Addressing an envelope:

Κος = Mr (Κύριος *keereeos*)
Κα = Mrs (Κυρία *keereea*)
Δις = Miss (Δεσποινίς *dhespeenees*)

Κα ΜΑΡΙΑ ΘΕΩΡΟΥ —— Name
ΟΡΦΕΩΣ 22 —— Street and number
131 37 —— Postcode
ΑΘΗΝΑ —— Town/City (Athens)

Greek web-sites end in *.gr*. Rates at Internet cafes vary so ask beforehand about the price.

 The Greek for 'at' is παπάκι *papakee* (literally 'little duck').

www. www is as in English and 'dot' is *teleea*.

Key Talk

Greek people frequently say 'hello' and 'how are you?'. Υειά σου (ya soo), means 'hi' and 'bye', among friends and young people. The formal or plural 'hello' and 'goodbye' is γεια (ya sas). When entering shops etc it is rude not to first greet the owner.
Greek people use 'thank you' less than us. It's OK to say καλά (kala) ('fine') instead.

Καλώς ήλθατ

yes	**no**	**that's fine/ok!**
ne	okhee	endaksee
ναι	όχι	εντάξει

please	**thank you**	**don't mention it**
parakalo	efkhareesto	parakalo
παρακαλώ	ευχαριστώ	παρακαλώ

hello/goodbye	**hello**	**good night**
ya sas	kherete	kalee neekhta
γεια σας	χαίρετε	καλή νύχτα

good morning	**good evening**	**excuse me/sorry!**
kaleemera	kaleespera	seeghnomee
καλημέρα	καλησπέρα	συγνώμη

Here's an easy way to ask for things ... just add **parakalo** (please)

a...	**a coffee**	**2 coffees**
enan... ('o' words)	enan kafe	dheeo kafedhes
έναν...	έναν καφέ	δύο καφέδες

	a beer	**2 beers**
meea... ('η' words)	meea beera	dheeo beeres
μία...	μία μπίρα	δύο μπίρες

	a bottle	**2 bottles**
ena... ('το' words)	ena bookalee	dheeo bookaleea
ένα...	ένα μπουκάλι	δύο μπουκάλια

a coffee and two beers, please
enan kafe ke dheeo beeres parakalo
έναν καφέ και δύο μπίρες, παρακαλώ

Key Talk

I'd like...
tha **ee**thela...
θα ήθελα...

we'd like...
tha the**la**me...
θα θέλαμε...

I'd like an ice cream
tha **ee**thela ena paghot**o**
θα ήθελα ένα παγωτό

we'd like to go to Athens
tha the**la**me na p**a**me steen ath**ee**na
θα θέλαμε να πάμε στην Αθήνα

do you have...?
e**khe**te...?
έχετε...;

do you have any milk?
e**khe**te gh**a**la
έχετε γάλα;

do you have stamps?
e**khe**te ghramat**o**seema
έχετε γραμματόσημα;

do you have a map?
e**khe**te ena khart**ee**?
έχετε ένα χάρτη;

do you have fruit?
e**khe**te fr**oo**ta?
έχετε φρούτα;

how much is it?
p**o**so k**a**nee
πόσο κάνει;

how much does ... cost?
p**o**so kost**ee**zee o/ee/to...?
πόσο κοστίζει ο/η/το...;

how much is the wine?
p**o**so k**a**nee to kras**ee**
πόσο κάνει το κρασί;

how much does the ticket cost?
p**o**so kost**ee**zee to eeseet**ee**reeo
πόσο κοστίζει το εισιτήριο;

how much is a kilo?
p**o**so k**a**nee to keel**o**
πόσο κάνει το κιλό;

how much is one?
p**o**so k**a**nee to **e**na
πόσο κάνει το ένα;

- Έχει (*ekhee*) and **υπάρχει** (*eeparkhee*) both mean 'there is', or 'is there?' if you put a question mark in your voice.
- If you ask a question and the person speaks too fast for you to understand, try **πιο σιγά παρακαλώ** (*pyo seegha parakalo*).
- A younger person may well reply in English.

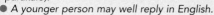

where is/are...?
poo **ee**ne...
πού είναι...;

where is the toilet?
poo **ee**ne ee tooa**le**ta
πού είναι η τουαλέτα;

where are the children?
poo **ee**ne ta pe**dya**
πού είναι τα παιδιά;

is there...?
eep**ar**khee...
υπάρχει...;

are there...?
eep**ar**khoon...
υπάρχουν...;

is there a taverna?
eep**ar**khee m**ee**a tav**er**na
υπάρχει μία ταβέρνα;

are there any rooms?
eep**ar**khoon dhom**a**teea
υπάρχουν δωμάτια;

is there a swimming pool?
eep**ar**khee pees**ee**na
υπάρχει πισίνα;

there is/are no...
dhen eep**ar**khee/eep**ar**khoon...
δεν υπάρχει/υπάρχουν...

there is no...
dhen **e**khee...
δεν έχει...

there is...
ekhee...
έχει...

there is no hot water
dhen **e**khee zes**to** ne**ro**
δεν έχει ζεστό νερό

there is no bread
dhen **e**khee pso**mee**
δεν έχει ψωμί

I need...
khree**a**zome...
χρειάζομαι...

I need a doctor
khree**a**zome **e**nan yat**ro**
χρειάζομαι έναν γιατρό

I need a taxi
khree**a**zome tak**see**
χρειάζομαι ταξί

Key Talk

can I...?	**can we...?**
boro na...	boroome na ...
μπορώ να...;	μπορούμε να...;

can I pay?	**can we eat?**	**where can I...?**
boro na pleeroso	boroome na fame	poo boro na...
μπορώ να πληρώσω;	μπορούμε να φάμε;	πού μπορώ να...;

where can I buy bread?	**where can I get tickets?**
poo boro na aghoraso psomee	poo boro na aghoraso eeseeteereea
πού μπορώ να αγοράσω ψωμί;	πού μπορώ να αγοράσω εισιτήρια;

when?	**at what time...?**
pote	tee ora...
πότε;	τι ώρα...;

when does it leave?	**when does it arrive?**
pote fevyee	pote ftanee
πότε φεύγει;	πότε φτάνει;

when does it open?	**when does it close?**
pote aneeyee	pote kleenee
πότε ανοίγει;	πότε κλείνει;

yesterday	**today**	**tomorrow**
khtes	seemera	avreeo
χτες	σήμερα	αύριο

this morning	**this afternoon**	**tonight**
seemera to proee	seemera to apoyefma	apopse
σήμερα το πρωί	σήμερα το απόγευμα	απόψε

is it open?	**is it closed?**
eene aneekto	eene kleesto
είναι ανοικτό;	είναι κλειστό;

Key Talk

κα ΜΑΡΙΑ ΘΕΩΔΡΟΥ
ΟΡΦΕΩΣ 22
131 37
ΑΘΗΝΑ

● Greeks tend to address each other politely as 'Sir/Mr' κύριε (keeree-e), 'Madam/Mrs' κυρία (keereea) and 'Miss' δεσποινίς (dhespeenees).

● It will always be appreciated if you learn even a few phrases of Greek to show goodwill. Most Greeks will be friendly and patient.

how are you?
tee kanete
τι κάνετε;

fine, thanks, and you?
kala, efkhareesto, esees
καλά, ευχαριστώ, εσείς;

my name is...
me lene...
με λένε...

what is your name?
pos sas lene
πώς σας λένε;

I don't understand
dhen katalaveno
δεν καταλαβαίνω

do you speak English?
meelate angleeka
μιλάτε αγγλικά;

this is my husband
apo dho o seezeeghos moo
από 'δω ο σύζυγός μου

this is my wife
apo dho ee seezeeghos moo
από 'δω η σύζυγός μου

the meal was delicious
to fa-yeeto eetan nosteemotato
το φαγητό ήταν νοστιμότατο

thank you very much
sas efkhareesto polee
σας ευχαριστώ πολύ

you have a beautiful home
ekhete oreo speetee
έχετε ωραίο σπίτι

thanks for your hospitality
efkhareesto ya tee feelokseneea
ευχαριστώ για τη φιλοξενία

this is a gift for you
eene ena dhoro ya sas
είναι ένα δώρο για σας

I've enjoyed myself very much
perasa polee orea
πέρασα πολύ ωραία

we must stay in touch
na dhee-ateereesoome epeekeenoneea
να διατηρήσουμε επικοινωνία

Money – changing

● Banks are generally open 8am to 2pm Mon–Thur, 8am to 1pm Fri. ATM's are widespread, with instructions in English.
  ● Cash is the preferred method of payment and you can sometimes negotiate a reduction if you pay in cash.
  ● Greece is in the eurozone. Euro is ευρώ (evro) and cent is λεπτό (lepto), plural λεπτά (lepta).

where can I change money?
poo bor**o** na al**a**kso khr**ee**mata
πού μπορώ να αλλάξω χρήματα;

where is there a bank?
poo **ee**ne m**ee**a tr**a**peza
πού είναι μία τράπεζα;

where is there a bureau de change?
poo **ee**ne **e**na enalakt**ee**reeo seenal**a**ghmatos
πού είναι ένα εναλλακτήριο συναλλάγματος;

when does the bank open?
p**o**te an**ee**yee ee tr**a**peza
πότε ανοίγει η τράπεζα;

when does the bank close?
p**o**te kl**ee**nee ee tr**a**peza
πότε κλείνει η τράπεζα;

where is there a cash dispenser?
poo **e**khee **e**na ey tee em
πού έχει ένα ΑΤΜ;

I want to cash these traveller's cheques
tha **ee**thela na al**a**kso aft**a** ta takseedhyoteek**a** tsek
θα ήθελα να αλλάξω αυτά τα ταξιδιωτικά τσεκ

what is the rate for...?
py**a ee**ne ee eesoteem**ee**a ya...
ποια είναι η ισοτιμία για...;

pounds
tee l**ee**ra vretan**ee**as
τη λίρα Βρετανίας

dollars
to dhol**a**reeo
το δολάριο

I want to change £50
tha **ee**thela na al**a**kso pen**ee**nda l**ee**res vretan**ee**as
θα ήθελα να αλλάξω 50 λίρες Βρετανίας

spending – Money

- If you are visiting more remote areas, away from tourist spots, carry enough cash to get by, particularly at the weekend, in case banks and bureaux de change close early on a Friday.
- If you do get stranded in the wilds, hotels and restaurants may change money.
- Take your bank's phone number in case of problems.

Μόνο 1.230 € το άτομο

how much is it?
poso kanee
πόσο κάνει;

where do I pay?
poo pleerono
πού πληρώνω;

pay at the cash desk
pleeroste sto tameeo
πληρώστε στο ταμείο

I want to pay
thelo na pleeroso
θέλω να πληρώσω

how much do I have to pay?
poso prepee na pleeroso
πόσο πρέπει να πληρώσω;

can I pay by credit card?
boro na pleeroso me peestoteekee karta
μπορώ να πληρώσω με πιστωτική κάρτα;

do you accept traveller's cheques?
dhekheste takseedhyoteeka tsek
δέχεστε ταξιδιωτικά τσεκ;

how much is it...?	**per person**	**per night**	**per kilo**
poso kanee...	kathe atomo	kathe neekhta	to keelo
πόσο κάνει...;	κάθε άτομο	κάθε νύχτα	το κιλό

I need a receipt
khreeazome teen apodheeksee
χρειάζομαι την απόδειξη

do I need to pay a deposit?
khreeazete na dhoso prokatavolee
χρειάζεται να δώσω προκαταβολή;

Airport

- The new Venizelos Airport in Athens has excellent amenities. It's quite a way from central Athens but there's a shuttle bus, and also plenty of taxis. Signs are in Greek and English. English is spoken by most airport staff.
- There are regular internal flights from Venizelos to Thessaloniki, Corfu, Yannina, Heraklion etc.

to the airport, please
sto aerodhromeeo parakalo
στο αεροδρόμιο, παρακαλώ

how do I get to the town centre?
pos boro na pao sto kendro tees polees
πώς μπορώ να πάω στο κέντρο της πόλης;

where do I get the bus to the town centre?
apo poo perno to leoforeeo ya to kendro tees polees
από πού παίρνω το λεωφορείο για το κέντρο της πόλης;

how much is it...? | **to the centre** | **to the airport**
poso kanee... | sto kendro | sto aerodhromeeo
πόσο κάνει...; | στο κέντρο | στο αεροδρόμιο

where do I check in for...?
poo eene o elengkhos eeseeteereeon ya...
πού είναι ο έλεγχος εισιτηρίων για...;

which gate is it for the flight to...?
pya eene ee eksodhos tees pteesees ya...
ποια είναι η έξοδος της πτήσης για...;

boarding at gate number...
epeeveevasee steen eesodho...(number)
επιβίβαση στην είσοδο...

last call
teleftea kleesee
τελευταία κλήση

the flight is delayed
ee pteesee eene katheestereemenee
η πτήση είναι καθυστερημένη

Customs & Passports

● There is no restriction on goods purchased in another EU country provided they are for your own personal use (this covers gifts). Check guidelines on **www.hmce.gov.uk**.
● The price of alcohol and cigarettes is generally less in supermarkets than at the airport duty-free.
● Cyprus is not a member of the EU so customs restrictions apply.

I have nothing to declare
dhen **e**kho t**ee**pote ya dh**ee**losee
δεν έχω τίποτε για δήλωση

here is...	**my passport**	**my visa**
edh**o ee**ne...	to dheeavat**ee**ree**o** moo	ee v**ee**za moo
εδώ είναι...	το διαβατήριό μου	η βίζα μου

do I have to pay duty on this?
pr**e**pee na pleer**o**so f**o**ro yee aft**o**
πρέπει να πληρώσω φόρο γι' αυτό;

it's for my own personal use
eene ya prosopeek**ee** khr**ee**see
είναι για προσωπική χρήση

the children are on this passport
ta pedy**a ee**ne se aft**o** to dheeavat**ee**reeo
τα παιδιά είναι σε αυτό το διαβατήριο

this is the baby's passport
aft**o ee**ne to dheeavat**ee**reeo too mor**oo**
αυτό είναι το διαβατήριο του μωρού

I'm...	**British** (m/f)	**Australian** (m/f)
eeme...	vretan**o**s/vretan**ee**dha	afstral**o**s/afstral**ee**dha
είμαι...	Βρετανός/Βρετανίδα	Αυστραλός/Αυστραλίδα

Asking the Way – questions

● You can buy street maps at the kiosks (= **περίπτερο** peereeptero) where they may well help you with directions too. Otherwise just ask a passer-by for help.
● Remember, you can just name the place you want and add **παρακαλώ** (parakalo = please).

excuse me	**where is...?**	**where is the nearest...?**
seeghnomee	poo **ee**ne...	poo **ee**ne to kondeen**o**tero...
συγνώμη	πού είναι...;	πού είναι το κοντινότερο...;

how do I get to...?
pos bor**o** na p**a**o sto (with o and το words)/stee (with η words)...
πώς μπορώ να πάω στο/στη...;

is this the right way to...?
eeme sto sost**o** dhr**o**mo ya...
είμαι στο σωστό δρόμο για...;

the... | **is it far?**
o (masc.)/ee (fem.)/to (neuter)... | **ee**ne makree**a**
ο/η/το... | είναι μακριά;

can I walk there?
eene kond**a** me ta p**o**dheea
είναι κοντά με τα πόδια;

is there a bus that goes there?
eeparkhee kapyo leofor**ee**o poo peeyenee ek**ee**
υπάρχει κάποιο λεωφορείο που πηγαίνει εκεί;

we're looking for...
ps**a**khnoome ya to (with o and το words)/tee (with η words)...
ψάχνουμε για το/τη ...

we're lost | **can you show me on the map?**
khath**ee**kame | bor**ee**te na moo to dh**ee**ksete sto khart**ee**
χαθήκαμε | μπορείτε να μου το δείξετε στο χάρτη;

answers – Asking the Way

It's no use being able to ask the way if you're not going to understand the directions you get. We've tried to anticipate the likely answers, so listen out for: **στενό** (steno) sidestreet, **πριν** (preen) before, **μετά** (meta) after, **κέντρο** (kendro) centre, **κοντά** (konta) near, **δίπλα** (dheepla) next to, **απέναντι** (apenandee) opposite, **διασταύρωση** (dheeastavrosee) crossroads.

ΟΔΟΣ
ΗΠΙΤΟΥ
ΓΡΙΤΟΥ
ΑΠΟ 8 → 2

keep going straight ahead
eftheea brosta
ευθεία μπροστά

you have to turn round
prepee na yereesete peeso
πρέπει να γυρίσετε πίσω

turn...
streepste...
στρίψτε...

right
dheksya
δεξιά

left
areestera
αριστερά

go...
peeyenete...
πηγαίνετε...

towards...
pros...
προς...

keep going...
seenekheeste...
συνεχίστε...

as far as...
eos...
έως...

take...
parte...
πάρτε...

the first road on the right
ton proto dhromo dheksya
τον πρώτο δρόμο δεξιά

the second road on the left
ton dheftero dhromo areestera
τον δεύτερο δρόμο αριστερά

cross...
dheeaskheeste...
διασχίστε...

the square
teen plateea
την πλατεία

it's after the traffic lights
eene meta ta fanareea
είναι μετά τα φανάρια

Bus

- Buy tickets in advance at newspaper kiosks, tobacconists or at bus company ticket booths.
- When you board the bus, stamp your ticket in the orange machine situated at the front or rear doors.
- In Athens the same ticket covers both bus and trolley-bus. Special tickets are bought on the Airport bus and underground

where is the bus station?
poo **ee**ne o stathm**o**s leofor**ee**on
πού είναι ο σταθμός λεωφορείων;

I want to go...	**to the station**	**to the museum**
th**e**lo na p**a**o...	sto stathm**o**	sto moos**ee**o
θέλω να πάω...	στο σταθμό	στο μουσείο
	to the Acropolis	**to the Plaka**
	steen akr**o**polee	steen pl**a**ka
	στην Ακρόπολη	στην Πλάκα

does this bus go to...?
af**to** to leofor**ee**o peey**e**nee sto/stee...
αυτό το λεωφορείο πηγαίνει στο/στη...;

which bus do I take?
py**o** leofor**ee**o tha par**o**
ποιο λεωφορείο θα πάρω;

where does the bus go from?
ap**o** poo f**e**vyee to leofor**ee**o
από πού φεύγει το λεωφορείο;

how often are the buses?
k**a**the p**o**te **e**khee leofor**ee**o
κάθε πότε έχει λεωφορείο;

at what time does it arrive/leave?
tee **o**ra ft**a**nee/f**e**vyee
τι ώρα φτάνει/φεύγει;

can you please tell me when to get off?
bor**ee**te na moo p**ee**te p**o**te na kat**e**vo
μπορείτε να μου πείτε πότε να κατέβω;

For long-distance bus travel buy your ticket in the local bus agency. In small places this is often in the **καφενείον** *(*kafen**ee**on*), the coffee shop.*

The Greek bus service for long-distance routes is called **ΚΤΕΛ** *(KTEL). Note that smoking is prohibited on their services. Tickets usually have designated seat numbers.*

where is the KTEL office?
poo **ee**ne to praktor**ee**o too ktel
πού είναι το πρακτορείο του ΚΤΕΛ;

1 ticket	**2 tickets**
ena eeseet**ee**reeo	dh**ee**o eeseet**ee**reea
ένα εισιτήριο	δύο εισιτήρια

a return ticket
ena eeseet**ee**reeo me epeestrof**ee**
ένα εισιτήριο με επιστροφή

to Thessaloniki	**to Patra**
stee thesalon**ee**kee	steen patra
στη Θεσσαλονίκη	στην Πάτρα

how much does it cost to...?
p**o**so kost**ee**zee ya...
πόσο κοστίζει για...;

are there any discounts for students?
ekhee eedhe**e**ka eeseet**ee**reea ya feete**e**t**e**s
έχει ειδικά εισιτήρια για φοιτητές;

where does the coach leave?
ap**o** poo pern**a** to leofor**ee**o
από πού περνά το λεωφορείο;

when does the coach leave
p**o**te pern**a** to leofor**ee**o
πότε περνά το λεωφορείο;

how long does it take to...?
pyee **o**ra ka**n**ee ya...
ποιη ώρα κάνει για...;

Train

● *There is only a fairly small network of trains on mainland Greece. Tickets are sold at stations and some travel agents.*
● *Faster Intercity trains connect Athens with Thessaloniki and Patras.*
● *Slower local trains run in the Peloponnese, Thessaly and Macedonia.*

to the station, please
sto stathmo parakalo
στο σταθμό παρακαλώ

where is the station?
poo **ee**ne o stathmos trenoo
πού είναι ο σταθμός τρένου;

a single to...
ena ap**lo** eeseet**ee**reeo ya...
ένα απλό εισιτήριο για...

2 singles to...
dh**ee**o apl**a** eeseet**ee**reea ya...
δύο απλά εισιτήρια για...

a return to...
ena eeseet**ee**reeo me epeestrof**ee** ya...
ένα εισιτήριο με επιστροφή για...

2 returns to...
dh**ee**o eeseet**ee**reea me epeestrof**ee** ya...
δύο εισιτήρια με επιστροφή για...

1st/2nd class
pro**tee**/dh**ef**teree th**esee**
πρώτη/δεύτερη θέση

smoking
kapneest**on**
καπνιστών

non smoking
mee kapneest**on**
μη καπνιστών

is this the train for...?
eene af**to** to treno ya...
είναι αυτό το τρένο για...;

is the seat free?
eene ee th**esee** el**ef**theree
είναι η θέση ελεύθερη;

Underground

● The 'old' Athens underground is called **Ηλεκτρικό**
(*eelektreeko*) and runs to the port of Piraeus.
● The impressive new metro (**Αττικό μετρό** *ateeko metro*)
operates 5.30am to midnight. Tickets are valid for a single
journey of any length. Multi-trip Metro tickets (24-hr) are also
valid for buses and trolley-buses.

where is the metro station?
poo **ee**ne o stathm**o**s too metr**o**
πού είναι ο σταθμός του μετρό;

(for old electric line)
too eelektreek**oo**
του ηλεκτρικού;

a ticket/4 tickets, please
ena eeseet**ee**reeo/**te**ssera eeseet**ee**reea parakal**o**
ένα εισιτήριο/τέσσερα εισιτήρια παρακαλώ

a one-day ticket
enan olo**ee**mero eeseet**ee**reeo
έναν ολόμερο εισητήριο

2 one-day tickets
dh**ee**o olo**ee**mera eeseet**ee**reea
δύο ολόμερα εισητήρια

do you have an underground map?
ekhete **e**nan khartee me tees ghramm**e**s too metr**o**
έχετε έναν χάρτη με τις γραμμές του μετρό;

I want to go to...
th**e**lo na pao sto/stee...
θέλω να πάω στο/στη...

can I go by underground?
bor**o** na pao me to metr**o**
μπορώ να πάω με το μετρό;

do I have to change?
pr**e**pee na alakso tr**e**no
πρέπει να αλλάξω τρένο;

where?
poo
πού;

which line do I take?
pya ghramm**ee** prepee na paro
ποια γραμμή πρέπει να πάρω;

which is the station for Syntagma?
py**o**s **ee**ne o stathm**o**s ya to s**ee**ndagma
ποιος είναι ο σταθμός για το Σύνταγμα;

Taxi

● *Taxis are yellow in Athens, other colours elsewhere.*
● *Ask someone at the airport/hotel about prices of taxis so you know the approximate fare in advance.*
● *You can flag down a taxi – people often share.*
● *Make sure the meter is on zero to start (tariff 1 for daytime, 2 after midnight). Tipping is not necessary but is appreciated.*

to the airport, please
sto aerodhromeeo parakalo
στο αεροδρόμιο, παρακαλώ

please take me to this address
se afteen tee dheeeftheensee parakalo
σε αυτην τη διεύθυνση, παρακαλώ

how much will it cost?
poso kosteezee
πόσο κοστίζει;

it's too much
eene polee akreeva
είναι πολύ ακριβά

how much is it to the centre?
poso kosteezee ya to kendro
πόσο κοστίζει για το κέντρο;

where can I get a taxi?
poo boro na vro taksee
πού μπορώ να βρω ταξί;

please order me a taxi
parakalo kaleste ena taksee
παρακαλώ καλέστε ένα ταξί

can I have a receipt?
boreete na moo dhosete apodheeksee
μπορείτε να μου δώσετε απόδειξη;

I'm afraid I don't have change
dheesteekhos dhen ekho pseela
δυστυχώς δεν έχω ψηλά

keep the change
krateeste ta resta
κρατήστε τα ρέστα

Boat/Ferry

There are extensive ferry-services to the Greek islands. Ask about different classes of tickets. There are standard ferries and hydrofoils or 'Flying Dolphins' (*eeptameno dhelfeenee*). Foot passengers don't usually have to book in advance, but it's wise to pre-book if you have a car, motorbike or bicycle. Hydrofoils are faster but are more expensive.

1 ticket	2 tickets	single	round trip
ena eeseeteereeo	dheeo eseeteereea	apla	me epeestrofee
ένα εισιτήριο	δύο εισιτήρια	απλά	με επιστροφή

is there a tourist ticket?
eeparkhee eedheeko tooreesteeko eeseeteereeo
υπάρχει ειδικό τουριστικό εισιτήριο;

is there a ticket for students/pensioners?
ekhee eedheeko eeseeteereeo ya feeteetes/seendaksyookhoos
έχει ειδικό εισιτήριο για φοιτητές/συνταξιούχους;

do you have a timetable?
ekhete ena dromologheeo
έχετε ένα δρομολόγιο;

when does the ferry leave?
pote fevyee to pleeo
πότε φεύγει το πλοίο;

is there a restaurant on board?
ekhee esteeatoreeo mesa
έχει εστιατόριο μέσα;

can we hire a boat?
boroome na neekyasoome meea varka
μπορούμε να νοικιάσουμε μία βάρκα;

are there any boat trips?
eeparkhoon dheeadhromes me teen varka
υπάρχουν διαδρομές με την βάρκα;

Car – driving/parking

● *To drive in Greece, visitors must be at least 18 years old and have an EU licence or international driving licence.*
  ● *Tolls are payable on motorways. Keep your receipt in case you're stopped by the motorway police.*
  ● *Roadside parking is often OK outside cities, but check! In cities, find a PARKING with fixed rates.*

can I park here?
boro na parkaro edho
μπορώ να παρκάρω εδώ;

where is the ticket machine?
poo eene to parkometro
πού είναι το παρκόμετρο;

where can I park?
poo boro na parkaro
πού μπορώ να παρκάρω;

is there a car park near here?
eeparkhee kapyo parking edho konda
υπάρχει κάποιο πάρκινγκ εδώ κοντά;

how long can I park here?
ya posee ora boro na parkaro edho
για πόση ώρα μπορώ να παρκάρω εδώ;

we're going to....
peeyenoome sto/stee...
πηγαίνουμε στο/στη...

what's the best route?
pos tha pame kaleetera
πώς θα πάμε καλύτερα;

is the road open?
eene o dhromos aneektos
είναι ο δρόμος ανοικτός;

is the road good?
eene o dhromos kalos
είναι ο δρόμος καλός;

how do I get to the motorway?
pos tha pao steen ethneekee odho
πως θα παω στην εθνική οδό;

which exit is it for....?
pya eene ee exodhos ya...
ποια είναι η έξοδοs για...;

petrol station – Car

is there a petrol station near here?
eeparkhee venzeenadheeko edho konda
υπάρχει βενζινάδικο εδώ κοντά;

fill it up, please
yemeeste to parakalo
γεμίστε το, παρακαλώ

unleaded
amoleevdhee
αμόλυβδη

20 euros of unleaded
eekosee evro amoleevdhee
είκοσι ευρώ αμόλυβδη

where is the air line?
poo ekhee aera
πού έχει αέρα;

can you wash the windscreen?
boreete na pleenete to parbreez
μπορείτε να πλήνετε το παρμπρίζ;

please check...
boreete na eleghkhete...
μπορείτε να ελέγχετε...

the tyre pressure
teen peeyesee sta lasteekha
την πίεση στα λάστιχα

the oil
ta ladheea
τα λάδια

the water
to nero
το νερό

everything is ok
ola endaksee
όλα εντάξει

Car – problems/breakdown

● If you break down on the motorway use the emergency phones for assistance or get hold of one of the automobile assistance services **ΕΛΠΑ** (ELPA) tel: 104 or Express Service tel: 154. Ask them their rates before asking them to come.
● Off the motorway, small garages **συνεργείο** (seenergh**ee**o) can be found.

I've broken down
kh**a**lase to aftok**ee**neet**o** moo
χάλασε το αυτοκίνητό μου

I'm on my own *(female)*
eeme m**o**nee moo
είμαι μόνη μου

I have children in the car
ekho pedy**a** sto aftok**ee**neeto
έχω παιδιά στο αυτοκίνητο

where is the nearest garage? *(for repairs)*
poo **ee**ne to py**o** kond**ee**no seenergh**ee**o
πού είναι το πιο κοντινό συνεργείο;

is it serious?
eene sovar**o**
είναι σοβαρό;

I don't have a spare tyre
dhen **e**kho rez**e**rva
δεν έχω ρεζέρβα

have you the parts?
ekhete ta andalakteek**a**
έχετε τα ανταλλακτικά;

when will it be ready?
p**o**te tha **ee**ne et**ee**mo
πότε θα είναι έτοιμο;

how much will it cost?
p**o**so tha kost**ee**see
πόσο θα κοστίσει;

the car won't start
ee meekhan**ee** dhen ksek**ee**n**a**
η μηχανή δεν ξεκινά

the battery is flat
ee batar**ee**a **ee**ne adh**ee**a
η μπαταρία είναι άδεια

the engine is overheating
afks**a**nete ee thermokras**ee**a tees mekhan**ee**s
αυξάνεται η θερμοκρασία της μηχανής

I have a flat tyre
me **e**pyase last**ee**kho
με έπιασε λάστιχο

can you replace the windscreen?
bor**ee**te na ftyaksete to parbr**ee**z
μπορείτε να φτιάξετε το παρμπρίζ;

hire – Car

To hire a car in Greece you must be over 21 and have held a full driving licence for at least a year.
The price of car-hire varies a lot from company to company, so shop around. Car rental can be booked online in the UK before you go.
Check you've been told the total price – beware of hidden extras.

I want to hire a car
thelo na neekyaso ena aftokeeneeto
θέλω να νοικιάσω ένα αυτοκίνητο

for one day
ya meea mera
για μία μέρα

for ... days
ya ... meres
για ... μέρες

what is included in the insurance?
tee pereelamvanete steen asfaleea
τι περιλαμβάνεται στην ασφάλεια;

I want to take out additional insurance
thelo na paro prosthetee asfaleea
θέλω να πάρω πρόσθετη ασφάλεια

I prefer a...
proteemo ena...
προτιμώ ένα ...

large
meghalo
μεγάλο

small
meekro
μικρό

car
aftokeeneeto
αυτοκίνητο

what do we do if we break down?
tee prepee na kanoome se pereeptosee provleematos
τι πρέπει να κάνουμε σε περίπτωση προβλήματος;

where do I have to return the car to?
poo prepee na epeestrepso to aftokeeneeto
πού πρέπει να επιστρέψω το αυτοκίνητο;

by what time?
tee ora
τι ώρα;

I'd like to leave it in...
tha eethela na to afeeso sto/stee...
θα ήθελα να το αφήσω στο/στη...

where are the documents?
poo eene ta kharteea
που είναι τα χαρτιά;

Shopping – holiday

- *Shops open 8/9am till 1/2pm, evenings approx. 5–8 pm. Many close in afternoons, on Sat evenings and Sundays. They open longer in tourist areas.*
  - *Kiosks open till late and have a wide selection including phonecards.*
- *In Cyprus some shops close on Wed and Sat afternoons.*

do you sell/have...?
ekhete...
έχετε...;

stamps
ghrammatoseema
γραμματόσημα

batteries for this
batareees yee afto
μπαταρίες γι' αυτό

where can I find...?
poo na vro...
πού να βρω...;

a colour film
ena film eghkhromo
ένα φιλμ έγχρωμο

10 stamps
dheka ghramatoseema
δέκα γραμματόσημα

for postcards
ya kartes
για κάρτες

to Britain
ya angleea
για Αγγλία

a tape for this camcorder, please
meea kaseta ya afteen teen kamera parakalo
μία κασέτα για αυτήν την κάμερα, παρακαλώ

I'm looking for a present
psakhno ya ena dhoro
ψάχνω για ένα δώρο

have you something cheaper?
ekhete katee pyo ftheeno
έχετε κάτι πιο φθηνό;

it's a gift
eene ya dhoro
είναι για δώρο

please wrap it up *(as a gift)*
dheeploste to ya dhoro parakalo
διπλώστε το για δώρο, παρακαλώ

is there a market?
ekhee la-eekee aghora
έχει λαϊκή αγορά;

which day?
pya mera
ποια μέρα;

clothes – Shopping

In Greece you'll find the whole spectrum of fashion retailers, from exclusive city shops to cut price stores and market stalls. There are department stores too – national and international. The Hondos Centre is a popular chain.

Credit cards are accepted in the larger and more modern shops, but less often in smaller places.

can I try this on?
boro na to dhokeemaso
μπορώ να το δοκιμάσω;

I like it
moo aresee
μου αρέσει

I don't like it
dhen moo aresee
δεν μου αρέσει

it's too big for me
moo eene meghalo
μου είναι μεγάλο

have you a smaller one?
ekhete meekrotero noomero
έχετε μικρότερο νούμερο;

it's too small for me
moo eene polee steno
μου είναι πολύ στενό

have you a larger one?
ekhete meghaleetero noomero
έχετε μεγαλύτερο νούμερο;

it's too expensive
eene polee akreevo
είναι πολύ ακριβό

do you have this in my size?
ekhete afto sto noomero moo
έχετε αυτό στο νούμερό μου;

I'll take this one
tha to paro
θα το πάρω

can you give me a discount?
tha moo kanete kaleeteree teemee
θα μου κάνετε καλύτερη τιμή;

I take a size...
foro noomero...
φορώ νούμερο...

what size are you?
tee noomero forate
τι νούμερο φοράτε;

what shoe size do you take?
tee noomero papootsyoo forate
τι νούμερο παπουτσιού φοράτε;

Shopping – food

● Most towns will have a market at least one day a week where you can buy fresh fruit, vegetables and other local produce.
● Markets are usually open from early morning till about 1.30pm.
● The price of food starts to fall the nearer it gets to closing time.

where can I buy...?
poo boro na aghoraso...
πού μπορώ να αγοράσω...;

fruit	**bread**	**milk**
froota	psomee	ghala
φρούτα	ψωμί	γάλα

where is the supermarket?
poo eene to supermarket
πού είναι το σουπερμάρκετ;

where is the market?
poo eene ee la-eekee aghora
πού είναι η λαϊκή αγορά;

when is the market?
pote ekhee la-eekee aghora
πότε έχει λαϊκή αγορά;

it's me next
ekho seera
έχω σειρά

that's enough
ftanee
φτάνει

4 cakes
teserees pastes
τέσσερις πάστες

a loaf of bread
ena psomee
ένα ψωμί

a litre of...	**milk**	**wine**	**olive oil**
ena leetro...	ghala	krasee	eleoladho
ένα λίτρο...	γάλα	κρασί	ελαιόλαδο

a bottle of...	**water**	**sparkling**	**still**
ena bookalee...	nero	a-eryookho	mee a-eryookho
ένα μπουκάλι...	νερό	αεριούχο	μη αεριούχο

a can of...	**beer**	**coke**	**orangeade**
ena kootee...	beera	coca cola	portokaladha
ένα κουτί...	μπίρα	κόκα κόλα	πορτοκαλάδα

food – Shopping

Units of weight are kilos and grams.
Remember that many shops close approx. 2–5pm and most close on Sundays.
Bread is best bought daily at the bakers.
Supermarkets do not usually sell medicines – go to the pharmacy for these.

250g of...	**taramosalata**	**cheese**	**ham**	**butter**
ena tetarto...	taramosalata	teeree	zambon	vooteero
ένα τέταρτο...	ταραμοσαλάτα	τυρί	ζαμπόν	βούτυρο

half a kilo of...	**tomatoes**	**green beans**
meeso kilo	domates	fasolakya
μισό κιλό	ντομάτες	φασολάκια

a kilo of...	**potatoes**	**apples**
ena keelo...	patates	meela
ένα κιλό...	πατάτες	μήλα

two cheese pies	**three spinach pies**
dheeo teeropeetes	trees spanakopeetes
δύο τυρόπιτες	τρεις σπανακόπιτες

a portion of...	**meat balls**	**spaghetti**
meea mereedha...	keftedhes	makaroneea
μία μερίδα...	κεφτέδες	μακαρόνια

a packet of...	**biscuits**	**sugar**
ena paketo...	beeskota	zakharee
ένα πακέτο...	μπισκότα	ζάχαρη

a tin of tomatoes	**a jar of honey**
ena kootee domates	ena dhokheeo melee
ένα κουτί ντομάτες	ένα δοχείο μέλι

can I help you?	**anything else?**
tee tha thelate	katee allo
τι θα θέλατε;	κάτι άλλο;

Sightseeing

● Opening hours of ancient sites and museums vary greatly.
● Monasteries may well open morning and evening, closing i
the afternoon – so it's important to check first.
● At religious sites there will probably be a dress code,
e.g. no shorts (for men or women), short skirts, etc. It's best
to dress carefully in such places anyway, to avoid offence.

where is the tourist office?
poo **ee**ne to tooreesteek**o** ghraf**ee**o
πού είναι το τουριστικό γραφείο;

we'd like to visit...
thel**oo**me na epeeskeft**oo**me...
θέλουμε να επισκεφτούμε...

have you any leaflets?
ekhete odheey**ee**es
έχετε οδηγίες;

do you have a town guide?
ekhete odheegh**o** tees p**o**lees
έχετε οδηγό της πόλης;

in English
sta angleek**a**
στα αγγλικά

we want to go to...
thel**oo**me na p**a**me sto/stee...
θέλουμε να πάμε στο/στη...

how much is it to get in?
p**o**so kost**ee**zee ee seemetokh**ee**
πόσο κοστίζει η συμμετοχή;

is it open to the public?
eene aneekt**o** sto keen**o**
είναι ανοικτό στο κοινό;

are there any excursions?
eeparkhoon orghanom**e**nes ekdhrom**e**s
υπάρχουν οργανωμένες εκδρομές;

when do they leave?
p**o**te fevgh**oo**n
πότε φεύγουν;

where do they leave from?
ap**o** poo fevgh**oo**n
από που φεύγουν;

● At popular tourist beaches you can hire sun-beds and
umbrellas and there may be showers. Beach cafes/restaurants
abound and you'll often find watersports on offer.
● Greece is still known and loved for its secluded unspoilt
beaches with minimal facilities – they still exist!
● Beware of spiky black sea-urchins: **αχινοί** (akheen**ee**).

do you know a quiet beach?
ks**e**rete k**a**pya **ee**seekhee paral**ee**a
ξέρετε κάποια ήσυχη παραλία;

is there a swimming pool?
ekhee pees**ee**na
έχει πισίνα;

can we use the swimming pool?
bor**oo**me na khreeseemopy**ee**soome teen pees**ee**na
μπορούμε να χρησιμοποιήσουμε την πισίνα;

can we swim in the lake?
bor**oo**me na koleemb**ee**soome stee l**ee**mnee
μπορούμε να κολυμπήσουμε στη λήμνη;

is it deep?
eene vathy**a**
είναι βαθιά;

is the water clean?
eene to ner**o** kathar**o**
είναι το νερό καθαρό;

is it dangerous?
eene epeek**ee**ndheeno
είναι επικίνδυνο;

are there currents?
m**ee**pos **e**khee r**e**vmata
μήπως έχει ρεύματα;

where can we...?
poo bor**oo**me na...
πού μπορούμε να...;

hire a beach umbrella
neeky**a**soome m**ee**a ombr**e**la thal**a**ssees
νοικιάσουμε μία ομπρέλα θαλάσσης;

windsurf
kan**oo**me w**ee**nds**e**rfeeng
κάνουμε γουιντσέρφινγκ

waterski
kan**oo**me thal**a**seeo skee
κάνουμε θαλάσσιο σκι

Sport

● Most tourist offices have information on local sports facilities eg tennis, swimming, horse-riding, cycling, watersports etc.
● You can play golf at Glifada, in Athens.
● There are many gyms in towns and cities.
● Walking and mountaineering are well organised, with clearly-marked trails; rafting/canoeing are available too.

where can we...?
poo bor**oo**me na...
πού μπορούμε να...;

play tennis
p**e**ksoome t**e**nnis
παίξουμε τέννις

play golf
p**e**ksoome golf
παίξουμε γκολφ

hire bikes
neeky**a**soome podh**ee**lata
νοικιάσουμε ποδήλατα

go fishing
psar**e**psoome
ψαρέψουμε

go riding
k**a**noome eepas**ee**a
κάνουμε ιππασία

how much is it...?
p**o**so kost**ee**zee...
πόσο κοστίζει...;

per hour
teen **o**ra
την ώρα

per day
tee m**e**ra
τη μέρα

how do I book a court?
pos tha k**a**no krat**ee**see yeep**e**doo
πώς θα κάνω κράτηση γηπέδου;

can I hire...?
bor**o** na neeky**a**so...
μπορώ να νοικιάσω...;

raquets
rak**e**tes
ρακέτες

golf clubs
bast**oo**neea too golf
μπαστούνια του γκολφ

is there a football match?
ekhee podhosfere**e**k**o** agh**o**na
έχει ποδοσφαιρικό αγώνα;

who is playing
py**o**s p**e**zee
ποιος παίζει;

where is there a sports shop?
poo **ee**ne **e**na katast**ee**ma me **ee**dhee athle**e**teek**a**
πού είναι ένα κατάστημα με είδη αθλητικά;

● Greece's best-kept secret is its ski resorts which offer all the usual amenities at very reasonable rates.
● From approx. Dec to April you can ski on Mount Parnassus near Delphi (2 hours drive from Athens) or at resorts in Northern Greece and the Peloponnese.
● In Cyprus, skiing is available in the Troodos region.

can I hire skis?
boro na neekyaso skee
μπορώ να νοικιάσω σκι;

I'm a beginner
eeme arkhareeos
είμαι αρχάριος

what is the snow like today?
pos eene to khyonee seemera
πώς είναι το χιόνι σήμερα;

is there a map of the ski runs?
eeparkhee khartees me tees dheeadhromes
υπάρχει χάρτης με τις διαδρομές;

how much is a daily pass?
poso kosteezee ee karta teen eemera
πόσο κοστίζει η κάρτα την ημέρα;

which are easy runs?
pyes eene efkoles dheeadhromes
ποιες είναι εύκολες διαδρομές;

my skis are...
ta skee moo eene...
τα σκι μου είναι...

too long
polee makreea
πολύ μακριά

too short
polee konda
πολύ κοντά

my bindings are...
ee seendhesmee eene...
οι σύνδεσμοι είναι...

too loose
khalaree
χαλαροί

too tight
polee sfeekhtee
πολύ σφιχτοί

what is your boot size?
tee noomero eene ee botes sas
τι νούμερο είναι οι μπότες σας;

there is danger of avalanches
eeparkhee keendheenos khyonosteevadhas
υπάρχει κίνδυνος χιονοστιβάδας

Nightlife – popular

● *A list of cultural events is available in English-language newspapers in Greece.*
● *Special weekly publications list entertainment for the whole week, including bars and restaurants for every taste.*
● *Cinemas/theatres are found in cities and bigger towns.*
● *In clubs the admission charge often includes your first drink.*

what can we do tonight?
tee tha kanoome apopse
τι θα κάνουμε απόψε;

which is a good bar?
pyo bar eene kalo
ποιο μπαρ είναι καλό;

is it in a safe area?
eene se asfalee pereeokhee
είναι σε ασφαλή περιοχή;

which is a good disco?
pya deeskotek eene kalee
ποια ντισκοτέκ είναι καλή;

is it expensive?
eene akreevee
είναι ακριβή;

where do local people go at night?
poo seeneetheesoon na dheeaskedhazoon ee dopyee to vradhee
πού συνηθίζουν να διασκεδάζουν οι ντόπιοι το βράδυ;

are there any concerts?
ekhee kapya seenavleea
έχει κάποια συναυλία;

do you want to dance?
thelees na khorepsees
θέλεις να χορέψεις;

where are you from?
apo poo eese
από που είσαι;

what's your name?
pos se lene
πώς σε λένε;

I'm Giorgo
me lene yorgo
με λένε Γιώργο

no thanks, I don't want to
okhee efkhareesto dhen thelo
όχι ευχαριστώ, δεν θέλω

cultural – Nightlife

- *Most places have an annual summer festival of music, dancing, food and wine. The Athens festival includes shows at the ancient theatres of Herodes Atticus and Epidaurus.*
- *Other festival evenings (throughout Greece) include August 15th (Feast of Virgin Mary), Greek Easter (check dates), and Carnival απόκριες (apokree-es) in Feb/Mar (especially at Patras).*

is there a list of cultural events?
eeparkhee meea leesta me tees ekdheelosees
υπάρχει μία λίστα με τις εκδηλώσεις;

are there any local festivals?
ekhee kapyo topeeko paneeyeeree
έχει κάποιο τοπικό πανηγύρι;

we'd like to go...	**to the theatre**	**to a concert**
tha thelame na pame...	sto theatro	se meea seenavleea
θα θέλαμε να πάμε...;	στο θέατρο	σε μία συναυλία

to a performance in an ancient theatre
se meea parastasee se arkheo theatro
σε μία παράσταση σε αρχαίο θέατρο

what's on?	**how much are the tickets?**
tee ekdheelosees eeparkhoon	poso kosteezoon ta eeseeteereea
τι εκδηλώσεις υπάρχουν;	πόσο κοστίζουν τα εισιτήρια;

do I need to book?
khreeazete na kleeso eeseeteereea
χρειάζεται να κλείσω εισιτήρια;

2 tickets...	**for tonight**	**for tomorrow night**
dheeo eeseeteereea...	ya apopse	ya avreeo vradhee
δύο εισιτήρια...	για απόψε	για αύριο βράδυ

when does the performance end?
pote telyonee ee parastasee
πότε τελειώνει η παράσταση;

Hotel

● Tourist offices will be able to give you information on accommodation and help you make a booking.
● Large towns have every class of hotel. Smaller towns and villages have hotels ξενοδοχείο (ksenodhokheeo) and rooms δωμάτιο (dhomateeo). Breakfast may or may not be included.
● Accommodation in private homes does not exist in Cyprus.

have you a room for tonight?
ekhete ena dhomateeo ya apopse
έχετε ένα δωμάτιο για απόψε;

a single room
ena monokleeno
ένα μονόκλινο

a double room
ena dheekleeno
ένα δίκλινο

a family room
ena dhomateeo ya eekoyenya
ένα δωμάτιο για οικογένεια

with bathroom
me banyo
με μπάνιο

with shower
me doos
με ντους

how much is it?
poso kosteezee
πόσο κοστίζει;

is breakfast included?
to proeeno eene steen teemee
το πρωινό είναι στην τιμή;

I booked a room
ekho kanee meea krateesee
έχω κάνει μία κράτηση

my name is...
to onoma moo eene...
το όνομά μου είναι...

I'd like to see the room
tha eethela na dho to dhomateeo
θα ήθελα να δω το δωμάτιο

is there anything cheaper?
ekhete teepota ftheenotero
έχετε τίποτα φθηνότερο;

what time is...?
tee ora serveerete...
τι ώρα σερβίρεται...;

breakfast
to proeeno
το πρωινό

dinner
to vradheeno
το βραδυνό

we'll be back late tonight
tha epeestrepsoome argha apopse
θα επιστρέψουμε αργά απόψε

the key, please
to kleedhee, parakalo
το κλειδί, παρακαλώ

can you keep these in the safe?
boreete na krateesete afta sto khreematakeevotyo
μπορείτε να κρατήσετε αυτά στο χρηματακιβώτιο;

come in!
peraste
περάστε

please come back later
parakalo elate arghotera
παρακαλώ ελάτε αργότερα

can we have breakfast in our room?
boroome na paroome proeeno sto dhomateeo
μπορούμε να πάρουμε πρωινό στο δωμάτιο;

please bring...
parakalo na ferete...
παρακαλώ να φέρετε...

ashtray
ena tasakee
ένα τασάκι

soap
ena sapoonee
ένα σαπούνι

towels
petsetes
πετσέτες

a glass
ena poteeree
ένα ποτήρι

please clean...
parakalo na kathareesete...
παρακαλώ να καθαρίσετε...

my room
to dhomateeo moo
το δωμάτιό μου

the bathroom
to banyo
το μπάνιο

I would like a wake-up call...
tha eethela ena teelefoneema na kseepneeso...
θα ήθελα ένα τηλεφώνημα να ξυπνήσω...

at 7 o'clock
stees epta
στις επτά

is there a laundry service in the hotel?
ekhee pleendeereeo to ksenodhokheeo
έχει πλυντήριο το ξενοδοχείο;

I'm leaving tomorrow
fevgho avreeo
φεύγω αύριο

please prepare the bill
parakalo eteemasete to logharyasmo
παρακαλώ ετοιμάσετε το λογαριασμό

Self-catering

- You'll find plenty of self-catering accommodation, in large or small apartments (deeam**e**reesma) or just rooms (dhom**a**teeo) with en-suite bathrooms.
- The voltage in Greece is 220 V (2 pin plugs). Make sure you take an adaptor with you.
- Rubbish is collected from skips in the street, not from houses.

which is the key for this door?
py**o** **ee**ne to kleedh**ee** yee aft**ee**n teen p**o**rta
ποιο είναι το κλειδί γι' αυτήν την πόρτα;

where are the fuses?
poo **e**khee asf**a**lyes
πού έχει ασφάλειες;

can you show me how it works?
bor**ee**te na moo dh**ee**ksete pos leetoor-y**ee**
μπορείτε να μου δείξτε πώς λειτουργεί;

how does ... work?	**the dishwasher**	**the cooker**
pos leetoor-y**ee**...	to pleend**ee**reeo py**a**ton	ee kooz**ee**na
πώς λειτουργεί...;	το πλυντήριο πιάτων	η κουζίνα
	the washing machine	**the waterheater**
	to pleend**ee**reeo	o thermos**ee**fonas
	το πλυντήριο	ο θερμοσίφωνας

who do I speak to if there are any problems?
se py**o**n meel**a**o an eep**a**rkhee k**a**pyo pr**o**vleema
σε ποιόν μιλάω αν υπάρχει κάποιο πρόβλημα;

where do I put the rubbish?
poo pet**a**me ta skoop**ee**dhya
πού πετάμε τα σκουπίδια;

the gas has run out	**what do I do?**
ee fy**a**lee too gaz**yoo** tel**ee**ose	tee na k**a**no
η φιάλη του γκαζιού τελείωσε	τι να κάνω;

Camping & Caravanning

● Free camping is now illegal and you can be fined. People do, however, still camp wild in quiet places off the beaten track.
● There are plenty of well-equipped, reasonably-priced campsites in Greece. Ask the tourist office for help or look for the tent-and-caravan sign with CAMPING written in English.
● There are six campsites on Cyprus.

we're looking for a campsite
psakhnoome ya thesee kamping
ψάχνουμε για θέση κάμπινγκ

have you a list of campsites?
ekhete leesta me ta kamping
έχετε λίστα με τα κάμπινγκ;

have you any vacancies?
ekhete thesees
έχετε θέσεις;

how much is it per night?
poso kosteezee ee vradya
πόσο κοστίζει η βραδιά;

how far is the beach?
poso makreea eene ee paraleea
πόσο μακριά είναι η παραλία;

we'd like to stay for ... nights
theloome na meenoome ... vradya
θέλουμε να μείνουμε ... βράδυα

do you have sites in the shade?
ekhete thesees stee skeea
έχετε θέσεις στη σκιά;

this site is very muddy
aftee ee thesee ekhee laspee
αυτή η θέση έχει λάσπη

is there another site?
ekhete alee thesee
έχετε άλλη θέση;

can we park our caravan here overnight?
boroome na afeesoome to trokhospeeto mas edho teen neekhta
μπορούμε να αφήσουμε το τροχόσπιτό μας εδώ την νύχτα;

can we put our tent here?
boroome na valoome edho teen skeenee mas
μπορούμε να βάλουμε εδώ την σκηνή μας;

Children

● Greeks love children and will make a fuss of yours! Greek children are usually polite and well-behaved and eat along with their parents – a children's menu is rare.
● Children aged 10 and over have to pay adult fare on public transport.
● Babies and small children must travel in car safety seats.

a child's ticket
ena pedheeko eeseeteereeo
ένα παιδικό εισητήριο

he/she is ... years old
eene ... khronon
είναι ... χρονών

is there a reduction for children?
eeparkhee eedheekee teemee ya pedya
υπάρχει ειδική τιμή για παιδιά;

have you...?
ekhete...
έχετε...;

a high chair
meea pedheekee karekla
μία παιδική καρέκλα

a cot
ena pedheeko krevatee
ένα παιδικό κρεββάτι;

is it ok to bring children?
eeparkhee provleema an feroome ta pedhya
υπάρχει πρόβλημα αν φέρουμε τα παιδιά;

what is there for children to do?
tee boroon na kanoon ta pedhya
τι μπορούν να κάνουν τα παιδιά;

where is a play park?
poo eene ee pedheekee khara
πού είναι η παιδική χαρά;

I have lost...
ekhasa...
έχασα...

my child
to pedhee moo
το παιδί μου

my children
ta pedhya moo
τα παιδιά μου

is it safe for children?
eene asfales ya ta pedhya
είναι ασφαλές για τα παιδιά;

is it dangerous
eene epeekeendheeno
είναι επικίνδυνο;

I have two children
ekho dheeo pedhya
έχω δύο παιδιά

do you have children?
ekhete pedhya
έχετε παιδιά;

Special Needs

- There are good facilities for the disabled on the Metro and at Athens (Venizelos) airport. Elsewhere, the situation is gradually improving.
- Disabled = ανάπηρος (anapeeros). Wheelchair = καροτσάκι (karotsakee).
- A very useful website is **www.greecetravel.com/handicapped**.

is it possible to visit ... with a wheelchair?
eene dheenato na epeeskefthoome ... me anapeereeko karotsakee
είναι δυνατό να επισκεφθούμε ... με αναπηρικό καροτσάκι;

do you have toilets for the disabled?
ekhete tooaletes ya anapeeroos
έχετε τουαλέτες για αναπήρους;

I need a bedroom on the ground floor
khreeazome eepnodhomateeo sto eesoyeeo
χρειάζομαι υπνοδωμάτιο στο ισόγειο

is there a lift?
ekhee asanser
έχει ασανσέρ;

where is the lift?
poo eene to asanser
πού είναι το ασανσέρ;

are there many steps?
ekhee pola skalya
έχει πολλά σκαλιά;

is there an entrance for wheelchairs?
eeparkhee eedheekee eesodho ya anapeereeko karotsakee
υπάρχει ειδική είσοδο για αναπηρικό καροτσάκι;

is there a place on this train for a wheelchair?
eeparkhee thesee sto treno ya anapeereeko karotsakee
υπάρχει θέση στο τρένο για αναπηρικό καροτσάκι;

is there a reduction for the disabled?
eeparkhee eedheekee teemee ya anapeeroos
υπάρχει ειδική τιμή για αναπήρους;

Exchange Visitors

● *These phrases are intended for families hosting Greek-speaking visitors. We have used the informal form.*
● *Greek visitors may take a while to adjust to our meal-times, our taste in food and our lifestyle in general. Their way of life is more traditional and less frenetic than ours – so treat them gently!*

did you sleep well?
keemeetheekes kala
κοιμήθηκες καλά;

what would you like for breakfast?
tee tha eetheles ya proeeno
τι θα ήθελες για πρωινό;

what would you like to eat/drink?
tee thelees na pyees/fas
τι θέλεις να πιείς/φας;

what would you like to do today?
pos thelees na perasees teen eemera
πώς θέλεις να περάσεις την ημέρα;

would you like to go shopping?
thelees na pame ya psonya
θέλεις να πάμε για ψώνια;

I will pick you up at...
tha peraso na se paro stees...
θα περάσω να σε πάρω στις...

take care
na prosekhees
να προσέχεις

we'll be in bed when you get back
tha ekhoome paee ya eepno otan tha epeestrepsees
θα έχουμε πάει για ύπνο όταν θα επιστρέψεις

would you like to take a shower?
thelees na kanees ena doos
θέλεις να κάνεις ένα ντους;

do you eat...?
tros...
τρως...;

do you drink...?
peenees...
πίνεις...;

did you enjoy yourself?
perases kala
πέρασες καλά;

please be back by...
an thelees na epeestrepsees stees...
αν θέλεις να επιστρέψεις στις...

Exchange Visitors

- These phrases are intended for those people staying with Greek-speaking families. We have used the formal form.
- Greek people are very proud of their food. They will feed you well and will value your praise and interest.
- Don't try to help with the washing-up; this is the task of the lady of the house!

I like...
moo ar**e**see...
μου αρέσει...

I don't like...
dhen moo ar**e**see...
δεν μου αρέσει...

it was delicious
eetan n**o**steemo
ήταν νόστιμο

may I phone home?
bor**o** na teelefon**ee**so sto sp**ee**tee
μπορώ να τηλεφωνίσω στο σπίτι;

can I have a key?
bor**o** na **e**kho **e**na kleedh**ee**
μπορώ να έχω ένα κλειδί;

can you take me by car?
bor**ee**te na me p**a**te me to aftok**ee**neeto
μπορείτε να με πάτε με το αυτοκίνητο;

can I borrow...?
bor**o** na dhan**ee**so...
μπορώ να δανείσω...;

an iron
ena s**ee**dhero
ένα σίδερο

a hairdryer
ena peestol**a**kee
ένα πιστολάκι

what time do I have to get up?
tee **o**ra pr**e**pee na kseepn**ee**so
τι ώρα πρέπει να ξυπνήσω;

how long are you staying?
p**o**son ker**o** tha m**e**nete
πόσον καιρό θα μένετε;

I'm leaving in a week
f**e**vgho se m**ee**a evdhom**a**dha
φεύγω σε μία εβδομάδα

thanks for everything
efkhare**e**st**o** ya **o**la
ευχαριστώ για όλα

I've had a great time
p**e**rasa p**a**ra pol**ee** or**e**a
πέρασα πάρα πολύ ωραία

Problems

- Greeks are generally friendly and helpful and keen to lend a hand to people in distress.
  - It will go down well if you try to speak a little Greek on these occasions!
  - Greece was crime-free but recently it is on the increase.
- For most problems, go to the tourist police station.

can you help me?
boreete na me voeetheesete
μπορείτε να με βοηθήσετε;

I don't speak Greek
dhen meelao eleeneeka
δεν μιλάω Ελληνικά

do you speak English?
meelate angleeka
μιλάτε Αγγλικά;

does anyone speak English?
meelaee kapyos angleeka
μιλάει κάποιος Αγγλικά;

I'm lost
ekho khathee
έχω χαθεί

I need to get to...
prepee na pao sto/stee...
πρέπει να πάω στο/στη...

I've missed...
ekhasa...
έχασα...

my connection
teen andapokreesee moo
την ανταπόκρισή μου

my plane
to aeroplano
το αεροπλάνο

I've lost...
ekhasa...
έχασα...

my passport
to dheeavateereeo moo
το διαβατήριό μου

my money
ta lefta moo
τα λεφτά μου

I have no money
dhen ekho lefta
δεν έχω λεφτά

my suitcase isn't here
ee valeetsa moo dhen eene edho
η βαλίτσα μου δεν είναι εδώ

I've left my bag...
ksekhasa teen tsanda moo...
ξέχασα την τσάντα μου...

on the coach
sto leoforeeo
στο λεωφορείο

leave me alone! *(female)*
afeese me eeseekhee
άφησέ με ήσυχη

go away!
fee-ye
φύγε

Complaints

- Greek people react to complaints in a variety of ways – it's best to try to be good-natured but firm.
- Refunds can be difficult to negotiate.
- Queuing can be tricky – you have to be assertive at times!
- Laws about noise-levels are haphazard – ask a reliable local.
- If a serious problem arises, go to the tourist police.

the light
to fos
το φως

the telephone
to teelefono
το τηλέφωνο

...doesn't work
...dhen leetoor-yee
...δεν λειτουργεί

the toilet
ee tooaleta
η τουαλέτα

the heating
ee thermansee
η θέρμανση

the room is dirty
to dhomateeo eene vromeeko
το δωμάτιο είναι βρώμικο

the bath is dirty
to banyo eene vromeeko
το μπάνιο είναι βρώμικο

it's too noisy
ekhee polee thoreevo
έχει πολύ θόρυβο

I don't like the room
dhen moo aresee to dhomateeo
δεν μου αρέσει το δωμάτιο

I didn't order this
dhen zeeteesa afto
δεν ζήτησα αυτό

I want to complain
thelo na kano parapona
θέλω να κάνω παράπονα

we've been waiting for a very long time
pereemenoome polee ora
περιμένουμε πολλή ώρα

we're in a hurry
eemaste vyasteekee
είμαστε βιαστικοί

there is a mistake
ekhete kanee lathos
έχετε κάνει λάθος

this is broken
afto eene khalasmeno
αυτό είναι χαλασμένο

can you repair it?
boreete na to epeedheeorthosete
μπορείτε να το επιδιορθώσετε;

Emergencies

- If you experience a theft or other crime, go to the police and make a report. Keep a copy of the report for any related insurance claim.
- To call an emergency ambulance, dial **166** and report the emergency along with your name and location.
- The health system in Greece is very good.

help!
voeetheea
βοήθεια

can you help me?
boreete na me voeetheesete
μπορείτε να με βοηθήσετε;

there's been an accident
ekhee yeenee ateekheema
έχει γίνει ατύχημα

someone is injured
eeparkhoon travmatee-es
υπάρχουν τραυματίες

please call...
parakalo kaleste...
παρακαλώ καλέστε...

the police
teen asteenomeea
την αστυνομία

an ambulance
ena asthenoforo
ένα ασθενοφόρο

he was going too fast
etrekhe me meghalee takheeteeta
έτρεχε με μεγάλη ταχύτητα

that man keeps following me
ekeenos o andras me akoloothee seenekhos
εκείνος ο άντρας με ακολουθεί συνεχώς

where's the police station?
poo eene to asteenomeeko tmeema
πού είναι το αστυνομικό τμήμα;

I want to report a theft
thelo na dheeloso meea klopee
θέλω να δηλώσω μία κλοπή

I've been robbed
ekho pesee theema klopees
έχω πέσει θύμα κλοπής

I've been attacked
ekho pesee theema epeethesee
έχω πέσει θύμα επίθεση

Emergencies

● *Key words and phone numbers:*
Police **αστυνομία** asteenom**ee**a *100,*
Ambulance **ασθενοφόρο** asthenof**o**ro *166,*
Fire Brigade **πυροσβεστική** peerosvesteek**ee** *199.*
Hospital **νοσοκομείο** nosokom**ee**o, Doctor **γιατρός** yatr**o**s,
Fire **φωτιά** fot**ya**, Accident **ατύχημα** at**ee**kheema.

my car has been broken into
parav**ee**asan to aftok**ee**neet**o** moo
παραβίασαν το αυτοκίνητό μου

my car has been stolen
ekl**e**psan to aftok**ee**neet**o** moo
έκλεψαν το αυτοκίνητό μου

I've been raped
me v**ee**asan
με βίασαν

I need a report for my insurance
khre**e**azome khart**ee** pereeghraf**ee**s seemv**a**ndon ya teen
asfal**ee**a moo
χρειάζομαι χαρτί περιγραφής συμβάντων για την ασφάλειά μου

how much is the fine?
p**o**so **ee**ne to pr**o**steemo
πόσο είναι το πρόστιμο;

where do I pay it?
poo bor**o** na to pleer**o**so
πού μπορώ να το πληρώσω;

I would like to phone the British Consulate
th**e**lo na teelefon**ee**so sto vretane**e**k**o** proksen**ee**o
θέλω να τηλεφωνίσω στο βρετανικό προξενείο

I have no money
dhen **e**kho left**a**
δεν έχω λεφτά

we're on our way
erkh**o**maste am**e**sos
ερχόμαστε αμέσως

Health

● EU citizens are entitled to free emergency care in Greece.
You need to take form E111 with you, completed and
stamped at a post office in the UK. You will still need medical
insurance cover for non-emergency treatment.
● You'll get free treatment at health centres and some
hospitals – it's best to ask about this at the outset.

have you something for...?
ekhete katee ya...
έχετε κάτι για...;

car sickness
zalee sto aftokeeneeto
ζάλη στο αυτοκίνητο

diarrhoea
dheeareea
διάρροια

is it safe to give children?
eene asfales ya ta pedhya
είναι ασφαλές για τα παιδιά;

I feel ill
dhen esthanome kala
δεν αισθάνομαι καλά

I need a doctor
khreeazome yatro
χρειάζομαι γιατρό

my son is ill
o yos moo eene arostos
ο γιος μου είναι άρρωστος

my daughter is ill
ee koree moo eene arostee
η κόρη μου είναι άρρωστη

I'm on this medication
perno afta ta farmaka
παίρνω αυτά τα φάρμακα

my blood group is...
ekho omadha ematos...
έχω ομάδα αίματος...

I have high blood pressure
ekho eepertasee
έχω υπέρταση

I'm diabetic (m/f)
eeme dheeaveeteekos/ee
είμαι διαβητικός/ή

I'm pregnant
eeme engeeos
είμαι έγγυος

I'm on the pill
perno anteeseeleepteeka
παίρνω αντισυλληπτικά

I'm allergic to penicillin
ekho aler-yeea steen peneekeeleenee
έχω αλλεργία στην πενικιλλίνη

Health

I'm breastfeeding
theelazo to moro moo
θηλάζω το μωρό μου

is it safe to take when breastfeeding?
eene asfales kata teen ghalookheea
είναι ασφαλές κατά την γαλουχία;

will he/she have to go to hospital?
prepee na bee sto nosokomeeo
πρέπει να μπει στο νοσοκομείο;

where is the hospital?
poo eene to nosokomeeo
πού είναι το νοσοκομείο;

I need to go to casualty
prepee na pao sta epeeghonda pereestateeka
πρέπει να πάω στα επείγοντα περιστατικά

when are visiting hours?
pote ekhee epeeskepteereeo
πότε έχει επισκεπτήριο;

which ward?
pyo dhomateeo
ποιο δωμάτιο;

I need a dentist
khreeazome odhondeeatro
χρειάζομαι οδοντίατρο

I have toothache
ekho ponodhondo
έχω πονόδοντο

the filling has come out
moo efee-ye to sfra-yeesma
μου έφυγε το σφράγισμα

do I have to pay now?
prepee na pleeroso tora
πρέπει να πληρώσω τώρα;

I have an abscess in the tooth
ekho ena aposteema sto dondee
έχω ένα απόστημα στο δόντι

it hurts
me pona-ee
με πονάει

can you repair my dentures?
boreete na moo epeedheeorthosete teen odhondosteekheea
μπορείτε να μου επιδιορθώσετε την οδοντοστοιχία;

Business

● *Office hours vary but the lunch-time break may well be a long one and not all offices operate in the afternoon. Mornings are the best times to tackle any issues of business or officialdom – the earlier the better, as you sometimes have a long wait.*
● *Private companies often open for longer than public offices*
● *Greek web-sites and e-mail addresses end in* **.gr***.*

here's my card
krat**ee**ste teen k**a**rta moo
κρατήστε την κάρτα μου

I'm from the Smith Company
eeme ap**o** teen eter**ee**a Smith
είμαι από την εταιρία Smith

I want to make an appointment
tha **ee**thela **e**na randev**oo**
θα ήθελα ένα ραντεβού

with Mr/Ms...
me ton k**ee**reeo/teen keer**ee**a...
με τον κύριο/την κυρία...

for April 4th at 11 o'clock in the morning
ya tees t**e**serees apreel**ee**oo stees **e**ndeka to pro**ee**
για τις τέσσερις Απριλίου στις έντεκα το πρωί

can we meet at a restaurant?
bor**oo**me na seenandeeth**oo**me se **e**na esteeat**o**reeo
μπορούμε να συναντηθούμε σε ένα εστιατόριο;

I will send an e-mail to confirm
tha st**ee**lo **e**na e-mail ya na epeeveve**o**so
θα στείλω ένα e-mail για να επιβεβαιώσω

I'm staying at Hotel...
m**e**no sto ksenodhokh**ee**o...
μένω στο ξενοδοχείο...

how do I get to your office?
pos bor**o** na **e**rtho sto ghraf**ee**o sas
πώς μπορώ να έρθω στο γραφείο σας;

here is some information about my company
krat**ee**ste mer**ee**kes pleerofor**ee**yes ya teen eter**ee**a moo
κρατήστε μερικές πληροφορίες για την εταιρεία μου

do you have an appointment?
ekhete randev**oo**
έχετε ραντεβού;

I have an appointment with...
ekho randev**oo** me ton/teen...
έχω ραντεβού με τον/την...

delighted to meet you!
kh**e**ro pol**ee**
χαίρω πολύ

my Greek isn't very good
ta eleeneek**a** moo dhen **ee**ne pol**ee** kal**a**
τα ελληνικά μου δεν είναι πολύ καλά

what is the name of the managing director
pos l**e**yete o dhee-evtheent**ee**s
πώς λέγεται ο διευθυντής

I would like some information about your company
tha **ee**thela mereek**e**s pleerofor**ee**yes ya teen eter**ee**a sas
θα ήθελα μερικές πληροφορίες για την εταιρεία σας

do you have a press office?
ekhete tm**ee**ma t**ee**poo
έχετε τμήμα τύπου;

I need an interpreter
khree**a**zome **e**na dhee-ermeen**e**a
χρειάζομαι ένα διερμηνέα

can you photocopy this?
bor**ee**te na fototeep**ee**sete aft**o**
μπορείτε να φωτοτυπήσετε αυτό;

where is the conference room?
poo **ee**ne ee **e**thoosa seesk**e**pseon
πού είναι η αίθουσα συσκέψεων;

at what time?
tee **o**ra
τι ώρα;

at ... o'clock
stees...
στις...

Phoning

● Card-operated public phones are much more common than coinbox ones. They are very easy to use. Cards are on sale at kiosks, supermarkets and some petrol stations. Ask for a **τηλεκάρτα** (teelekarta) for 3 or 6 euros.
● To call the UK, dial 00 44 then the area code without the first 0. For USA dial 00 1, for Australia 00 61.

a phonecard
meea teelekarta
μία τηλεκάρτα

I want to make a phone call
thelo na kano ena teelefoneema
θέλω να κάνω ένα τηλεφώνημα

Mr Raptis, please
ton keereeo Raptee parakalo
τον κύριο Ράπτη, παρακαλώ

extension ..., please
esotereeko ... parakalo
εσωτερικό ... παρακαλώ

can I speak to...?
boro na meeleeso ston/steen...
μπορώ να μιλήσω στον/στην...;

Jim Brown here
Jim Brown edho
Jim Brown εδώ

I'll call later
tha teelefoneeso arghotera
θα τηλεφωνήσω αργότερα

I'll call back tomorrow
tha ksanateelefoneeso avreeo
θα ξανατηλεφωνήσω αύριο

can I have an outside line, please
boro na ekho meea eksotereekee ghrammee parakalo
μπορώ να έχω μία εξωτερική γραμμή, παρακαλώ

do you have a mobile?
ekhete keeneeto
έχετε κινητό;

what is the number?
pyo eene to noomero
ποιο είναι το νούμερο;

where can I recharge my mobile phone?
poo boro na forteeso to keeneeto moo
πού μπορώ να φορτίσω το κινητό μου;

hello
leyete
λέγεται

who is calling?
pyos eene
ποιος είναι;

it's engaged
meelaee
μιλάει

68

Faxing/E-mail

- There are plenty of internet cafes in cities, large towns and tourist areas. See **www.netcafeguide.com**.
- Greek websites and email addresses often end in **.gr** and @ is called **παπάκι** (papakee) meaning 'little duck'.
- You can fax from/to private offices displaying FAX in their list of services or from OTE offices (telephone exchanges).

is there an internet cafe near here?
eeparkhee internet cafe edho konta?
υπαρχει internet cafe εδώ κοντά;

I want to send an e-mail
thelo na steelo ena e-mail
θέλω να στείλω ένα e-mail

what's your e-mail address?
pyo eene to e-mail sas
ποιο είναι το e-mail σας;

did you get my e-mail?
peerate to e-mail moo
πήρατε το e-mail μου;

my e-mail address is...
to e-mail moo eene...
το e-mail μου είναι...

the website is www.collins.co.uk
to website eene www.collins.co.uk
to website είναι www.collins.co.uk

caro.smith@any.co.uk
caro.smith@any.co.uk
caro teleea smith papakee any teleea co teleea uk

I want to send a fax
thelo na steelo ena fax
θα στείλω ένα φαξ

what's your fax number?
pyo eene to noomero too fax sas
ποιο είναι το νούμερο του φαξ σας;

did you get my fax?
lavate to fax moo
λάβατε το φαξ μου;

do you have a fax?
ekhete fax
έχετε φαξ;

where can I send a fax from?
apo poo boro na steelo ena fax
από πού μπορώ να στείλω ένα φαξ;

Numbers

0	μηδέν *meedhen*
1	ένα *ena*
2	δύο *dheeo*
3	τρία *treea*
4	τέσσερα *tesera*
5	πέντε *pende*
6	έξι *eksee*
7	επτά *epta*
8	οκτώ *okto*
9	εννέα *enea*
10	δέκα *dheka*
11	έντεκα *endeka*
12	δώδεκα *dhodheka*
13	δεκατρία *dhekatreea*
14	δεκατέσσερα *dhekatesera*
15	δεκαπέντε *dhekapende*
16	δεκαέξι *dhekaeksee*
17	δεκαεφτά *dhekaefta*
18	δεκαοκτώ *dhekaokto*
19	δεκαεννέα *dhekaenea*
20	είκοσι *eekosee*
21	είκοσι ένα *eekosee ena*
22	είκοσι δύο *eekosee dheeo*
30	τριάντα *treeanda*
40	σαράντα *saranda*
50	πενήντα *peneenda*
60	εξήντα *ekseenda*
70	εβδομήντα *evdhomeenda*
80	ογδόντα *oghdhonda*
90	ενενήντα *eneneenda*
100	εκατό *ekato*
110	εκατόν δέκα *ekaton dheka*
200	πεντακόσια *pendakosya*
1,000	χίλια *kheelya*
2,000	δύο χιλιάδες *dheeo kheeleeadhes*
1,000,000	ένα εκατομμύριο *ena ekatomeereeo*

1st	πρώτος *protos*
2nd	δεύτερος *dhefteros*
3rd	τρίτος *treetos*
4th	τέταρτος *tetartos*
5th	πέμπτος *pemptos*
6th	έκτος *ektos*
7th	έβδομος *evdhomos*
8th	όγδοος *oghdho-os*
9th	ένατος *enatos*
10th	δέκατος *dhekatos*

Monday	Δευτέρα dheftera
Tuesday	Τρίτη treetee
Wednesday	Τετάρτη tetartee
Thursday	Πέμπτη pemptee
Friday	Παρασκευή paraskevee
Saturday	Σάββατο savato
Sunday	Κυριακή keereeakee

January	Ιανουάριος eeanooareeos
February	Φεβρουάριος fevrooareeos
March	Μάρτιος marteeos
April	Απρίλιος apreeleeos
May	Μάιος maeeos
June	Ιούνιος eeooneeos
July	Ιούλιος eeooleeos
August	Αύγουστος avghoostos
September	Σεπτέμβριος septemvreeos
October	Οκτώβριος oktovreeos
November	Νοέμβριος noemvreeos
December	Δεκέμβριος dhekemvreeos

what's the date?
tee eemeromeeneea ekhoome seemera
τι ημερομηνία έχουμε σήμερα;

which month?
pyos meenas
ποιος μήνας;

it's the 5th of August 2005
eene pende avghoostoo dheeo kheelyadhes pende
είναι πέντε αυγούστου δύο χιλιάδες πέντε

on Saturday
to savato
το Σάββατο

on Saturdays
ta savata
τα Σάββατα

every Saturday
kathe savato
κάθε Σάββατο

next Saturday
to epomeno savato
το επόμενο Σάββατο

last Saturday
to proeeghoomeno savato
το προηγούμενο Σάββατο

Time

● It helps to know the system a little: it's 10 to 8 = it's 8 minus 10. It's half past 8 = it's 8 and a half.
● Some keywords are: 'before' **πριν** pr**ee**n, 'after' **μετά** met**a**, 'now' **τώρα** t**o**ra, 'today' **σήμερα** s**ee**mera, 'yesterday' **χθες** khth**e**s, 'tomorrow' **αύριο** **a**vreeo, 'morning' **πρωί** pro**ee**, 'afternoon' **απόγευμα** ap**o**yevma, 'evening' **βράδυ** vr**a**dhee.

what time is it, please?
tee **o**ra **ee**ne parakal**o**
τι ώρα είναι, παρακαλώ;

am
pro meseemvr**ee**as
προ μεσημβρίας

pm
meta meseemvr**ee**as
μετά μεσημβρίας

at midday
to meseem**e**ree
το μεσημέρι

at midnight
ta mes**a**neekhta
τα μεσάνυχτα

it's 1 o'clock
eene m**ee**a ee **o**ra
είναι μία η ώρα

it's six o'clock
eene **e**ksee ee **o**ra
είναι έξι η ώρα

it's 10 to 8
eene okt**o** par**a** dh**e**ka
είναι οκτώ παρά δέκα

it is half past 8
eene okt**o** ke mees**ee**
είναι οκτώ και μισή

an hour
m**ee**a **o**ra
μία ώρα

half an hour
mees**ee o**ra
μισή ώρα

at 10 o'clock
stees dh**e**ka
στις δέκα

at 2200
stees dh**e**ka to vr**a**dhee
στις δέκα το βράδυ

soon
seend**o**ma
σύντομα

later
argh**o**tera
αργότερα

Greek Cuisine

The immense diversity you find in the Greek landscape is reflected in the variety of food to be found both on the islands and on the mainland. Greeks are perhaps the best exponents of the 'Mediterranean diet', with a great liking for salads well-seasoned with plenty of olive oil and vegetables also cooked in this golden liquid.

Greek food may not be presented as prettily as in other European countries, but it is unfussy, wholesome and healthy – with the emphasis on local produce and the season.

Classic Greek dishes include *moosakas* (layers of aubergine, meat and béchamel sauce); *soovlakeea* (pieces of pork grilled on a skewer like a shish kebab); *klefteeko* (lamb casserole); and *keftedhes* (herbed meat patties). These might be accompanied by Greek salad (*khoreeateekee salata*), including chunks of tomato, cucumber, onions and feta cheese; *tzatseekee* (yoghurt, cucumber, garlic and mint); or *taramosalata* (a purée of fish roes).

One way of sampling the many flavours, is by ordering *mezedhes* if they are on the menu in a Greek or Cypriot restaurant. These are savoury titbits and often include olives, pieces of cheese or meat, such as pork, seafood and small portions of various dishes (similar to Spanish tapas).

Breakfast for many Greeks is simply coffee, perhaps with a bowl of yoghurt and honey. If you prefer something substantial to start the day, fresh bread (*psomee*) with cheese (*teeree*), olives (*elyes*) or jam (*marmeladha*) is a common choice. You can buy it yourself from the bakery (*foorno*). Lunch is taken between 1 and 3pm, and is usually a cooked meal, though fairly light: typically one main dish, with salad or chips, followed by a simple dessert such as fruit or yoghurt. The evening meal, which is the main one of the day, is taken from as early as six until very late. It's accompanied by side-dishes and bread.

Ordering drinks

● All the usual soft and alcoholic drinks are available in Greece.
Measures of shorts can be large – beware!
● Greek coffee like Turkish is strong and in a small cup.
Specify gleeko (sweet), metreeo (medium-sugar) or sketo
(no sugar). Instant coffee is always 'Nescafe' (me ghala =
with milk; me zakharee= with sugar). Frape is iced coffee.

a coffee
ena neskafe
ένα νεσκαφέ

a Greek coffee
ena eleeneeko kafe
ένα ελληνικό καφέ

2 white coffees
dheeo kafedhes me ghala
δύο καφέδες με γάλα

a lager
meea beera
μία μπίρα

small
mekree
μικρή

large
meghalee
μεγάλη

a tea
ena tsaee
ένα τσάι

with milk
me ghala
με γάλα

with lemon
me lemonee
με λεμόνι

a bottle of mineral water
ena bookalee metaleeko nero
ένα μπουκάλι μεταλλικό νερό

sparkling
a-eryookho
αεριούχο

still
mee a-eryookho
μη αεριούχο

the wine list, please
ton katalogho krasyon parakalo
τον κατάλογο κρασιών, παρακαλώ

a carafe of house wine
meea karafa krasee
μία καράφα κρασί

a glass of wine
ena poteeree krasee
ένα ποτήρι κρασί

a bottle of wine
ena bookalee krasee
ένα μπουκάλι κρασί

red
kokeeno
κόκκινο

white
lefko
λευκό

would you like a drink?
thelete katee na pyeete
θέλετε κάτι να πιείτε;

what will you have?
tee tha thelate
τι θα θέλατε;

Ordering food

● The menu is more of a price-list so ask which items are available (tee ekhete seemera = what do you have today?)
● Greek people often order several dishes and share them. They tend not to eat in courses so you need to ask if you want food to be served in 'order' or it will arrive all at once.
● Tipping is completely up to you!

I'd like to book a table
thelo na krateeso ena trapezee
θέλω να κρατήσω ένα τραπέζι

for ... people
ya ... atoma
για ... άτομα

for tonight
ya apopse
για απόψε

at 8 pm
ya tees okto to vradhee
για τις οκτώ το βράδυ

the menu, please
ton katalogho parakalo
τον κατάλογο, παρακαλώ

is there a dish of the day?
ekhee pyato tees eemeras
έχει πιάτο της ημέρας;

I'll have this
tha paro afto
θα πάρω αυτό

what do you recommend?
tee proteenete
τι προτείνετε;

I don't eat meat
dhen tro-o kreas
δεν τρώω κρέας

do you have any vegetarian dishes?
ekhete katee ya khortofaghoos
έχετε κάτι για χορτοφάγους;

excuse me!
parakalo
παρακαλώ

please bring some...
fernete leegho...
φέρνετε λίγο...

bread
psomee
ψωμί

water
nero
νερό

the bill, please
to logharyasmo parakalo
το λογαριασμό παρακαλώ

enjoy your meal!
kalee oreksee
καλή όρεξη

Special requirements

● If you have very specific requirements, stick to large up-market restaurants where English is spoken, so that you can order exactly what you want.
● For vegetarians there are a range of vegetable and pasta dishes as well as cheese and dips.
● Greeks will now offer low-fat alternatives on their menus.

I'm vegetarian
eeme khortofaghos
είμαι χορτοφάγος

I don't eat meat
dhen troo kreas
δεν τρώω κρέας

I don't eat pork
dhen troo kheereeno
δεν τρώω χοιρινό

I don't eat fish/shellfish
dhen troo psaree / ostraka
δεν τρώω ψάρι / όστρακα

which dishes have no meat/fish?
peea fayeeta dhen ekhoon kreas / psaree
ποια φαγητά δεν έχουν κρέας / ψάρι;

I have an allergy to peanuts
ekho aleryeea sta feesteekeea
έχω αλλεργία στα φυστίκια

what is this made with?
me tee eene fteeaghmeno afto
με τι είναι φτιαγμένο αυτό;

I'm on a diet
kano dheeeta
κάνω δίαιτα

is it raw?
eene omo
είναι ωμό;

I don't drink alcohol
dhen peeno alkool
δεν πίνω αλκοόλ

SNACKS

Snacking is easy and convenient, with food available on every street corner: cheese, spinach or sausage pies (*teeropeetes, spanakopeetes, lookaneekopeetes*), toasted sandwiches (*sandveets*), pitta bread (*peeta*), small kebabs (*soovlakeea*) and so on, or for the sweet-toothed, *lookoomee* (Turkish delight) and such honey-based treats as *baklava* and *kataeefee*.

Pop-corn stands are popular.

buffet — ΚΥΛΙΚΕΙΟ
coffee — ΚΑΦΕ
soft drinks — ΑΝΑΨΥΚΤΙΚΑ
cheese & ham toasties — ΤΟSΤ
sandwiches — ΣΑΝΤΟΥΪΤΣ

PIES

cheese pies *teeropeetes*

spinach pie *spanakopeetes*

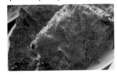

Eating places

RESTAURANTS

Restaurants in tourist resorts usually start serving food from midday or 1 pm until late at night. Greeks tend to have a large meal for lunch between 1 and 3 pm. If going out for dinner, they tend to do so after 8 or 9 pm. There may also be Greek dancing.

ΕΣΤΙΑΤΟΡΙΟ

Restaurant is *esteeatoreeo*.

GRILL *pseestareea*

ΣΟΥΒΛΑΤΖΙΔΙΚΟ

Soovlatzeedheeko is a take-away selling mainly pork kebabs (*soovlakee*) and chips.

It's a quick and easy sit-down or take-away place for a snack (doner kebab with slices of pork or chicken), wrapped up in a pitta bread with tomatoes, onions, chips and plain yogurt.

TAVERNA

ΤΑΒΕΡΝΑ

— traditional cuisine
— everything chargrilled
— views over the Ionian Sea

You are never far from a taverna. Look out for the traditional family-run ones, rather than the ones aimed mainly at tourists.

OUZO BAR

An **oo**zeree is a small bar serving ouzo and other traditional drinks. Ouzo is usually served with ice, and diluted to taste by the drinker, which makes the clear spirit turn cloudy. They may also serve mez**e**des (appetisers) such as olives, cheese, pieces of pork and seafood.

Baklava and kata**ee**fee are cakes made with nuts and honey.

ΖΑΧΑΡΟΠΛΑΣΤΕΙΟ

A zakharoplast**ee**o is a patisserie selling sweet Greek pastries either to take away or eat on the premises. It sometimes also serves coffee and soft drinks.

GREEK SALAD

A typical Greek salad (khor**ee**at**ee**kee sal**a**ta), includes chunks of tomato, cucumber, onions and feta cheese.

Bread (psom**ee**) is always served at Greek meals.

Reading the menu

Greek food tends to be cooked in large pots and you can go into the kitchen to see what is cooking. Greek people often order several dishes and share them. So although you might be ordering starters and main meals, the food tends to be brought as it has been cooked, rather than in order.

*Bree**amee*** –
potatoes, courgettes, aubergines, onions, tomato, garlic and herbs, simmered slowly in olive oil.

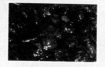

*Stee**fadho*** –
beef cooked in a rich sauce with onions, tomatoes, wine, peppercorns and spices.

Moussaka –
made with mince, aubergines and béchamel sauce.

*Past**eet**seeo* –
pasta bake with mince and white sauce.

Fasoladha –
white beans cooked with olive oil, onion, garlic, tomato purée and oregano.

*Fasolak**eea*** – green beans cooked with olive oil, onion, garlic, tomato purée and oregano.

*Ghee**gantes*** – butter bean stew cooked with oil, onion, garlic and vegetables.

TYPICAL GREEK MEALS

Tsatseekee
yogurt and
garlic dip

Fasolakeea
green beans

Kalamareea
fried squid

Domates yemeestes
stuffed tomatoes.
The filling is usually
rice, garlic, tomato
and herbs, sometimes
with mince.

Patates teeghaneetes
chips

*Khoreeateekee
salata*
Greek salad

Kotoleta kheereenee
pork in breadcrumbs

*see***mera today**

Often there will
also be an
English menu.

DESSERTS

Greek desserts tend to
be very sweet. Look out
for *ghleeka kootalyoo*
crystallized fruit in syrup.

Yoghurt and honey is
another popular dish.

Drinks & bills

GREEK COFFEE

Greek coffee (*eleeneekos kafes*), is strong, sweet and served in a tiny cup, like that of Turkey and the Arab countries. Instead of being filtered, it's ground very fine and brewed in a pot with the sugar included, rather than added afterwards. If you prefer yours without sugar, you will need to ask for a 'plain' coffee (*sketo kafe*). Sweet is *gleeko*, and medium is *metreeo*. If you want it white, specify *me ghala* (with milk).

The usual alternative to Greek coffee is instant, known by the name Nescafe regardless of brand, which can be served cold as a *frape*.

ICED COFFEE

INSTANT COFFEE

Coffee is often served with a glass of ice-cold water as a preliminary thirst-quencher, a welcome addition in a hot country. It is not common practice to finish a meal with coffee: in fact some restaurants do not serve it.

BEER

Beer, although not traditionally Greek, is popular. The major international lager brands are widely available, usually brewed in Greece under licence.

Wine in Greece is plentiful and cheap. You can buy a bottle, or ask for a glass, carafe or jug, straight from the barrel. You may be sceptical about the famous retsina (white wine flavoured with pine resin) but it is very refreshing, and can be diluted with soda, coke or iced water to quench your thirst. There are many fine wines to be found in Greece now, and a good restaurant will often have a selection of bottled vintages. Ask the restaurant-owner which wine he recommends.

Perhaps the best-known Greek spirits are ouzo (aniseed-flavoured – a little like French pastis) and Metaxa (Greek brandy). Ouzo is usually served with ice, and diluted to taste by the drinker, which makes the clear spirit turn cloudy. It can be found in ordinary bars or specialist ouzeris. Other famous Greek spirits include raki, from Crete, and *tseepooro*, an eau-de-vie distilled from the skins, stems, and pips of crushed grapes.

If you want the bill, ask for *to loghareeasmo, parakalo*. Tipping is completely up to you!

enjoy your meal!	cheers!
kalee oreksee	*ya mas*

MENU READER

α A

αγγούρι *angooree* cucumber
αγκινάρες *ankeenares* artichokes
αγκινάρες άλα πολίτα *ankeenares ala poleeta* artichokes with lemon juice and olive oil
αγριογούρουνο *aghreeoghooroono* wild boar
αεριούχο *aereeookho* fizzy, sparkling
αθερίνα *athereena* whitebait, usually fried
αλάτι *alatee* salt
αλεύρι *alevree* flour
αλευρόπιτα *alevropeeta* pie made with cheese, milk and eggs
αμύγδαλα *ameegdala* almonds
άνηθος *aneethos* dill
αρακάς *arakas* peas
αρνί *arnee* lamb
αρνί γιουβέτσι *arnee gyoovetsee* roast lamb with small pasta
αρνί γιουβέτσι *arnee lemonato* lamb braised in sauce with herbs and lemon juice
αρνί με βότανα *arnee me votana* lamb braised with vegetables and herbs
αρνίσιες μπριζόλες *arneesee-es breezoles* lamb chops
αρνί ψητό *arnee pseeto* roast lamb
αστακός *astakos* lobster (often served with lemon juice and olive oil)
άσπρο *aspro* white
άσπρο κρασί *aspro krasee* white wine
αυγά *avgha* eggs
αυγολέμονο *avgholemono* egg and lemon soup

αυγοτάραχο *avghotarakho* mullet roe (smoked)
αφέλια *afeleea* pork in red wine with seasonings (Cyprus)
αχινοί *akheenee* sea urchin roes
αχλάδι *akhladhee* pear
αχλάδι στο φούρνο *akhladhee sto foorno* baked pear in syrup sauce
αχνιστό *akhneesto* steamed

β B

βασιλικός *vaseeleekos* basil
βερίκοκο *vereekoko* apricot
βισινό κασέρι *veeseeno kaseree* sheep's cheese served with cherry preserve
βλίτα *vleeta* wild greens (like spinach, eaten with olive oil and lemon)
βότκα *votka* vodka
βοδινό *vodheeno* beef
βουτήματα *vooteemata* biscuits to dip in coffee
βούτυρο *vooteero* butter
βραδινό *vradeeno* evening meal
βραστό *vrasto* boiled

γ Γ

γάλα *ghala* milk
γαλακτομπούρικο *ghalaktobooreeko* custard tart
γαλακτοπωλείο *ghalaktopoleeo* café/patisserie
γαρίδες *ghareedhes* shrimps; prawns
γαρίδες γιουβέτσι *ghareedhes yoovetsee* prawns in tomato sauce with feta

γαρύφαλλο *gareefalo* clove (spice)
γαύρος *gavros* sardine-type fish (if salted: anchovy)
γίδα βραστή *yeeda vrastee* goat soup
γεμιστά *yemeesta* stuffed vegetables
γιαούρτι *yaoortee* yoghurt
γιαούρτι με μέλι *yaoortee me melee* yoghurt with honey
γιαχνί *yakhnee* cooked in tomato sauce and olive oil
γίγαντες *yeeghantes* large butter beans
γιουβαρλάκια *yoovarlaka* meatballs in lemon sauce
γκαζόζα *ghazoza* fizzy drink
γλυκά *ghlyka* desserts
γλυκά κουταλιού *ghlyka kootalyoo* crystallized fruits in syrup
γλώσσα *ghlosa* sole
γόπες *ghopes* bogue, a type of fish
γραβιέρα *ghravyera* cheese resembling gruyère
γύρος *yeeros* doner kebab

δ Δ

δάφνη *dhafnee* bay leaf
δάκτυλα *dhakteela* almond cakes
δαμάσκηνα *dhamaskeena* prunes with cream in wine sauce
δείπνο *dheepno* dinner
δεντρολίβανο *dendroleevano* rosemary
δίπλες *dheeples* pastry with honey and walnuts
δολμάδες *dholmadhes* vine leaves, rolled up and stuffed with minced meat and rice

ε E

ελάχιστα ψημένο *elakheesta pseemeno* rare (meat)

ελαιόλαδο *eleoladho* olive oil
ελιές *elyes* olives
ελιές τσακιστές *elyes tsakeestes* cracked green olives with coriander seeds and garlic (Cyprus)
ελιοτή *elyotee* olive bread
εξοχικό *eksokheeko* stuffed pork or beef with vegetables and cheese
εστιατόριο *esteeatoreeo* restaurant

ζ Z

ζαμπόν *zambon* ham
ζαχαροπλαστείο *zakharoplasteeo* cake shop
ζάχαρη *zakharee* sugar
ζελατίνα *zelateena* brawn
ζεστή σοκολάτα *zestee sokolata* hot chocolate
ζεστό *zesto* hot, warm

θ Θ

Θαλασσινά *thalaseena* seafood
Θυμάρι *theemaree* thyme

ι I

Ιμάμ μπαϊλντί *eemam baeeldee* stuffed aubergines (eggplants)

κ K

κάβα *kava* wine shop
κάβουρας *kavooras* boiled crab
καγιανάς με παστό κρέας *kayanas me pasto kreyas* salted pork with cheese, tomatoes and eggs
κακαβιά *kakaveea* fish soup
κακάο *kakow* hot chocolate
καλαμάκια *kalamakya* small skewers or straws

καλαμάρια *kalamareea* squid
καλαμάρια τηγανιτά *kalamareea teeghaneeta* fried squid
καλαμπόκι *kalambokee* corn on the cob
καλαμποκόπιτα *kalambokopeeta* corn bread
καλοψημένο *kalopseemeno* well done (meat)
κανέλα *kanella* cinnamon
κάπαρι *kaparee* pickled capers
καπνιστό *kapneesto* smoked
καραβίδα *karaveedha* crayfish
καράφα *karafa* carafe
καρέκλα *karekla* chair
καρότο *karoto* carrot
καρπούζι *karpoozee* watermelon
καρύδι *kareedhee* walnut
καρυδόπιτα *kareedhopeeta* walnut cake
καρύδα *kareedha* coconut
κασέρι *kaseree* sheep's milk cheese, often served fried
κάστανα *kastana* chestnuts
καταΐφι *kataeefee* small shredded pastry drenched in syrup
κατάλογος *kataloghos* menu
κατάλογος κρασιών *kataloghos krasyon* wine list
καταψυγμένο *katapseeghmeno* frozen
κατσίκι *katseekee* roast kid
καφενείο *kafeneeo* café
καφές *kafes* coffee (Greek-style)
καφέδες *kafedhes* coffees (plural)
καφές γλυκύς *kafes ghleekees* very sweet coffee
καφές μέτριος *kafes metreeos* medium-sweet coffee
καφές σκέτος *kafes sketos* coffee without sugar
κεράσια *keraseea* cherries

κεφαλοτύρι *kefaloteeree* type of cheese, often served fried in olive oil
κεφτέδες *keftedhes* meat balls
κιδώνι *keedhonee* quince
κιδώνι στο φούρνο *keedhonee sto foorno* baked quince
κιμάς *keemas* mince
κλέφτικο *klefteeko* casserole with lamb, potatoes and vegetables
κοκορέτσι *kokoretsee* traditional spit-roasted dish of spiced liver and other offal
κοκτέιλ *kokteyl* cocktail
κολατσιό *kolatsyo* brunch, elevenses
κολοκότες *kolokotes* pastries with pumpkin seeds and raisins
κολοκυθάκια *kolokeethakeea* courgettes, zucchini
κολοκυθόπιτα *kolokeethopeeta* courgette/zucchini pie
κολοκυθόπιτα γλυκιά *kolokeethopeeta gleekya* sweet courgette/zucchini pie
κονιάκ *konyak* brandy, cognac
κοντοσούβλι *kontosoovlee* spicy pieces of lamb, pork or beef, spit-roasted
κοτόπουλο *kotopoolo* chicken
κοτόπουλο ριγανάτο *kotopoolo reeghanato* grilled basted chicken with herbs
κοτόπουλο καπαμά *kotopoolo kapama* chicken casseroled with red peppers, onions, cinnamon and raisins
κουκιά *kookya* broad beans
κουλούρια *koolooreea* bread rings
κουνέλι *koonelee* rabbit
κουνουπίδι *koonoopeedhee* cauliflower
κουπέπια *koopepeea* stuffed vine leaves (Cyprus)
κουπές *koopes* meat pasties

κουραμπιέδες *koorambyedhes* small almond cakes eaten at Christmas

κρασί *krasee* wine

κρέας *kreas* meat

κρέμα *krema* cream

κρεμμύδια *kremeedheea* onions

κρητική σαλάτα *kreeteekee salata* watercress salad

κρύο *kreeo* cold

κυδώνια *keedhoneea* type of clams, cockles

κυνήγι *keeneeyee* game

κύριο πιάτο *keereeo pyato* main course

λ Λ

λαβράκι *lavrakee* sea-bass

λαγός *lagos* hare

λαδερά *ladhera* vegetable casserole

λάδι *ladhee* oil

λαδότυρο *ladoteero* soft cheese with olive oil

λάχανα *lakhana* green vegetables

λαχανικά *lakhaneeka* vegetables (menu heading)

λάχανο *lakhano* cabbage, greens

λεμονάδα *lemonadha* lemon drink

λεμόνι *lemonee* lemon

λευκό *lefko* white (used for wine as well as **άσπρο**)

λίγο *leegho* a little, a bit

λουκάνικα *lookaneeka* type of highly seasoned sausage

λουκουμάδες *lookoomadhes* small fried dough balls in syrup

λουκούμι *lookoomee* Turkish delight

λουκούμια *lookoomeea* shortbread served at weddings

λούντζα *loondza* loin of pork, marinated and smoked

μ Μ

μαγειρίτσα *mayeereetsa* soup made of lamb offal, special Easter dish

μαϊντανός *maeedanos* parsley

μακαρόνια *makaronya* spaghetti

μακαρόνια με κιμά *makaronya me keema* spaghetti bolognese

μαρίδες *mareedhes* small fish like sprats, served fried

μαρούλι *maroolee* lettuce

μαρτίνι *marteenee* martini

μαύρο κρασί *mavro krasee* red wine (although you'll hear *kokeeno krasee* more often)

μανιτάρια *maneetareea* mushrooms

μαυρομάτικα *mavromateeka* black-eyed peas

μεγάλο *megalo* large, big

μεζές *mezes* (plural **μεζέδες** *mezedhes*) selection of little snacks served free of charge with ouzo or retsina selection of small portions of Greek dishes for a group to share (available in some restaurants)

μεζεδοπωλείο *mezedhopoleeo* taverna/shop selling mezedhes

μέλι *melee* honey

μελιτζάνα *meleetzana* aubergine (eggplant)

μελιτζάνες ιμάμ *meleetzanes eemam* aubergines (eggplants) stuffed with tomato and onion

μελιτζανοσαλάτα *meleetzanosalata* aubergine (eggplant) mousse (dip)

μελιτζανάκι γλυκό *meleetzanakee gleeko* crystallized sweet in syrup, made from aubergine/eggplant μεσημεριανό *meseemereeano* lunch

μεταλλικό νερό *metaleeko nero* mineral water

μεταξά *metaksa* Metaxa (Greek brandy-type spirit)

μέτρια ψημένο *metreea pseemeno* medium (grilled meat)

μη αεριούχο *mee aereeookho* still, not fizzy

μήλα *meela* apples

μηλόπιτα *meelopeeta* apple pie

μίλκο *meelko* chocolate milk

μιλκσέικ *meelkseik* milkshake

μικρό *meekro* small, little

μοσχάρι *moskharee* beef

μοσχάρι κοκινιστό *moskharee kokeeneesto* beef in wine sauce with tomatoes and onions

μουσακάς *moosakas* moussaka, layers of aubergine (eggplant), minced meat and potato, with white sauce

μπακαλιάρος *bakaleearos* cod

μπακαλιάρος παστός *bakaleearos pastos* salt cod

μπακλαβάς *baklavas* filo-pastry with nuts soaked in syrup

μπάμιες *bameeyes* okra, ladies' fingers (vegetable)

μπαράκι *barakee* bar

μπαρμπούνι *barboonee* red mullet

μπέικον *baykon* bacon

μπίρα, μπύρα *beera* beer (lager-type)

μπιφτέκι *beeftekee* beef rissole/burger

μπουγάτσα *bougatsa* cheese or custard pastry sprinkled with sugar and cinnamon

μπουκάλι *bookalee* bottle

μπουρέκι *boorekee* cheese potato and courgette pie

μπουρέκια *boorekeea* puff pastry filled with meat and cheese (Cyprus)

μπουρδέτο *boordheto* fish or meat in a thick sauce of onions, tomatoes and red peppers

μπριάμ(ι) *breeam(ee)* ratatouille

μπριζόλα *breezola* steak/chop

μπριζόλα αρνίσια *breezola arneeseea* lamb chop

μπριζόλα μοσχαρίσια *breezola moskhareeseea* beef steak/chop

μπριζόλα χοιρινή *breezola kheereenee* pork chop

μύδια *meedheea* mussels

ν N

νες, νεσκαφέ *nes, nescafe* instant coffee (of any brand)

με γάλα *me ghala* with milk

νερό *nero* water

ντολμάδες *dolmadhes* vine leaves, rolled up and stuffed with rice and sometimes mince

ντομάτες *domates* tomatoes

ντομάτες γεμιστές *domates yemeestes* tomatoes stuffed with rice and herbs, and sometimes with mince

ξ Ξ

ξιφίας *kseefeeas* swordfish

ξύδι *kseedhee* vinegar

ο O

οβελιστήριο *oveleesteereeo* shop selling souvlakia and doner kebabs

οινοπωλείο *eenopoleeo* wine shop

ομελέτα *omeletta* omelette

ορεκτικά *orekteeka* first courses/starters (menu heading)

ούζερι *oozeree* small bar selling ouzo and other drinks, maybe with mezedhes (μεζέδες)

ούζο **oo**zo ouzo (traditional aniseed-flavoured spirit)

ουίσκι **wee**skee whisky

οχταπόδι okht**a**podhee octopus (see also χταπόδι)

οχταπόδι κρασάτο okht**a**podhee kras**a**to octopus in red wine sauce

π Π

παγάκια pag**a**kya ice-cubes

παγωτό pagho**to** ice-cream

παϊδάκια paeedh**a**keea grilled lamb chops

παντζάρια pandz**a**reea beetroot with seasonings

παξιμάδια pakseem**a**dheea crispy bread (baked twice)

παξιμαδοκούλουρα pakseemadhok**oo**loora tomato and cheese bread

παπουτσάκια papoots**a**keea stuffed aubergines (eggplants)

πασατέμπο pasat**e**mpo pumpkin seeds

πάστα p**a**sta cake, pastry

παστό past**o** salted

παστιτσάδα pasteets**a**da beef with tomatoes, onions, red wine, herbs, spices and pasta

παστίτσιο pasteets**ee**o baked pasta dish with a middle layer of meat and white sauce

πατσάς pats**a**s tripe soup

πατάτες pat**a**tes potatoes

πατάτες τηγανιτές pat**a**tes teeghan**ee**tes chips, fries

πεπόνι pep**o**nee melon

πέστροφα p**e**strofa trout

πηλιορίτικο μπουμπάρι peeleeor**ee**teeko boob**a**ree spicy sausage

πιάτο της ημέρας py**a**to tees e**e**meras dish of the day

πιλάφι peel**a**fee rice

πιπέρι peep**e**ree pepper

πιπεριές peeper**ye**s peppers

πιπεριές γεμιστές peeper**ye**s yem**ee**stes stuffed peppers with rice, herbs and sometimes mince

πίτα or πίττα p**ee**ta pitta flat envelope of unleavened bread or a pitta either a flat envelope of unleavened bread, or a pie with different fillings, such as meat, cheese, vegetables

πλακί plak**ee** fish in tomato sauce

πορτοκαλάδα portokal**a**dha orangeade

πορτοκάλια portok**a**lya oranges

πουργούρι poorgh**oo**ree cracked wheat (Cyprus)

πουργούρι πιλάφι poorgh**oo**ree peel**a**fee salad made of cracked wheat (Cyprus)

πράσα με σησάμι pr**a**sa me seesam**ee** leeks baked and sprinkled with sesame seeds

πρωινό proeen**o** breakfast

ρ Ρ

ραβιόλι ravee**o**lee pastry stuffed with cheese (Cyprus)

ραδίκια radh**ee**keea chicory

ρακή, ρακί rak**ee** raki, strong spirit a bit like schnapps

ρεβίθια rev**ee**theea chickpeas

ρέγγα r**e**nga herring

ρέγγα καπνιστή r**e**nga kapneest**ee** smoked herring, kipper

ρετσίνα rets**ee**na retsina, traditional resinated white wine

ρίγανη r**ee**ghanee oregano

ροδάκινο rodh**a**keeno peach

ροζέ κρασί roz**e** kras**ee** rosé wine

ρολό με κιμά rol**o** me keem**a** meatloaf

ρύζι r**ee**zee rice

89

ρυζόγαλο *reezoghalo* rice
   pudding
ρώσσικη σαλάτα *roseekee salata*
   Russian salad (pieces of egg,
   potatoes, gherkins, peas and
   carrots in mayonnaise)

σς Σ

σαγανάκι *saghanakee* cheese
   coated in flour and fried in olive
   oil
σαλάτα *salata* salad
σαλατικά *salateeka* salads (menu
   heading)
σαλάχι *salakhee* ray
σαλιγκάρια *saleengaree*a snails
σαλιγκάρια γιαχνί *saleengaree*a
   yakhnee snails in tomato sauce
σάντουιτς *sandweets* sandwich
   (sometimes a filled roll,
   sometimes a toasted sandwich
   with your own chosen
   combination of fillings)
σαραγλί *saranglee* pastry with
   walnuts, sesame seeds and
   syrup; sometimes chocolate too
σαρδέλλες *sardheles* sardines
σέλινο *seleeno* celery
σεφταλιά *seftalya* minced pork
   pasty
σικαλέσιο ψωμί *seekaleseeo*
   psomee rye bread
σικώτι *seekotee* liver
σκορδαλιά *skordhalya* garlic and
   potato mash
σκορδαλιά με ψάρι τηγανιτό
   skordhalya me psaree
   teeghaneeto fried fish served
   with garlic and potato mash
σκόρδο *skordho* garlic
σόδα *sodha* soda
σουβλάκι *soovlakee* meat kebab
σουβλατζίδικο *soovlatseedeeko*
   shop selling souvlakia, doner
   kebabs, etc

σούπα *soopa* soup
σουπιά *soopya* cuttlefish
σουτζουκάκια *sootzookakeea*
   highly seasoned meat balls
σοφρίτο *sofreeto* meat stew with
   creamy garlic sauce (Corfu)
σπανάκι *spanakee* spinach
σπανακόπιτα *spanakopeeta*
   spinach pie
σπαράγγι *sparangee* asparagus
σπαράγγια και αγγινάρες
   sparangeea ke angeenares
   asparagus and artichokes with
   lemon
σπαράγγια σαλάτα *sparangeea*
   salata asparagus salad
σταφύλια *stafeeleea* grapes
στη σούβλα *stee soovla* spit-
   roasted
στιφάδο *steefadho* braised meat
   in spicy onion and tomato
   sauce
στο φούρνο *sto foorno* baked in
   the oven
στρείδια *streedheea* oysters
σύκα *seeka* figs
σύκα στο φούρνο με μαυροδάφνη
   seeka sto foorno me
   mavrodafnee figs cooked in red
   wine sauce with spices
σχάρας *skharas* grilled

τ Τ

ταραμοσαλάτα *taramosalata*
   mousse of cod roe
ταχίνι *takheenee* sesame seed
   paste
τζατζίκι *tzatzeekee* yoghurt,
   garlic and cucumber dip
τόννος ψητός *tonos pseetos*
   grilled tuna with vegetables
τραπανός *trapanos* soup made of
   cracked wheat and yoghurt
   (Cyprus)

τσάι *tsaee* tea

τσιπούρα *tseepoora* type of sea bream

τσουρέκι *tsoorekee* festive bread

τυρί *teeree* cheese

τυροκαυτερή *teerokafteree* spicy dip made of cheese and peppers

τυρόπιτα *teeropeeta* cheese pie

τυροσαλάτα *teerosalata* starter made of cream cheese and herbs

φ Φ

φάβα *fava* yellow split peas or lentils, served in a purée with olive oil and capers

φαγγρί *fangree* sea bream

φακές *fakes* lentils

φασολάδα *fasoladha* soup made with white beans and vegetables, eaten with lemon

φασολάκια *fasolakeea* green beans

φασόλια *fasoleea* haricot beans

φέτα *feta* feta cheese, tangy white cheese used in salads and other dishes

φλαούνες *flaoones* Easter cheese cake (Cyprus)

φράουλες *fraooles* strawberries

φραπέ *frappe* iced coffee

φρούτα *froota* fruit

φυστίκια *feesteekya* peanuts

φυστίκια Αιγίνης *feesteekya eyeenees* pistacchios

χ Χ

χαλβάς *khalvas* sesame seed sweet

χαλούμι *khaloomee* ewe's- or goat's-milk cheese, often grilled

χέλι καπνιστό *khelee kapneesto* smoked eel

χοιρινό *kheereeno* pork

χοιρινό κρητικό *kheereeno kreeteeko* baked pork chops (Crete)

χοιρομέρι *kheeromeree* marinated, smoked ham

χόρτα *khorta* wild greens (similar to spinich) eaten cold with oil and lemon

χορτοφάγος *khortofaghos* vegetarian

χούμους *khoomoos* dip made with puréed chickpeas, hummus

χταπόδι *khtapodhee* octopus, grilled or as a side-salad

χωριάτικη σαλάτα *khoreeateekee salata* salad, Greek-style, with tomatoes, feta cheese, cucumber, onions, olives and oregano

ψ Ψ

ψάρι *psaree* fish

ψάρια καπνιστά *psareea kapneesta* smoked fish

ψάρια πλακί *psareea plakee* baked whole fish with vegetables and tomatoes

ψαρόσουπα *psarosoopa* seafood soup

ψαροταβέρνα *psarotaverna* fish taverna

ψησταριά *pseestareea* grill house

ψητό *pseeto* roast/grilled

ψωμάκι *psomakee* bread roll, bread bun

ψωμί *psomee* bread

ψωμί ολικής αλέσεως *psomee oleekees aleseos* wholemeal bread

PHONETIC MENU READER

A

aereeookho fizzy, sparkling
afeleea pork in red wine with seasonings (Cyprus)
agreeogooroono wild boar
akheenee sea urchin roes
akhladhee pear
  akhladhee sto foorno baked pear with syrup sauce
akhneesto steamed
alatee salt
alevree flour
alevropeeta pie made with cheese, milk and eggs
ameegdala almonds
aneethos dill
angeenares artichokes
angeenares ala poleeta artichokes with lemon juice and olive oil
angooree cucumber
arakas peas
arnee lamb
  arnee gyoovetsee roast lamb with small pasta
  arnee lemonato lamb braised in sauce with herbs and lemon juice
  arnee me votana lamb braised with vegetables and herbs
  arneesee-es breezoles lamb chops
  arnee pseeto roast lamb
aspro white
aspro krasee white wine
astakos lobster (often served with lemon juice and olive oil)
athereena whitebait, usually fried
avgha eggs
avgholemono egg and lemon soup
avghotarakho mullet roe (smoked)

B

bakaleearos cod
bakaleearos pastos salt cod
baklavas filo-pastry with nuts soaked in syrup
bameeyes okra (vegetable)
barakee bar
barboonee red mullet
baykon bacon
beeftekee meat rissole/burger
beera beer (lager-type)
bookalee bottle
boordeto fish or meat in a thick sauce of onions, tomatoes and red peppers
boorekee cheese, potato and courgette pie
boorekeea puff pastry filled with meat and cheese (Cyprus)
bougatsa cheese or custard pastry sprinkled with sugar and cinnamon
breeam(ee) ratatouille
breezola steak, chop
breezola arneeseea lamb chop
breezola moskhareeseea beef steak/chop
breezola kheereenee pork chop

D

dafnee bay leaf
dhakteela almond cakes
dhamaskeena prunes with cream in wine sauce

92

dheepno dinner
dendroleevano rosemary
dheeples pastry with honey and walnuts
dolmadhes vine leaves, rolled up and stuffed with rice and sometimes mince
domates tomatoes
  domates yemeestes tomatoes stuffed with rice and herbs, and sometimes with mince

E

eemam baeeldee stuffed aubergines (eggplants)
eenopoleeo wine shop
eksokheeko stuffed pork or beef with vegetables and cheese
elakheesta pseemeno rare (grilled meat)
eleoladho olive oil
elyes olives
elyes tsakeestes cracked green olives with coriander seeds and garlic (Cyprus)
elyotee olive bread
esteeatoreeo restaurant

F

fakes lentils
fangree sea bream
fasoladha soup made with white beans and vegetables, eaten with lemon
fasolakeea green beans
fasoleea haricot bean casserole
fava yellow split peas or lentils, served in a purée with olive oil and capers
feesteekya peanuts
feesteekya eyeenees pistacchios
feta feta cheese, used in salads and other dishes

flaoones Easter cheese cake (Cyprus)
fraooles strawberries
frappe iced coffee
freska froota fresh fruit
froota fruit

G

gareefalo clove (spice)
gavros sardine-type fish (if salted: anchovy)
ghala milk
ghalaktobooreko custard tart
galaktopoleeo café/patisserie
ghareedhes shrimps; prawns
  ghareedhes yoovetsee prawns in tomato sauce with feta
ghazoza fizzy drink
ghlosa sole
ghlyka desserts
ghlyka kootalyoo crystallised fruits in syrup
ghopes bogue, a type of fish
ghravyera cheese resembling gruyère

K

kafeneeo café
kafes coffee (Greek-style)
  kafedhes coffees (plural)
  kafes ghleekees very sweet coffee
  kafes me ghala milky coffee
  kafes metreeos medium-sweet coffee
  kafes sketos coffee without sugar
kakaveea fish soup
ka-kow hot chocolate
kalamakya small skewers, straws
kalamareea squid
kalamareea teeghaneeta fried squid

kalambokee corn on the cob
kalambokopeeta corn bread
kalopseemeno well done (grilled meat)
kanella cinnamon
kaparee pickled capers
kapneesto smoked
karafa carafe
karaveedha crayfish
kareedhee walnut
kareedhopeeta walnut cake
kareedha coconut
karekla chair
karoto carrot
karpoozee watermelon
kaseree sheep's milk cheese, often served fried
kastana chestnuts
kataeefee small pastry drenched in syrup
kataloghos menu
kataloghos krasyon wine list
katapseegmeno frozen
katseekee roast kid
kava wine shop
kavooras boiled crab
kayanas me pasto kreas salted pork with cheese, tomatoes and eggs
keedhonee quince
keedhoneea a type of clams
keedhonee sto foorno baked quince
keemas mince
keeneeyee game
keereeo pyato main course
kefaloteeree type of cheese, often served fried in olive oil
keftedhes meat balls
keraseea cherries
khalvas sesame seed sweet, halva
khaloomee ewe's or goat's milk cheese, often grilled, halloumi
kheereeno pork
kheereeno kreeteeko baked pork chops (Crete)

kheeromeree marinated, smoked ham
khelee kapneesto smoked eel
khoomoos dip made with puréed chickpeas
khorta wild greens eaten cold with oil and lemon
khoreeateekee salata salad, Greek style, with tomatoes, feta cheese, cucumber and onions
khortofaghos vegetarian
klefteeko casserole with lamb, potatoes and vegetables
kokoretsee traditional spit-roasted dish of spiced liver and other offal
kokteyl cocktail
kolatsyo brunch, elevenses
kolokeethakeea courgettes, zucchini
kolokeethopeeta courgette/zucchini pie
kolokeethopeeta gleekya sweet courgette/zucchini pie
kolokotes pastries with pumpkin seeds and raisins
kontosoovlee spicy pieces of lamb, pork or beef, spit-roasted
konyak brandy, cognac
kookya broad beans
koolooreea bread rings
koonelee rabbit
koonoopeedhee cauliflower
koopepeea stuffed vine leaves (Cyprus)
koopes meat pasties
koorambyedhes small almond cakes eaten at Christmas
kotopoolo chicken
kotopoolo reeghanato grilled basted chicken with herbs
kotopoolo kapama chicken casseroled with red peppers, onions, cinnamon and raisins
krasee wine
kreas meat

kreeo cold
kreeteekee salata watercress salad
krema cream
kremeedheea onions
kseedhee vinegar
kseefeeas swordfish
khtapodhee octopus, often grilled or as a side-salad

L

ladhee oil
ladhera dishes cooked in olive oil (menu heading)
ladoteero soft cheese with olive oil
lagos hare
lakhaneeka vegetables
lakhano cabbage
lavrakee sea-bass
leegho a little, a bit
lemonadha lemonade
lemonee lemon
lefko white
lookaneeka type of highly seasoned sausage
lookoomadhes small fried dough balls in syrup
lookoomee Turkish delight
lookoomeea shortbread served at weddings
loondza loin of pork, marinated and smoked

M

maeedanos parsley
makaroneea spaghetti
makaroneea me keema spaghetti bolognese
maneetareea mushrooms
mareedhes small fish like sprats, served fried
maroolee lettuce

marteenee martini
mavro black
  mavro krasee red wine (although you'll hear *kokeeno krasee* more often)
mavromateeka black-eyed peas
mayeereetsa soup made of lamb offal, special Easter dish
mee aereeookho still, not fizzy
meedheea mussels
meekro small, little
meela apples
meelopeeta apple pie
meelko chocolate milk
megalo large, big
melee honey
meleetzana aubergine
meleetzanakee gleeko crystallized sweet in syrup, made from aubergine (eggplant)
meleetzanes eemam aubergines stuffed with tomato and onion
meleetzanosalata aubergine mousse (dip)
meseemereeano lunch
metaleeko nero mineral water
metaxa Metaxa (Greek brandy-type spirit)
metreea pseemeno medium (grilled meat)
mezedhopoleeo mezés shop
mezes (plural *mezedhes*) selection of little snacks (served free of charge with ouzo or retsina), or a selection of small portions of Greek dishes for a group to share (available in some restaurants)
moskharee beef
moskharee kokeeneesto beef in wine sauce with tomatoes and onions
moosakas moussaka, layered aubergine, meat and potato, with white sauce

N

nes, nescafé instant coffee
  (of any brand)
  me ghala with milk
nero water

O

okhtapodhee octopus
okhtapodhee krasato octopus
  in red wine sauce
omeletta omelette
oozeree small bar selling ouzo
  and other drinks, maybe with
  mezedhes
oozo ouzo (traditional aniseed-
  flavoured spirit)
orekteeka first courses/starters
oveleesteereeo shop selling
  souvlakia and doner kebabs

P

pagakya ice-cubes
paghoto ice-cream
paeedhakeea grilled lamb chops
pakseemadheea crispy bread
  (baked twice)
pakseemadhokooloora tomato
  and cheese bread
pandzareea beetroot with
  seasonings
papootsakeea stuffed aubergines
pasatempo pumpkin seeds
pasta cake, pastry
pasto salted
pasteetsada beef with tomatoes,
  onions, red wine, herbs, spices
  and pasta
pasteetseeo baked pasta dish
  with a middle layer of meat and
  white sauce
patsas tripe soup

patates potatoes
patates teeghaneetes chips, fries
peelafee pilau rice
peeleeooreeteeko boobaree
  spicy sausage
peeperee pepper
peeperyes peppers
peeperyes yemeestes stuffed
  peppers with rice and
  sometimes meat
peeta pitta (flat envelope of
  unleavened bread); pie with
  different fillings, such as meat,
  cheese, vegetables etc.
peponee melon
pestrofa trout
plakee fish in tomato sauce
poorghooree cracked wheat
  (Cyprus)
poorghooree peelafee salad
  made of cracked wheat
  (Cyprus)
portokaladha orange drink
portokalya oranges
prasa me seesamee leeks baked
  and sprinkled with sesame
  seeds
proeeno breakfast
psaree fish
psareea kapneesta smoked fish
psareea plakee baked whole fish
  with vegetables and tomatoes
psarosoopa seafood soup
psarotaverna fish taverna
pseestareea grill house
pseeto roast
psomakee bread roll
psomee bread
psomee oleekees aleseos
  wholemeal bread

Q

pyato tees eemeras dish of the
  day

R

radheekeea chicory

rakee raki, strong spirit a bit like schnapps

raveeolee pastry stuffed with cheese (Cyprus)

reeghanee oregano

renga herring

renga kapneestee smoked herring, kipper

retseena retsina, traditional resinated white wine

reveetheea chickpeas

rolo me keema meatloaf

rodakeeno peach

roze krasee rosé wine

reezee rice

reezoghalo rice pudding

roseekee salata Russian salad (pieces of egg, potatoes, gherkins, peas and carrots in mayonnaise)

S

saghanakee cheese coated in flour and fried in olive oil

salata salad

salakhee ray/skate

salates salads (on menu)

saleengareea snails

saleengareea yakhnee snails in tomato sauce

sandweets sandwich (sometimes a filled roll, sometimes a toasted sandwich with your own chosen combination of fillings)

saranglee pastry with walnuts, sesame seeds and syrup; sometimes chocolate too

sardhelles sardines

seeka figs

seekaleseeo psomee rye bread

seeka sto foorno me mavrodafnee figs cooked in red wine sauce with spices

seekotee liver

seftalya minced pork pasty

seleeno celery

skharas grilled

skordhalya garlic and potato mash

skordhalya me psaree teeghaneeto fried fish served with garlic and potato mash

skordho garlic

sodha soda

sofreeto beef in creamy garlic sauce (Corfu)

soopa soup

soopya cuttlefish

soovlakee meat kebab

soovlatseedeeko shop selling souvlakia, doner kebabs, etc

sootzookakeea highly seasoned meat balls

spanakee spinach

spanakopeeta spinach pie

sparangee asparagus

sparangeea ke angeenares asparagus and artichokes with lemon

sparangeea salata asparagus salad

stafeeleea grapes

steefadho braised meat in onion and tomato sauce

stee soovla spit-roasted

sto foorno baked in the oven

streedheea oysters

T

takheenee sesame seed paste

taramosalata mousse of cod roe

teeree cheese

teerokafteree spicy dip made of cheese and peppers

teeropeeta cheese pie
teerosalata starter made of cheese and herbs
thalaseena seafood
theemaree thyme
tonos tuna
trapanos soup made of cracked wheat and yoghurt (Cyprus)
tsaee tea
tseepoora type of sea bream
tsoorekee festive bread
tzatzeekee yoghurt, garlic and cucumber dip

V

vaseeleekos basil
veeseeno kaseree sheep's cheese served with cherry preserve
vereekoko apricot
vleeta wild greens (like spinach, eaten with olive oil and lemon)
vooteemata biscuits to dip in coffee
vooteero butter
votka vodka
vradeeno evening meal
vrasto boiled

W

weeskee whisky

Y

yakhnee cooked in tomato sauce and olive oil
yaoortee yoghurt
yaoortee me melee yoghurt with honey
yeeda vrastee goat soup
yeeghantes large butter beans
yeeros doner kebab
yemeesta stuffed vegetables
yoovarlakya meatballs in lemon sauce

Z

zakharee sugar
zakharoplasteeo cake shop
zambon ham
zestee sokolata hot chocolate
zesto hot, warm

DICTIONARY
English-Greek
Greek-English

A

a ένας *enas* (masculine o words)
μία *meea* (feminine η words)
ένα *ena* (neuter το words)

abbey το μοναστήρι *to monasteeree*

abortion η άμβλωση *ee amvlosee*

about: *a book about Athens* ένα βιβλίο για την Αθήνα *ena veevleeo ya teen Atheena*
at about ten o'clock περίπου στις δέκα *pereepoo stees dheka*

above πάνω από *pano apo*

abscess το απόστημα *to aposteema*

accident το ατύχημα *to ateekheema*

accommodation το κατάλυμα *to kataleema*

ache ο πόνος *o ponos*

Acropolis η Ακρόπολη *ee Akropolee*

activities οι δραστηριότητες *ee dhrasteereeoteetes*

adaptor ο μετατροπέας *o metatropeas*

address η διεύθυνση *ee dheeeftheensee*
what is your address? ποια είναι η διεύθυνσή σας; *pya eene ee -dhee-eftheensee sas*

address book η ατζέντα *ee atzenda*

adhesive tape η συγκολλητική ταινία *ee seengoleeteekee teneea*

admission charge η είσοδος *ee eesodhos*

adult ο ενήλικος *o eneeleekos*

advance: *in advance* προκαταβολικώς *prokatavoleekos*

Aegean Sea το Αιγαίο (πέλαγος) *to eyeo (pelaghos)*

after μετά *meta*

afternoon το απόγευμα *to apoyevma*

aftershave το αφτερσέιβ *to aftershave*

afterwards αργότερα *arghotera*

again πάλι *palee*

ago: *a week ago* πριν μια βδομάδα *preen meea vdhomadha*

AIDS ΕΙΤΖ *e-eetz*

airbag ο αερόσακος *o aerosakos*

air conditioning ο κλιματισμός *o kleemateesmos*

air freshener το αποσμητικό χώρου *to aposmeeteeko khoroo*

airline η αεροπορική εταιρία *ee aeroporeekee etereea*

air mail αεροπορικώς *aeroporeekos*

air mattress το στρώμα για τη θάλασσα *to stroma ya tee thalasa*

airplane το αεροπλάνο *to aeroplano*

airport το αεροδρόμιο *to aerodhromeeo*

airport bus το λεωφορείο για το αεροδρόμειο *to leoforeeo ya to aerodhromeeo*

air ticket το αεροπορικό εισιτήριο *to aeroporeeko eeseeteereeo*

aisle (in aircraft) ο διάδρομος *o dheeadhromos*

alarm (emergency) ο συναγερμός *o seenayermos*

alarm clock το ξυπνητήρι *to kseepneeteeree*

alcohol το αλκοόλ *to alko-ol*

alcohol-free χωρίς αλκοόλ *khorees alko-ol*

alcoholic οινοπνευματώδης *eenopnevmatodhees*

all όλος *olos*
all the milk όλο το γάλα *olo to ghala*
all the time όλον τον καιρό *olon ton kero*

allergic to αλλεργικός σε *aleryeekos se*

alley το δρομάκι *to dhromakee*

allowance: *duty-free allowance* η επιτρεπόμενη ποσότητα *ee epeetrepomenee posoteeta*

all right *(agreed)* εντάξει *endaksee*

almond το αμύγδαλο *to ameeghdhalo*

also επίσης *epeesees*

always πάντα *panda*

am *see* (to be) GRAMMAR

ambulance το ασθενοφόρο *to asthenoforo*

America η Αμερική *ee amereekee*

American ο Αμερικανός / η Αμερικανίδα *o amereekanos / ee amereekaneedha*

amphitheatre το αμφιθέατρο *to amfeetheatro*

anaesthetic το αναισθητικό *to anestheeteeko*

anchor η άγκυρα *ee ankeera*

anchovy η αντζούγια *ee andzooya*

and και *ke*

angina η στηθάγχη *ee steethangkhee*

angry θυμωμένος *theemomenos*

another άλλος *alos*
another beer άλλη μία μπίρα *alee meea beera*

answer η απάντηση *ee apandeesee*

to answer απαντώ *apando*

answerphone ο αυτόματος τηλεφωνητής *o aftomatos teelefoneetees*

antacid το αντιόξινο *to andeeokseeno*

antibiotics τα αντιβιοτικά *ta andeeveeoteeka*

antihistamine το αντισταμινικό *to andeestameeneeko*

antiques οι αντίκες *ee anteekes*

antiseptic το αντισηπτικό *to andeeseepteeko*

anywhere οπουδήποτε *opoodheepote*

apartment το διαμέρισμα *to dheeamereesma*

apartment block η πολυκατοικία *ee poleekateekeea*

aperitif το απεριτίφ *to apereeteef*

apple το μήλο *to meelo*

appendicitis η σκωληκοειδίτιδα *ee skoleekoeedheeteedha*

application form η αίτηση *ee eteesee*

appointment το ραντεβού *to randevoo*

apricot το βερίκοκο *to vereekoko*

archaeology η αρχαιολογία *ee arkheoloyeea*

architecture η αρχιτεκτονική *ee arkheetektoneekee*

are *see* (to be) GRAMMAR

arm το μπράτσο *to bratso*

armbands *(for swimming)* τα μπρατσάκια *ta bratsakya*

around γύρω *yeero*

to arrest συλλαμβάνω *seelamvano*

arrivals οι αφίξεις *ee afeeksees*

to arrive φτάνω *ftano*

art gallery η πινακοθήκη *ee peenakotheekee*

arthritis η αρθρίτιδα *ee arthreeteedha*

artichoke η αγκινάρα *ee angeenara*

ashtray το τασάκι *to tasakee*

asparagus το σπαράγγι *to sparangee*

aspirin η ασπιρίνη *ee aspeereenee*
soluble aspirin διαλυόμενη ασπιρίνη *dheealeeomenee aspeereenee*

asthma το άσθμα *to asthma*

at σε (στο / στη / στο) *se (sto / stee / sto)*

atlas ο άτλαντας *o atlandas*

attractive *(person)* ελκυστικός *elkeesteekos*

aubergine η μελιτζάνα *ee meleetzana*

aunt η θεία *ee theea*

Australia η Αυστραλία *ee afstraleea*

Australian ο Αυστραλός / η Αυστραλίδα *o afstralos / ee afstraleedha*

automatic αυτόματος *aftomatos*

autoteller το ΑΤΜ *to ey tee em*

autumn το φθινόπωρο *to ftheenoporo*

avalanche η χιονοστιβάδα *ee khyonosteevadha*

avocado το αβοκάντο *to avokado*

awful φοβερός *foveros*

B

baby το μωρό *to moro*

baby food οι βρεφικές τροφές *ee vrefeekes trofes*

baby milk το βρεφικό γάλα *to vrefeeko ghala*

baby's bottle το μπιμπερό *to beebero*

baby seat *(in car)* το παιδικό κάθισμα *to pedheeko katheesma*

baby-sitter η μπεϊμπισίτερ *ee babysitter*

baby wipes τα υγρά μαντηλάκια για μωρά *ta eeghra mandeelakya ya mora*

back *(of a person)* η πλάτη *ee platee*

backpack το σακκίδιο *to sakeedheeo*

bad *(of food)* χαλασμένος *khalasmenos*
(of weather) κακός *kakos*

bag *(small)* η τσάντα *ee tsanda*
(suitcase) η βαλίτσα *ee valeetsa*

baggage οι αποσκευές *ee aposkeves*

baggage reclaim η παραλαβή αποσκευών *ee paralavee aposkevon*

bait *(for fishing)* το δόλωμα *to dholoma*

baker's ο φούρνος *o foornos*

balcony το μπαλκόνι *to balkonee*

bald *(person, tyre)* φαλακρός *falakros*

ball η μπάλα *ee bala*

banana η μπανάνα *ee banana*

band *(musical)* η ορχήστρα *ee orkheestra*

bandage ο επίδεσμος *o epeedhesmos*

bank η τράπεζα *ee trapeza*

banknote το χαρτονόμισμα *to khartonomeesma*

bar το μπαρ *to bar*

barbecue η ψησταριά *ee pseestarya*

barber ο κουρέας *o kooreas*

barrel το βαρέλι *to varelee*

basil ο βασιλικός *o vaseeleekos*

basket το καλάθι *to kalathee*

basketball το μπάσκετ *to basket*

bath (tub) το μπάνιο *to banyo*
  to take a bath κάνω μπάνιο *kano banyo*

bathing cap ο σκούφος του μπάνιου *o skoofos too banyoo*

bathroom το μπάνιο *to banyo*

battery η μπαταρία *ee batareea*

to be see (to be) GRAMMAR

beach η πλαζ *ee plaz* // η παραλία *ee paraleea*

bean (haricot) το φασόλι *to fasolee*
  (broad) το κουκί *to kookee*
  (green) το φασολάκι *to fasolakee*
  (soya) η σόγια *ee soya*

beautiful όμορφος *omorfos*

bed το κρεββάτι *to krevatee*
  double bed διπλό κρεββάτι *dheeplo krevatee*
  single bed μονό κρεββάτι *mono krevatee*
  twin beds δύο μονά κρεββάτια *dheeo mona krevatya*
  sofa bed καναπές κρεββάτι *kanapes krevatee*

bedding τα κλινοσκεπάσματα *ta kleenoskepasmata*

bedroom η κρεββατοκάμαρα *ee krevatokamara*

beef το βοδινό *to vodheeno* // το μοσχάρι *to moskharee*

beer η μπίρα *ee beera*

beetroot το παντζάρι *to pandzaree*

before (time) πριν (από) *preen (apo)*
  (place) μπροστά από *brosta apo*

to begin αρχίζω *arkheezo*

behind πίσω από *peeso apo*

to believe πιστεύω *peestevo*

bell (electric) το κουδούνι *to koodhoonee*

below κάτω από *kato apo*

belt η ζώνη *ee zonee*

beside δίπλα *dheepla*

best ο καλύτερος *o kaleeteros*

better (than) καλύτερος (από) *kaleeteros (apo)*

between μεταξύ *metaksee*

bib η σαλιάρα *ee salyara*

bicycle το ποδήλατο *to podheelato*

big μεγάλος *meghalos*

bigger μεγαλύτερος *meghaleeteros*

bikini το μπικίνι *to beekeenee*

bill ο λογαριασμός *o logharyasmos*

bin το καλάθι των αχρήστων *to kalathee ton akhreeston*

bin liner η σακούλα σκουπιδιών *ee sakoola skoopeedhyon*

binoculars τα κιάλια *ta kyalya*

bird το πουλί *to poolee*

birth η γέννηση *ee yeneesee*

birth certificate το πιστοποιητικό γεννήσεως *to peestopyeetiko yeneeseos*

birthday τα γενέθλια *ta yenethleea*
  happy birthday! χρόνια πολλά *khronya pola*

biscuit το μπισκότο *to beeskoto*

bit: *a bit (of)* λίγο *leegho*

bite *(insect)* το τσίμπημα *to tseebeema*

bitten: *I have been bitten* με δάγκωσε *me dhangose*

bitter πικρός *peekros*

black μαύρος *mavros*

blackcurrant το μαύρο φραγκοστάφυλο *to mavro frangostafeelo*

blanket η κουβέρτα *ee kooverta*

bleach το λευκαντικό *to lefkandeeko*

to bleed αιμορραγώ *emoragho*

blister η φουσκάλα *ee fooskala*

blocked *(pipe)* βουλωμένος *voolomenos*
(nose) κλειστή *kleestee*

blood group η ομάδα αίματος *ee omadha ematos*

blood pressure η πίεση αίματος *ee peeyesee ematos*

blouse η μπλούζα *ee blooza*

blow-dry στέγνωμα *steghnoma*

blue γαλάζιος *ghalazeeos*

boarding card το δελτίο επιβιβάσεως *to dhelteeo epeeveevaseos*

boarding house η πανσιόν *ee pansyon*

boat *(small)* η βάρκα *ee varka*
(ship) το πλοίο *to pleeo*

boat trip η βαρκάδα *ee varkadha*

to boil βράζω *vrazo*

boiled βραστός *vrastos*
boiled water βραστό νερό *vrasto nero*

bone το κόκκαλο *to kokalo*
(fishbone) το αγκάθι *to angkathee*

book n το βιβλίο *to veevleeo*

to book *(room, tickets)* κλείνω *kleeno*

booking: *to make a booking* κλείνω θέση *kleeno thesee*

booking office *(railways, airlines, etc.)* το εκδοτήριο *to ekdhoteereeo*
(theatre) το ταμείο *to tameeo*

bookshop το βιβλιοπωλείο *to veevleeopoleeo*

boots οι μπότες *ee botes*

border *(frontier)* τα σύνορα *ta seenora*

boring βαρετός *varetos*

boss ο / η προϊστάμενος *o / ee proeestamenos*

both και οι δυο *ke ee dheeo*

bottle το μπουκάλι *to bookalee*

bottle-opener το ανοιχτήρι *to aneekhteeree*

bowl το μπωλ *to bol*

box *(container)* το κιβώτιο *to keevotyo*
(cardboard) το κουτί *to kootee*

box office το ταμείο *to tameeo*

boy το αγόρι *to aghoree*

boyfriend ο φίλος *o feelos*

bra το σουτιέν *to sootyen*

bracelet το βραχιόλι *to vrakheeolee*

to brake φρενάρω *frenaro*

brake fluid το υγρό των φρένων *to eeghro ton frenon*

brake light τα φώτα πεδήσεως *ta fota pedheeseos*

brakes τα φρένα *ta frena*

brandy το κονιάκ *to konyak*

bread το ψωμί to psomee (wholemeal) ψωμί ολικής αλέσεως psomee oleekees aleseos

to break σπάζω spazo

breakdown η βλάβη ee vlavee

breakdown van το συνεργείο διασώσεως to seeneryeeo dheeasoseos

breakfast το πρωινό to proeeno

breast το στήθος to steethos

to breathe αναπνέω anapneo

bride η νύφη ee neefee

bridegroom ο γαμπρός o ghambros

briefcase ο χαρτοφύλακας o khartofeelakas

to bring φέρνω ferno

Britain η Βρετανία ee vretaneea

British ο Βρετανός / η Βρετανίδα o vretanos / ee vretaneedha

brochure η μπροσούρα ee brosoora

broken σπασμένος spasmenos **broken down** χαλασμένος khalasmenos

bronze μπρούντζινος broondzeenos

brooch η καρφίτσα ee karfeetsa

brother ο αδελφός o adhelfos

brown καφέ kafe

bruise η μελανιά ee melaneea

brush η βούρτσα ee voortsa

bucket ο κουβάς o koovas

buffet ο μπουφές o boofes

buffet car το βαγόνι εστιατόριο to vaghonee esteeatoreeo

bulb (light) ο γλόμπος o ghlobos

bumbag η τσαντάκι μέσης ee tsantakee mesees

buoy η σημαδούρα ee seemadhoora

bureau de change (bank) ξένο συνάλλαγμα kseno seenalaghma

to burn καίω keo

burnt καμένος kamenos

to burst σκάζω skazo

bus το λεωφορείο to leoforeeo

business η δουλειά ee dhoolya

bus station ο σταθμός του λεωφορείου o stathmos too leoforeeoo

bus stop η στάση του λεωφορείου ee stasee too leoforeeoo

bus terminal το τέρμα του λεωφορείου to terma too leoforeeoo

bus tour η εκδρομή με λεωφορείο ee ekdhromee me leoforeeo

busy απασχολημένος apaskholeemenos

but αλλά ala

butcher's το κρεοπωλείο to kreopoleeo

butter το βούτυρο to vooteero

button το κουμπί to koombee

to buy αγοράζω aghorazo

bypass η παρακάμψη ee parakampsee

C

cab το ταξί to taksee

cabbage το καμπρολάχανο to kambrolakhano

cabin η καμπίνα ee kabeena

cable car το τελεφερίκ to telefereek

cable TV η δορυφορική τηλεώραση ee dhoreeforeekee teeleorasee café το καφενείο to kafeneeo

cake το γλύκισμα o ghleekeesma

cake shop το ζαχαροπλαστείο to zakharoplasteeo

calculator ο υπολογιστής o eepoloyeestees

calendar το ημερολόγιο to eemeroloyo

to call φωνάζω fonazo

call n (telephone) η κλήση ee kleesee
long-distance call η υπεραστική κλήση ee eeperasteekee kleesee

calm ήσυχος eeseekhos

camcorder η βιντεοκάμερα ee veedeokamera

camera η φωτογραφική μηχανή ee fotoghrafeekee meekhanee

to camp κατασκηνώνω kataskeenono

camping gas το γκαζάκι to gazakee

camping stove το πετρογκάζ to petrogas

campsite το κάμπινγκ to camping

to can vb : I can μπορώ boro
you can μπορείς borees
he can μπορεί boree
we can μπορούμε boroome

can (of food) η κονσέρβα ee konserva
(for oil) ο τενεκές o tenekes

Canada ο Καναδάς o kanadhas

Canadian ο Καναδός / η Καναδή o Kanadhos / ee Kanadhee

candle το κερί to keree

to cancel ακυρώνω akeerono

canoe το κανό to kano

can-opener το ανοιχτήρι to aneekhteeree

cappuccino το καπουτσίνο to kapootseeno

car το αυτοκίνητο to aftokeeneeto

car alarm ο συναγερμός o seenayermos

car ferry το φεριμπότ to fereebot

car keys τα κλειδιά αυτοκινήτου ta kleedhya aftokeeneetoo

car park το πάρκινγκ to parking

car radio το ραδιόφωνο αυτοκινήτου to radhyofono aftokeeneetoo

car seat (for children) το παιδικό κάθισμα αυτοκινήτου to pedheeko katheesma aftokeeneetoo

car wash το πλυντήριο αυτοκινήτων to pleenteereeo aftokeeneeton

carafe η καράφα ee karafa

caravan το τροχόσπιτο to trokhospeeto

card η κάρτα ee karta

cardigan η ζακέτα ee zaketa

careful προσεκτικός prosekteekos

carpet το χαλί to khalee

carriage (railway) το βαγόνι to vaghonee

carrot το καρότο to karoto

to carry κουβαλώ koovalo

case (matter) η υπόθεση ee eepothesee
(suitcase) η βαλίτσα ee valeetsa

to cash (cheque) εξαργυρώνω eksaryeerono

cash τα μετρητά ta metreeta

cash desk το ταμείο to tameeo

cash dispenser το ATM to ey tee em

cashier ο ταμίας o tameeas

casino το καζίνο to kazeeno

cassette η κασέτα ee kaseta

castle το κάστρο to kastro

casualty department τα επείγοντα περιστατικά ta epeeghonda pereestateeka

cat η γάτα ee ghata

catalogue ο κατάλογος o kataloghos

to catch πιάνω pyano (bus, train, etc.) παίρνω perno

Catholic καθολικός katholikos

cauliflower το κουνουπίδι to koonoopeedhee

cave η σπηλιά ee speelya

CD το CD to see dee

celery το σέλινο to seleeno

cemetery το νεκροταφείο to nekrotafeeo

cents (euro) λεπτά lepta

centimetre το εκατοστό to ekastosto

central κεντρικός kendreekos

central locking (car) η αυτόματη κλειδαριά ee aftomatee kleedharya

centre το κέντρο to kendro

century ο αιώνας o eonas

certificate το πιστοποιητικό to peestopyeeteeko

chain η αλυσίδα ee aleeseedha

chair η καρέκλα ee karekla

champagne η σαμπάνια ee sambanya

change η αλλαγή ee alayee (money) τα ρέστα ta resta

to change αλλάζω alazo

changing room (beach, sports) το αποδυτήριο to apodheeteereeo

chapel το παρεκκλήσι to parekleesee

charcoal το ξυλοκάρβουνο to kseelokarvoono

charge η τιμή ee teemee

charter flight το τσάρτερ to tsarter

cheap φτηνός fteenos

cheap rate (for phone, etc) η φτηνή ταρίφα ee fteenee tareefa

cheaper φτηνότερος fteenoteros

to check ελέγχω elenkho

check in περνώ από τον έλεγχο εισιτηρίων perno apo ton elenkho eeseeteereeon

check-in desk ο έλεγχος εισιτηρίων o elenkhos eeseeteereeon

cheek το μάγουλο to maghoolo

cheerio! γεια ya

cheers! γεια μας! ya mas

cheese το τυρί to teeree

chemist's το φαρμακείο to farmakeeo

cheque η επιταγή ee epeetayee

cheque card η κάρτα επιταγών ee karta epeetaghon

cherry το κεράσι to kerasee

chestnut το κάστανο to kastano

chewing gum η τσίχλα ee tseekhla

chicken το κοτόπουλο to kotopoolo

chickenpox η ανεμοβλογιά ee anemovloya

chickpeas τα ρεβίθια ta reveetheea

child το παιδί to pedhee

children τα παιδιά ta pedhya

chilli το τσίλλι to tseelee

chilled: *is the wine chilled?* είναι κρύο το κρασί; *eene kreeo to krasee*

chips πατάτες τηγανητές *patates teeghaneetes*

chocolate η σοκολάτα *ee sokolata*

Christmas τα Χριστούγεννα *ta khreestooyena*
merry Christmas! καλά Χριστούγεννα *kala khreestooyena*

church η εκκλησία *ee ekleeseea*

cigar το πούρο *to pooro*

cigarette το τσιγάρο *to tseegharo*

cigarette paper το τσιγαρόχαρτο *to tseegharokharto*

cinema ο κινηματογράφος *o keeneematoghrafos*

cistern το καζανάκι *to kazanakee*

city η πόλη *ee polee*

clean καθαρός *katharos*

to clean καθαρίζω *kathareezo*

cleansing cream η κρέμα καθαρισμού *ee krema kathareesmoo*

client ο πελάτης / η πελάτισσα *o pelatees / ee pelateesa*

cliffs οι γκρεμοί *ee gremee*

climbing η ορειβασία *ee oreevaseea*

climbing boots οι μπότες ορειβασίας *ee botes oreevaseeas*

clingfilm το σελοφάν *to selofan*

cloakroom η γκαρνταρόμπα *ee gardaroba*

clock το ρολόι *to roloee*

to close κλείνω *kleeno*

close *adj (near)* κοντινός *kondeenos*
(weather) αποπνιχτικός *apopneekhteekos*

closed κλειστός *kleestos*

cloth το πανί *to panee*
(for floor) το σφουγγαρόπανο *to sfoongaropano*

clothes τα ρούχα *ta rookha*

clothes line το σκοινί για τα ρούχα *to skeenee ya ta rookha*

clothes peg το μανταλάκι *to mandalakee*

cloudy συννεφιασμένος *seenefyasmenos*

clove *(spice)* το γαρίφαλο *to ghareefalo*

club η λέσχη *ee leskhee*

coach *(railway)* το βαγόνι *to vaghonee*
(bus) το πούλμαν *to poolman*
(instructor) ο προπονητής *o proponeetees*

coach station ο σταθμός λεωφορείων *o stathmos leoforeeon*

coach trip το ταξίδι με πούλμαν *to takseedhee me poolman*

coast η ακτή *ee aktee*

coastguard η ακτοφυλακή *ee aktofeelakee*

coat το παλτό *to palto*

coat hanger η κρεμάστρα *ee kremastra*

cockroach η κατσαρίδα *ee katsareedha*

cocoa το κακάο *to kakao*

coffee ο καφές *o kafes*
black coffee σκέτος καφές *sketos kafes*
white coffee καφές με γάλα *kafes me ghala*

coin το νόμισμα *to nomeesma*

colander το σουρωτήρι *to sooroteeree*

cold κρύος *kreeos*
I have a cold είμαι κρυωμένος *eeme kreeomenos*
I'm cold κρυώνω *kreeono*

cold sore ο έρπητας *o erpeetas*

colour το χρώμα *to khroma*

colour blind δαλτωνικός *dhaltoneekos*

colour film το έγχρωμο φιλμ *to enkhromo feelm*

comb η χτένα *ee khtena*

to come έρχομαι *erkhome*

to come back γυρίζω *yeereezo*

to come in μπαίνω *beno*

comfortable αναπαυτικός *anapafteekos*

communion (holy) η Θεία κοινωνία *ee theea keenoneea*

company (firm) η εταιρία *ee etereea*

compartment (train) το διαμέρισμα *to dheeamereesma*

compass η πυξίδα *ee peekseedha*

to complain παραπονούμαι *paraponoome*

compulsory υποχρεωτικός *eepokhreoteekos*

computer ο κομπιούτερ *o computer*

computer software το software *to software*

concert η συναυλία *ee seenavleea*

concert hall το μέγαρο μουσικής *to megharo mooseekees*

condition η κατάσταση *ee katastasee*

condom το προφυλακτικό *to profeelakteeko*

conductor (bus) ο εισπράκτορας *o eespraktoras* (train) ο ελεγκτής *o elenktees*

conference η διάσκεψη *ee dheeaskepsee*

to confirm επιβεβαιώνω *epeeveveono*

congratulations! συγχαρητήρια *seenkhareeteereea*

connection (trains, etc) η σύνδεση *ee seendhesee*

to be constipated έχω δυσκοιλιότητα *ekho dheeskeeleeoteeta*

consulate το προξενείο *to prokseneeo*

to contact επικοινωνώ *epeekeenono*

contact lenses οι φακοί επαφής *ee fakee epafees*

contact lens cleaner το καθαριστικό διάλυμα *to kathareesteeko dheealeema*

contraceptives τα αντισυλληπτικά *ta andeeseeleepteeka*

contract το συμβόλαιο *to seemvoleo*

to cook μαγειρεύω *mayeerevo*

cooker η κουζίνα *ee koozeena*

cool δροσερός *dhroseros*

cool box (for picnics) το ψυγειάκι *to pseeyeeakee*

copper ο χάλκος *o khalkos*

to copy (photocopy) φωτοτυπώ *fototeepo*

copy n το αντίγραφο *to andeeghrafo*

coral το κοράλλι *to koralee*

corkscrew το τιρμπουσόν *to teerbooson*

corn (sweet corn) το καλαμπόκι *to kalambokee*

corner η γωνία *ee ghoneea*

cornflakes τα κορνφλέικς *ta cornflakes*

cortisone η κορτιζόνη *ee korteezonee*

cosmetics τα καλλυντικά *ta kaleendeeka*

to cost κοστίζω *kosteezo*
how much does it cost? πόσο κάνει; *poso kanee*

cotton το βαμβάκι *to vamvakee*

cotton buds οι μπατουέτες *ee batooetes*

cotton wool το βαμβάκι *to vamvakee*

couchette η κουκέτα *ee kooketa*

cough ο βήχας *o veekhas*

country η χώρα *ee khora*
(not town) η εξοχή *ee eksokhee*

couple (two people) το ζευγάρι *to zevgharee*

courgette το κολοκυθάκι *to kolokeethakee*

courier (for tourists) ο / η συνοδός *o / ee seenodhos*

course (meal) το πιάτο *to pyato*

cousin ο εξάδελφος / η εξαδέλφη *o eksadhelfos / ee eksadhelfee*

cover charge το κουβέρ *to koover*

crab το καβούρι *to kavooree*

cramp η κράμπα *o krampa*

to crash συγκρούομαι *seengkrooome*

crash η σύγκρουση *ee seengroosee*

crash helmet το κράνος *to kranos*

cream η κρέμα *ee krema*

credit card η πιστωτική κάρτα *ee peestoteekee karta*

crime το έγκλημα *to engkleema*

crisps τα πατατάκια *ta patatakya*

croquette η κροκέτα *ee kroketa*

cross ο σταυρός *o stavros*

to cross διασχίζω *dheeaskheezo*

crossroads το σταυροδρόμι *to stavrodhromee*

crowded γεμάτος *yematos*

cruise η κρουαζιέρα *ee krooazyera*

crutches οι πατερίτσες *ee patereetses*

cucumber το αγγούρι *to angooree*

cup το φλυτζάνι *to fleedzanee*

cupboard το ντουλάπι *to doolapee*

currant η σταφίδα *ee stafeedha*

current (electric) το ρεύμα *to revma*

cushion το μαξιλάρι *to makseelaree*

custard η κρέμα *ee krema*

customer ο πελάτης *o pelatees*

customs το τελωνείο *to teloneeo*

to cut κόβω *kovo*

cut το κόψιμο *to kopseemo*

cutlery τα μαχαιροπήρουνα *ta makheropeeroona*

to cycle ποδηλατώ *podheelato*

cyst η κύστη *ee keestee*

cystitis η κυστίτιδα *ee keesteeteedha*

D

daily ημερήσιος *eemereeseeos*

dairy products τα γαλακτοκομικά προϊόντα *ta ghalaktokomeeka proeeonda*

damage η ζημιά *ee zeemya*

damp υγρός *eeghros*

dance *n* ο χορός *o khoros*

to dance χορεύω *khorevo*

danger ο κίνδυνος *o keendheenos*

dangerous επικίνδυνος *epeekeendheenos*

dark *(colour)* σκούρο *skooro*
 it's dark είναι σκοτεινά *eene skoteena*

date η ημερομηνία *ee eemeromeeneea*
 what's the date? τι ημερομηνία είναι; *tee eemeromeeneea eene*

date of birth η ημερομηνία γεννήσεως *ee eemeromeeneea yeneeseos*

daughter η κόρη *ee koree*

day η μέρα *ee mera*

dead νεκρός *nekros*

dear αγαπητός *aghapeetos*
 (expensive) ακριβός *akreevos*

decaffeinated χωρίς καφεΐνη *khorees kafe-eenee*

deck chair η ξαπλώστρα *ee ksaplostra*

to declare δηλώνω *dheelono*

deep βαθύς *vathees*

deep freeze η κατάψυξη *ee katapseeksee*

to defrost ξεπαγώνω *ksepaghono*

delay η καθυστέρηση *ee katheestereesee*

delayed καθυστερισμένος *katheestereesmenos*

delicious νόστιμος *nosteemos*

dentist ο / η οδοντίατρος *o / ee odhondeeatros*

dentures η οδοντοστοιχία *ee odhondosteekheea*

deodorant το αποσμητικό *to aposmeeteeko*

department store το πολυκατάστημα *to poleekatasteema*

departure η αναχώρηση *ee anakhoreesee*

departure lounge η αίθουσα αναχωρήσεων *ee ethoosa anakhoreeseon*

deposit *(part payment)* η προκαταβολή *ee prokatavolee*

dessert το επιδόρπιο *to epeedhorpeeo*

details οι λεπτομέρειες *ee leptomereeyes*

detergent το απορρυπαντικό *to aporeepandeeko*

detour: to make a detour βγαίνω από το δρόμο *vyeno apo to dhromo*

to develop αναπτύσσω *anapteeso*

diabetic διαβητικός *dheeaveeteekos*

to dial παίρνω αριθμό *perno areethmo*

dialling code ο τηλεφωνικός κώδικας *o teelefoneekos kodheekas*

diamond το διαμάντι *to dheeamandee*

diapers οι πάνες *ee panes*

diarrhoea η διάρροια *ee dheeareea*

diary το ημερολόγιο *to eemeroloyo*

dictionary το λεξικό *to lekseeko*

diesel το ντίζελ *to deezel*

diet η δίαιτα *ee dhee-eta*
  I'm on a diet κάνω δίαιτα *kano dhee-eta*

different διαφορετικός *dheeaforeteekos*

difficult δύσκολος *dheeskolos*

digital camera η ψηφιακή φωτογραφική μηχανή *ee pseefeeakee fotografeekee meekhanee*

dinghy η μικρή βάρκα *ee meekree varka*

dining room η τραπεζαρία *ee trapezareea*

dinner το δείπνο *to dheepno*

direct άμεσος *amesos*

directory *(telephone)* ο τηλεφωνικός κατάλογος *o teelefoneekos kataloghos*

directory enquiries οι πληροφορίες καταλόγου *ee pleeroforeeyes kataloghoo*

dirty βρώμικος *vromeekos*

disabled ανάπηρος *anapeeros*

disco η ντισκοτέκ *ee deeskotek*

discount η έκπτωση *ee ekptosee*

dish το πιάτο *to pyato*

dish towel η πετσέτα πιάτων *ee petseta pyaton*

dishwasher το πλυντήριο πιάτων *to pleenteereeo pyaton*

disinfectant το απολυμαντικό *to apoleemandeeko*

disk *(floppy)* η δισκέτα *ee dheesketa*

distilled water το απεσταγμένο νερό *to apestaghmeno nero*

divorced ο χωρισμένος / η χωρισμένη *o khoreesmenos / ee khoreesmenee*

dizzy ζαλισμένος *zaleesmenos*

to do: *I do* κάνω *kano*
  you do κάνεις *kanees*

doctor ο / η γιατρός *o / ee yatros*

documents τα έγγραφα *ta engrafa*

dog το σκυλί *to skeelee*

doll η κούκλα *ee kookla*

dollar το δολάριο *to dholareeo*

door η πόρτα *ee porta*

donkey το γαϊδούρι *to ghaeedhooree*

donor card η κάρτα δότη *ee karta dhotee*

double διπλός *dheeplos*

double bed το διπλό κρεββάτι *to dheeplo krevate*

double room το δίκλινο δωμάτιο *to dheekleeno dhomateeo*

down: *to go down* κατεβαίνω *kateveno*

downstairs κάτω *kato*

drachmas δραχμές *dhrakhmes*

drain η αποχέτευση *ee apokhetefsee*

draught *(of air)* το ρεύμα *to revma*

draught lager η μπίρα από βαρέλι *ee beera apo varelee*

drawer το συρτάρι *to seertaree*

drawing το σχέδιο *to skhedheeo*

dress το φόρεμα *to forema*

to dress ντύνομαι *deenome*

dressing *(for salad)* το λαδολέμονο *to ladholemono*

dressing gown η ρόμπα *ee roba*

drill τρυπώ *treepo*

drink *n* το ποτό *to poto*
  to have a drink παίρνω ένα ποτό *perno ena poto*

to drink πίνω *peeno*

drinking water το πόσιμο νερό *to poseemo nero*

to drive οδηγώ *odheegho*

driver ο οδηγός *o odheeghos*

driving licence η άδεια οδήγησης *ee adheea odheeyeesees*

to drown πνίγομαι *pneeghome*

drug (illegal) το ναρκωτικό *to narkoteeko*

(medicine) το φάρμακο *to farmako*

drunk μεθυσμένος *metheesmenos*

dry n στεγνός *steghnos*

to dry στεγνώνω *steghnono*

dry-cleaners το καθαριστήριο *to kathareesteereeo*

duck η πάπια *ee papya*

due: when is the train due? πότε θα φτάσει το τραίνο; *pote tha ftasee to treno*

dummy η πιπίλα *ee peepeela*

during κατά τη διάρκεια *kata tee dheearkeea*

dust η σκόνη *ee skonee*

duvet το πάπλωμα *to paploma*

duvet cover η παπλωματοθήκη *ee paplomatotheekee*

E

each κάθε *kathe*

100 cents each εκατό ενρώ ο καθένας *ekato evro o kathenas*

ear το αυτί *to aftee*

earache: I have earache με πονάει το αυτί μου *me ponaee to aftee moo*

earlier νωρίτερα *noreetera*

early νωρίς *norees*

earrings τα σκουλαρίκια *ta skoolareekya*

earthquake ο σεισμός *o seesmos*

east η ανατολή *ee anatolee*

Easter το Πάσχα *to paskha*

easy εύκολος *efkolos*

to eat τρώω *tro-o*

eel το χέλι *to khelee*

egg το αβγό *to avgho*

fried eggs αβγά τηγανητά *avgha teeghaneeta*

boiled eggs αβγά βραστά *avgha vrasta*

poached eggs αβγά ποσέ *avgha pose*

either ... or ή ... ή *ee ... ee* // είτε ... είτε *eete ... eete*

elastic το λάστιχο *to lasteekho*

elastic band το λαστιχάκι *to lasteekhakee*

electrician ο ηλεκτρολόγος *o eelektrologhos*

electricity meter ο μετρητής ηλεκτρισμού *o metreetees eelektreesmoo*

electric razor η ξυριστική μηχανή *ee kseereesteekee meekhanee*

e-mail το e-mail *to e-mail*

e-mail address η e-mail διεύθυνση *ee e-mail dheeeftheensee*

embassy η πρεσβεία *ee presveea*

emergency: it's an emergency είναι επείγον περιστατικό *eene epeeghon pereestateeko*

empty άδειος *adheeos*

end το τέλος *to telos*

engaged (to marry)
αρραβωνιασμένος / η
aravonyasmenos / ee
(toilet) κατειλημμένη
kateeleemenee
(phone) μιλάει *meelaee*

engine η μηχανή *ee meekhanee*

England η Αγγλία *ee angleea*

English (thing) αγγλικός *angleekos*

Englishman / woman ο Άγγλος / η
Αγγλίδα *o anglos / ee angleedha*

to enjoy oneself διασκεδάζω
dheeaskedhazo

enough αρκετά *arketa*
enough bread αρκετό ψωμί
arketo psomee

enquiry desk / office το γραφείο
πληροφοριών *to ghrafeeo
pleeroforeeon*

to enter μπαίνω *beno*

entertainment η ψυχαγωγία *ee
pseekhaghoyeea*

entrance η είσοδος *ee eesodhos*

entrance fee η τιμή εισόδου *ee
teemee eesodhoo*

envelope ο φάκελος *o fakelos*

equipment ο εξοπλισμός *o
eksopleesmos*

escalator η κυλιόμενη σκάλα *ee
keelyomenee skala*

especially ειδικά *eedheeka*

essential απαραίτητος *apareteetos*

euro ενρώ *evro*

Europe η Ευρώπη *ee evropee*

even number ο ζυγός αριθμός *o
zeeghos areethmos*

evening το βράδυ *to vradhee*
this evening απόψε *apopse*
in the evening το βράδυ *to
vradhee*

every κάθε *kathe*

everyone όλοι *olee*

everything όλα *ola*

exact ακριβής *akreevees*

examination η εξέταση *ee
eksetasee*

excellent εξαιρετικός *eksereteekos*

except εκτός από *ektos apo*

excess luggage επί πλέον
αποσκευές *epee pleon aposkeves*

exchange rate η τιμή του
συναλλάγματος *ee teemee too
seenalaghmatos*

excursion η εκδρομή *ee
ekdhromee*

excuse me με συγχωρείτε *me
seenkhoreete*

exhaust pipe η εξάτμιση *ee
eksatmeesee*

exhibition η έκθεση *ee ekthesee*

exit η έξοδος *ee eksodhos*

expensive ακριβός *akreevos*

expert ο / η ειδικός *o / ee
eedheekos*

to expire λήγω *leegho*

expired έχει λήξει *ekhee leeksee*

to explain εξηγώ *ekseegho*

express (train) η ταχεία *ee takheea*

express letter το κατεπείγον
γράμμα *to katepeeghon ghrama*

extra: it costs extra κοστίζει
επιπλέον *kosteezee epeepleon*
extra money περισσότερα
χρήματα *pereesotera khreemata*

eyes τα μάτια *ta matya*

F

fabric το ύφασμα *to eefasma*

face το πρόσωπο *to prosopo*

facilities οι ευκολίες *ee efkoleeyes*

factory το εργοστάσιο *to erghostaseeo*

to faint λιποθυμώ *leepotheemo*

fainted λιποθύμησε *leepotheemeese*

fair *adj* ξανθός *ksanthos*

fair *n (commercial)* η έκθεση *ee ekthesee*
(fun fair) το λουνα-πάρκ *to loonapark*

to fall πέφτω *pefto*
he / she has fallen έπεσε *epese*

family η οικογένεια *ee eekoyenya*

famous διάσημος *dheeaseemos*

fan *(electric)* ο ανεμιστήρας *o anemeesteeras*

fan belt το λουρί του ψυγείου *to looree too pseeyeeoo*

far μακριά *makreea*

fare *(bus, train)* το εισιτήριο *to eeseeteereeo*

farm το αγρόκτημα *to aghrokteema*

fast γρήγορα *ghreeghora*

fat *adj* χοντρός *khondros*

fat *n* το λίπος *to leepos*

father ο πατέρας *o pateras*

father-in-law ο πεθερός *o petheros*

fault *(mistake)* το λάθος *to lathos*
it is not my fault δε φταίω εγώ *dhe fteo egho*

favourite ο πιο αγαπημένος *o pyo aghapeemenos*

fax το φαξ *fax*

feather *(of bird)* το φτερό *to ftero*

to feed ταΐζω *taeezo*

to feel αισθάνομαι *esthanome*
I feel sick θέλω να κάνω εμετό *thelo na kano emeto*

female θηλυκός *theeleekos*

ferry το φεριμπότ *to fereebot*

festival το φεστιβάλ *to festeeval*

to fetch φέρνω *ferno*

fever ο πυρετός *o peeretos*

few: a few μερικοί / μερικές / μερικά *mereekee (masculine) / mereekes (feminine) / mereeka (neuter)*

fiancé(e) ο αρραβωνιαστικός / η αρραβωνιαστικιά *o aravonyasteekos / ee aravonyasteekya*

field το χωράφι *to khorafee*

file *(nail)* η λίμα *ee leema*
(computer) το αρχείο *to arkheeo*

to fill γεμίζω *yemeezo*
fill it up! (car) γεμίστε το *yemeeste to*

fillet το φιλέτο *to feeleto*

filling *(in cake, etc.)* η γέμιση *ee yemeesee*
(in tooth) το σφράγισμα *to sfrayeesma*

film *(for camera)* το φιλμ *to feelm*
(in cinema) η ταινία *ee teneea*

filter το φίλτρο *to feeltro*

to finish τελειώνω *teleeono*

fire *(heater)* η θερμάστρα *ee thermastra*
fire! φωτιά! *fotya!*
fire brigade η πυροσβεστική *ee peerosvesteekee*
fire extinguisher ο πυροσβεστήρας *o peerosvesteeras*

fireworks τα πυροτεχνήματα *ta peerotekhneemata*

first πρώτος *protos*

first aid οι πρώτες βοήθειες *ee protes voeetheeyes*

first class (seat, etc.) η πρώτη θέση
ee pro**t**ee the**see**

first floor ο πρώτος όροφος ο
pro**t**os **o**rofos

first name το όνομα to **o**noma

fish το ψάρι to p**s**aree

to fish ψαρεύω psar**e**vo

fishing rod το καλάμι ψαρέματος
to kal**a**mee psar**e**matos

fit (healthy) υγιής eey**ee**-ees

to fix φτιάχνω ftee**a**khno
(arrange) κανονίζω kanon**ee**zo

fizzy (drink) αεριούχο aery**oo**kho

flash (on camera) το φλας to flas

flask το θερμός to ther**mo**s

flat (apartment) το διαμέρισμα to
dheeam**e**reesma

flat tyre: *I have a flat tyre* έχω
σκασμένο λάστιχο **e**kho
skas**me**no las**te**ekho

flea ο ψύλλος o ps**ee**los

flight η πτήση ee pt**ee**see

flippers (swimming) τα
βατραχοπέδιλα ta
vatrakhop**e**dheela

flood η πλημμύρα ee pleem**ee**ra

floor το πάτωμα to p**a**toma
(storey) ο όροφος o **o**rofos

flour το αλεύρι to al**e**vree

flower το λουλούδι to lool**oo**dhee

flu η γρίππη ee ghr**ee**pee

to fly πετώ pet**o**

fly η μύγα ee m**ee**gha

to follow ακολουθώ akoloth**o**

food το φαγητό to fa-yeet**o**

food poisoning η τροφική
δηλητηρίαση ee trofeek**ee**
dheeleeteer**ee**asee

foot το πόδι to p**o**dhee

football το ποδόσφαιρο to
podh**o**sfero

for για ya

foreign ξένος ks**e**nos

forest το δάσος to dh**a**sos

to forget ξεχνώ ksekhn**o**

fork το πηρούνι to peer**oo**nee
(in road) η διακλάδωση ee
dheeakl**a**dhosee

fortnight το δεκαπενθήμερο το
dhekapenth**ee**mero

fountain το σιντριβάνι to
seendreev**a**nee

fracture (of bone) το κάταγμα to
k**a**taghma

France η Γαλλία ee ghal**ee**a

free ελεύθερος el**e**ftheros
(costing nothing) δωρεάν dhore**a**n

to freeze (food) ψύχω pse**e**kho

freezer ο καταψύκτης ο
kataps**ee**ktees

French (thing) γαλλικός ghaleek**o**s

French beans τα φασολάκια ta
fasol**a**kya

frequent συχνός seekhn**o**s

fresh φρέσκος fr**e**skos

fridge το ψυγείο to pseey**ee**o

fried τηγανητός teeghaneet**o**s

friend ο φίλος / η φίλη o f**ee**los /
ee f**ee**lee

from από ap**o**

front (part) το μπροστινό (μέρος)
to brosteen**o** (m**e**ros)
in front μπροστά brost**a**

frozen (water) παγωμένος
pagho**me**nos
(food) κατεψυγμένος
katepseeghm**e**nos

fruit τα φρούτα *ta froota*

fruit juice ο χυμός φρούτων *o kheemos frooton*

fruit salad η φρουτοσαλάτα *ee frootosalata*

frying pan το τηγάνι *to teeghanee*

fuel τα καύσιμα *ta kafseema*

fuel pump η αντλία καυσίμων *ee andleea kafseemon*

full γεμάτος *yematos*

full board (η) πλήρης διατροφή *(ee) pleerees dheeatrofee*

fumes (of car) τα καυσαέρια *ta kafsaereea*

funeral η κηδεία *ee keedheea*

funny αστείος *asteeos*

fur η γούνα *ee ghoona*

furniture τα έπιπλα *ta epeepla*

fuse η ασφάλεια *ee asfaleea*

fuse box ο ηλεκτρικός πίνακας *o eelektreekos peenakas*

G

gallery (art) η πινακοθήκη *ee peenakotheekee*

game το παιγνίδι *to peghneedhee* (to eat) το κυνήγι *to keeneeyee*

garage (for parking car) το γκαράζ *to garaz*

garden ο κήπος *o keepos*

garlic το σκόρδο *to skordho*

gas το γκάζι *to gazee*

gas cooker η γκαζιέρα *ee ghazyera*

gas cylinder η φιάλη γκαζιού *ee feealee gazyoo*

gate (at airport) η έξοδος *ee eksodhos*

gears οι ταχύτητες *ee takheeteetes* *first gear* πρώτη *protee* *second gear* δεύτερη *dhefteree* *third gear* τρίτη *treetee* *fourth gear* τετάρτη *tetartee* *neutral* νεκρή *nekree* *reverse* όπισθεν *opeesthen*

gearbox το κιβώτιο ταχυτήτων *to keevotyo takheeteeton*

gents (toilet) Ανδρών *andhron*

genuine γνήσιος *ghneeseeos*

germs τα μικρόβια *ta meekroveea*

German measles η ερυθρά *ee ereethra*

to get παίρνω *perno* (fetch) φέρνω *ferno*

to get in (car, etc.) μπαίνω *beno*

to get off (from bus) κατεβαίνω από *kateveno apo*

to get on (bus) ανεβαίνω στο λεωφορείο *aneveno sto leoforeeo*

to get through (on the phone) συνδέομαι *seendheome*

gift το δώρο *to dhoro*

gift shop το κατάστημα δώρον *to katasteema dhoron*

gin το τζιν *to gin*

ginger το τζίντζερ *to dzeendzer*

girl το κορίτσι *to koreetsee*

girlfriend η φίλη *ee feelee*

to give δίνω *dheeno*

to give back επιστρέφω *epeestrefo*

glass (to drink from) το ποτήρι *to poteeree* *a glass of water* ένα ποτήρι νερό *ena poteeree nero*

glasses (spectacles) τα γυαλιά *ta yalya*

gloves τα γάντια *ta ghandeea*

glucose η γλυκόζη *ee ghleekozee*

glue n η κόλλα *ee kola*

to glue κολλώ *kolo*

to go πηγαίνω *peeyeno*
  I go / I am going πηγαίνω
  peeyeno
  you go / you are going πηγαίνεις
  peeyenees
  we go / we are going πηγαίνουμε
  peeyenoome

to go back γυρίζω πίσω *yeereezo*
peeso

to go down κατεβαίνω *kateveno*

to go in μπαίνω *beno*

to go out βγαίνω *vyeno*

to go up ανεβαίνω *aneveno*

goat η κατσίκα *ee katseeka*

goggles τα γυαλιά *ta yalya*

gold ο χρυσός *o khreesos*
(made of gold) χρυσός *khreesos*

golf το γκολφ *to golf*

golf course το γήπεδο του γκολφ
to yeepedho too golf

good καλός *kalos*

good afternoon χαίρετε *kherete*

goodbye αντίο *adeeo*

good day καλημέρα *kaleemera*

good evening καλησπέρα
kaleespera

good morning καλημέρα
kaleemera

good night καληνύχτα
kaleeneekhta

goose η χήνα *ee kheena*

gram το γραμμάριο *to ghramareeo*

grandfather ο παππούς *o papoos*

grandmother η γιαγιά *ee yaya*

grandparents ο παππούς και η
γιαγιά *o papoos ke ee yaya*

grapefruit το γκρέιπ-φρουτ *to*
grapefruit

grapes τα σταφύλια *ta stafeelya*

grated cheese το τυρί τριμένο *to*
teeree treemeno

grater ο τρίφτης *o treeftees*

greasy λιπαρός *leeparos*

great μεγάλος *meghalos*

Greece η Ελλάδα *ee eladha*

Greek (person) ο Έλληνας / η
Ελληνίδα *o eleenas / ee*
eleeneedha

Greek adj ελληνικός *eleeneekos*

green πράσινος *praseenos*

grey γκρίζος *greezos*

grilled της σχάρας *tees skharas*

grocer's το μπακάλικο *to*
bakaleeko //
το παντοπωλείο *to pandopoleeo*

ground n το έδαφος *to edhafos*

ground adj (coffee, etc.) αλεσμένος
alesmenos

ground floor το ισόγειο *to*
eesoyeeo

groundsheet ο μουσαμάς εδάφους
o moosamas edhafoos

group η ομάδα *ee omadha*

to grow μεγαλώνω *meghalono*

guarantee η εγγύηση *ee*
engeeyeesee

guard (on train) ο υπεύθυνος
τρένου *o eepeftheenos trenoo*

guest ο φιλοξενούμενος *o*
feeloksenoomenos

guesthouse ο ξενώνας *o ksenonas*

guide ο / η ξεναγός *o / ee*
ksenaghos

to guide ξεναγώ *ksenagho*

guidebook ο οδηγός *o odheeghos*

guided tour η περιήγηση με ξεναγό *ee peree-eeyeesee me ksenagho*

gym shoes τα αθλητικά παπούτσια *ta athleeteeka papootsya*

H

haemorrhoids οι αιμορροΐδες *ee emoroeedhes*

hair τα μαλλιά *ta malya*

hairbrush η βούρτσα *ee voortsa*

haircut το κούρεμα *to koorema*

hairdresser ο κομμωτής / η κομμώτρια *o komotees / ee komotreea*

hairdryer το πιστολάκι *to peestolakee*

half το μισό *to meeso*
half an hour μισή ώρα *meesee ora*

half board (η) ημιδιατροφή *(ee) eemeedheeatrofee*

half-bottle το μικρό μπουκάλι *to meekro bookalee*

half price μισή τιμή *meesee teemee*

ham το ζαμπόν *to zambon*

hamburger το χάμπουργκερ *to khamboorger*

hammer το σφυρί *to sfeeree*

hand το χέρι *to kheree*

handbag η τσάντα *ee tsanda*

handicapped ανάπηρος *anapeeros*

handkerchief το μαντήλι *to mandeelee*
(tissue) το χαρτομάντηλο *to khartomandeelo*

hand luggage οι χειραποσκευή *ee kheeraposkevee*

hand-made χειροποίητος *kheeropee-eetos*

to hang up *(phone)* κλείνω *kleeno*

to happen συμβαίνω *seemveno*
what happened? τι συνέβη; *tee seenevee*

happy χαρούμενος *kharoomenos*

harbour το λιμάνι *to leemanee*

hard *(difficult)* δύσκολος *dheeskolos*

hard-boiled *(egg)* σφιχτό *sfeekhto*

hardware shop το σιδηροπωλείο *to seedheeropoleeo*

harvest ο θερισμός *o thereesmos*

hat το καπέλο *to kapelo*

to have see GRAMMAR

hay fever η αλλεργική ρινίτιδα *ee aleryeekee reeneeteedha*

hazelnut το φουντούκι *to foondookee*

he αυτός *aftos*

head το κεφάλι *to kefalee*

headache: *I have a headache* έχω πονοκέφαλο *ekho ponokefalo*

headlights οι προβολείς του αυτοκινήτου *ee provolees too aftokeeneetoo*

headphones τα ακουστικά *ta akoosteeka*

to hear ακούω *akoo-o*

hearing aid το ακουστικό βαρηκοΐας *to akoosteeko vareekoeeas*

heart η καρδιά *ee kardhya*

heart attack η καρδιακή προσβολή *ee kardheeakee prosvolee*

heartburn η καούρα *ee kaoora*

119

heater η θερμάστρα *ee thermastra*

heating η θέρμανση *ee thermansee*

heavy βαρύς *varees*

hello γεια σας *ya sas*

helmet ο κράνος *o kranos*

to help βοηθώ *voeetho*
help! βοήθεια *voeetheea*

hepatitis η ηπατίτιδα *ee eepateeteedha*

herb το βότανο *to votano*

herbal tea το τσάι του βουνού *to tsaee too voonoo*

here εδώ *edho*

hernia η κήλη *ee keelee*

high ψηλός *pseelos*

high blood pressure η ψηλή πίεση *ee pseelee peeyesee*

high chair η ψηλή παιδική καρέκλα *ee pseelee pedheekee karekla*

hill ο λόφος *o lofos*
(slope) η πλαγιά *ee playa*

hill walking η ορειβασία *ee oreevaseea*

to hire νοικιάζω *neekyazo*

to hit χτυπώ *khteepo*

hitchhiking το οτοστόπ *to otostop*

HIV positive θετικός για ΕΙΤΖ *theteekos ya aids*

to hold κρατώ *krato*

hold-up η καθυστέρηση *ee katheestereesee*

hole η τρύπα *ee treepa*

holiday οι διακοπές *ee dheeakopes*

home το σπίτι *to speetee*
at home στο σπίτι *sto speetee*

honey το μέλι *to melee*

honeymoon ο μήνας του μέλιτος *o meenas too meleetos*

hook (fishing) το αγκίστρι *to angkeestree*

to hope ελπίζω *elpeezo*

hors d'œuvre τα ορεκτικά *ta orekteeka*

horse το άλογο *to alogho*

hospital το νοσοκομείο *to nosokomeeo*

hot ζεστός *zestos*
I'm hot ζεσταίνομαι *zestenome*
it's hot έχει ζέστη *ekhee zestee*
hot water το ζεστό νερό *to zesto nero*

hotel το ξενοδοχείο *to ksenodhokheeo*

hour η ώρα *ee ora*

house το σπίτι *to speetee*

housewife η νοικοκυρά *ee neekokeera*

house wine το κρασί χύμα *to krasee kheema*

how πώς *pos*
how long? πόση ώρα; *posee ora*
how much? πόσο; *poso*
how many? πόσα; *posa*
how are you? πώς είστε; *pos eeste*

hungry: I'm hungry πεινώ *peeno*

to hurry: I'm in a hurry βιάζομαι *vyazome*

to hurt: that hurts με πονά *me pona*

husband ο σύζυγος *o seezeeghos*

hydrofoil το ιπτάμενο δελφίνι *to eeptameno dhelfeenee*

hypodermic needle η υποδερμική βελόνα *ee eepodhermeekee velona*

I

I εγώ egho

ice ο πάγος o paghos

ice cream / ice lolly το παγωτό to
paghoto

iced (drink) παγωμένος
paghomenos

icon η εικόνα ee eekona

if αν an

ignition η ανάφλεξη ee anafleksee

ignition key το κλειδί μίζας to
kleedhee meezas

ill άρρωστος arostos

immediately αμέσως amesos

immunisation ο εμβολιασμός o
emvoleeasmos

important σπουδαίος spoodheos

impossible αδύνατο adheenato

in μέσα mesa
(with countries, towns) σε (στο /
στη / στο) se (sto / stee / sto)

included συμπεριλαμβάνεται
seembereelamvanete

indigestion η δυσπεψία ee
dheespepseea

indoors εσωτερικά esotereeka

infectious μεταδοτικός
metadhoteekos

information οι πληροφορίες ee
pleeroforeeyes

information office το γραφείο
πληροφοριών to ghrafeeo
pleeroforeeon

inhaler η συσκευή εισπνοής ee
seeskevee eespnoees

injection η ένεση ee enesee

injured τραυματισμένος
travmateesmenos

ink το μελάνι to melanee

inner tube η σαμπρέλα ee
sambrela

insect το έντομο to endomo

insect bite το τσίμπημα to
tseembeema

insect repellent το
εντομοαπωθητικό to
endomoapotheeteeko

inside n (interior) το εσωτερικό to
esotereeko
inside the car μέσα στο
αυτοκίνητο mesa sto aftokeeneeto
it's inside είναι μέσα eene mesa

instant coffee στιγμιαίος καφές
steeghmyeos kafes

instructor ο εκπαιδευτής o
ekpedheftees

insulin η ινσουλίνη ee
eensooleenee

insurance η ασφάλεια ee asfaleea

insurance certificate η βεβαίωση
ασφαλίσεως ee veveosee
asfaleeseos

insured ασφαλισμένος
asfaleesmenos

interesting ενδιαφέρων
endheeaferon

international διεθνής dhee-
ethnees

internet το ιντερνέτ to eenternet

interpreter ο / η διερμηνέας o / ee
dhee-ermeeneas

interval (theatre) το διάλειμμα to
dheealeema

into σε (στο / στη / στο) se (sto /
stee / sto)

invitation η πρόσκληση ee
proskleesee

to invite προσκαλώ proskalo

invoice το τιμολόγιο *to teemoloyo*

Ireland η Ιρλανδία *ee eerlandheea*

Irish *(person)* ο Ιρλανδός / η Ιρλανδή *o eerlandhos / ee eerlandhee*

iron *(for clothes)* το σίδερο *to seedhero*
(metal) ο σίδηρος *o seedheeros*

to iron σιδερώνω *seedherono*

ironmonger's το σιδηροπωλείο *to seedheeropoleeo*

is *see* **(to be)** GRAMMAR

island το νησί *to neesee*

it το *to*

Italy η Ιταλία *ee eetaleea*

itch η φαγούρα *ee faghoora*

itemised bill ο αναλυτικός λογαριασμός *o analeeteekos logharyasmos*

J

jack ο γρύλος *o ghreelos*

jacket το μπουφάν *to boofan*

jam η μαρμελάδα *ee marmeladha*

jammed στριμωγμένος *streemoghmenos*

jar το βάζο *to vazo*

jaundice ο ίκτερος *o eekteros*

jeans το τζιν *to jean*

jelly το ζελέ *to zele*

jellyfish η τσούχτρα *ee tsookhtra*

jersey το πουλόβερ *to poolover*

to jetski το jetski *to jetski*

jetty ο μώλος *o molos*

jeweller's το κοσμηματοπωλείο *to kosmeematopoleeo*

jewellery τα κοσμήματα *ta kosmeemata*

job η δουλειά *ee dhoolya*

to jog κάνω τζόκινγκ *kano jogging*

joint το άρθρωση *to arthrosee*

joke το αστείο *to asteeo*

journey το ταξίδι *to takseedhee*

jug η κανάτα *ee kanata*

juice ο χυμός *o kheemos*

jump leads τα καλώδια μπαταρίας *ta kalodheea batareeas*

junction *(crossroads)* η διασταύρωση *ee dheeastavrosee*

just: *just two* μόνο δύο *mono dheeo*
I've just arrived μόλις έφτασα *molees eftasa*

K

to keep κρατώ *krato*

kettle ο βραστήρας *o vrasteeras*

key το κλειδί *to kleedhee*

key-ring το μπρελόκ *to brelok*

kid *(meat)* το κατσικάκι *to katseekakee*

kidneys τα νεφρά *ta nefra*

kilo το κιλό *to keelo*

kilometre το χιλιόμετρο *to kheelyometro*

kind *n (sort)* το είδος *to eedhos*

kind *adj* ευγενικός *efyeneekos*

king ο βασιλιάς *o vaseelyas*

kiosk το περίπτερο *to pereeptero*

to kiss φιλώ *feelo*

kitchen η κουζίνα *ee koozeena*

kitchen paper το χαρτί κουζίνας *to khartee koozeenas*

kitten το γατάκι *to ghatakee*

kiwi fruit το ακτινίδιο *to akteeneedheeo*

knee το γόνατο *to ghonato*

knee highs οι κάλτσες *ee kaltses*

knickers (women's) η κυλότα *ee keelota*

knife το μαχαίρι *to makheree*

to knock down (by car) χτυπώ με αυτοκίνητο *khteepo me aftokeeneeto*

to knock over (vase, glass) ρίχνω κάτω *reekhno kato*

L

label η ετικέτα *ee eteeketa*

lace η δαντέλα *ee dhandela*

laces (of shoe) τα κορδόνια *ta kordhoneea*

ladder η σκάλα *ee skala*

ladies (toilet) Γυναικών *yeenekon*

lady η κυρία *ee keereea*

lager η μπίρα *ee beera*

lake η λίμνη *ee leemnee*

lamb το αρνάκι *to arnakee*

lamp η λάμπα *ee lamba*

to land (plane) προσγειώνω *prosyeeono*

landslide η καθίζηση *ee katheezeesee*

language η γλώσσα *ee ghlosa*

laptop το λάπτοπ *to laptop*

large μεγάλος *meghalos*

last τελευταίος *telefteos*

late (in the day) αργά *argha*
  I am late (for an appointment) έχω αργήσει *ekho aryeesee*

later αργότερα *arghotera*

laundrette το πλυντήριο *to pleendeereeo*

laundry service η υπηρεσία πλυντηρίου *ee eepeereeseea pleendeereeoo*

lavatory η τουαλέτα *ee tooaleta*

lawyer ο / η δικηγόρος *o / ee dheekeeghoros*

laxative το καθαρτικό *to katharteeko*

lay-by η βοηθητική λωρίδα *ee voeetheeteekee loreedha*

lazy τεμπέλης *tembelees*

lead (electric) το καλώδιο *to kalodheeo*

leader (guide) ο / η ξεναγός *o / ee ksenaghos*

leadfree αμόλυβδος *amoleevdhos*

leaf το φύλλο *to feelo*

leak η διαρροή *ee dheearoee*

to learn μαθαίνω *matheno*

least: at least τουλάχιστο *toolakheesto*

leather το δέρμα *to dherma*

leather goods τα δερμάτινα είδη *ta dhermateena eedhee*

to leave (go away) φεύγω *fevgho*

leek το πράσσο *to praso*

left: (on/to the) left αριστερά *areestera*

left-luggage (office) η φύλαξη αποσκευών *ee feelaksee aposkevon*

leg το πόδι *to podhee*

leggings οι περισκελίδες *ee pereeskeleedhes*

lemon το λεμόνι *to lemonee*

lemonade η λεμονάδα *ee lemonadha*

lemon tea το τσάι με λεμόνι *to tsaee me lemonee*

to lend δανείζω *dhaneezo*

length το μήκος *to meekos*

lens ο φακός *o fakos*

lentils οι φακές *ee fakes*

less: *less milk* λιγότερο γάλα *leeghotero ghala*

lesson το μάθημα *to matheema*

to let (allow) επιτρέπω *epeetrepo* (hire out) νοικιάζω *neekyazo*

letter το γράμμα *to ghrama*

letterbox το γραμματοκιβώτιο *to ghramatokeevotyo*

lettuce το μαρούλι *to maroolee*

level crossing η σιδηροδρομική διασταύρωση *ee seedheerodhromeekee dheeastavrosee*

library η βιβλιοθήκη *ee veevleeotheekee*

licence η άδεια *ee adheea*

to lie down ξαπλώνω *ksaplono*

lifeboat η ναυαγοσωστική λέμβος *ee navaghososteekee lemvos*

lifeguard ο ναυαγοσώστης *o navaghosostees*

life insurance η ασφάλεια ζωής *ee asfaleea zoees*

life jacket το σωσίβιο *to soseeveeo*

lift το ασανσέρ *to asanser*

lift pass (skiing) το εισιτήριο *to eeseeteereeo*

light το φως *to fos*

light bulb ο γλόμπος *o ghlobos*

lighter (to light a cigarette) ο αναπτήρας *o anapteeras*

lightning ο κεραυνός *o keravnos*

to like : *I like* μου αρέσει *moo aresee*

lilo το φουσκωτό στρώμα *to fooskoto stroma*

lime (fruit) το γλυκολέμονο *to ghleekolemono*

line η γραμμή *ee ghramee*

lip reading η χειλοανάγνωση *ee kheeloanaghnosee*

lip salve το προστατευτικό στικ *to prostatefteeko stick*

lipstick το κραγιόν *to krayon*

liqueur το λικέρ *to leeker*

to listen ακούω *akoo-o*

litre το λίτρο *to leetro*

litter τα σκουπίδια *ta skoopeedhya*

little μικρός *meekros* *a little* λίγο *leegho*

to live μένω *meno* *he lives in London* μένει στο Λονδίνο *menee sto londheeno*

liver το συκώτι *to seekotee*

living room το καθιστικό *to katheesteeko*

lizard η σαύρα *ee savra*

lobster ο αστακός *o astakos*

local τοπικός *topeekos*

lock η κλειδαριά *ee kleedharya*

to lock κλειδώνω *kleedhono* *I'm locked out* κλειδώθηκα έξω *kleedhotheeka ekso*

locker (luggage) η θήκη *ee theekee*

log book η άδεια κυκλοφορίας *ee adheea keekloforeeas*

lollipop το γλειφιτζούρι *to ghleefeedzooree*

London το Λονδίνο *to londheeno*

long μακρύς *makrees*

to look at κοιτάζω *keetazo*

to look after φροντίζω *frondeezo*

to look for ψάχνω *psakhno*

lorry το φορτηγό *to forteegho*

to lose χάνω *khano*

lost χαμένος *khamenos*
I've lost my wallet έχασα το πορτοφόλι μου *ekhasa to portofolee moo*
I am lost χάθηκα *khatheeka*

lost-property office το γραφείο απωλεσθέντων αντικειμένων *to ghrafeeo apolesthendon andeekeemenon*

lot: *a lot (of)* πολύς *polees*

lotion η λοσιόν *ee losyon*

loud δυνατός *dheenatos*

lounge *(at airport)* η αίθουσα *ee ethoosa*
(in hotel, house) το σαλόνι *to salonee*

to love αγαπώ *aghapo*

low χαμηλός *khameelos*

low-alcohol beer η μπίρα χαμηλή σε αλκοόλ *ee beera khameelee se alko-ol*

low-fat λάιτ *laeet*

luggage οι αποσκευές *ee aposkeves*

luggage allowance το επιτρεπόμενο βάρος αποσκευών *to epeetrepomeno varos aposkevon*

luggage rack ο χώρος αποσκευών *o khoros aposkevon*

luggage tag η ετικέτα *ee eteeketa*

luggage trolley το καροτσάκι αποσκευών *to karotsakee aposkevon*

lump η εξόγκωση *ee eksogosee*

lunch το μεσημεριανό *to meseemereeano*

lung ο πνεύμονας *o pnevmonas*

luxury η πολυτέλεια *ee poleeteleea*

M

machine η μηχανή *ee meekhanee*

mad τρελός *trelos*

magazine το περιοδικό *to pereeodheeko*

magnifying glass ο μεγενθυτικός φακός *o meyentheeteekos fakos*

maiden name το πατρώνυμο *to patroneemo*

main course *(of meal)* το κύριο πιάτο *to keereeo pyato*

mains *(electric)* ο κεντρικός αγωγός *o kendreekos aghoghos*

to make κάνω *kano*

make-up το μακιγιάζ *to makeeyaz*

male αρσενικός *arseneekos*

man *(mankind)* ο άνθρωπος *o anthropos*
(as opposed to woman) ο άντρας *o andras*

manager ο διαχειριστής *o dheeakheereestees*

many πολλοί *polee*
many people πολλοί άνθρωποι *polee anthropee*

map ο χάρτης *o khartees*

marble το μάρμαρο *to marmaro*

margarine η μαργαρίνη *ee marghareenee*

marina η μαρίνα *ee mareena*

market η αγορά *ee aghora*

market day η μέρα της αγοράς *ee mera tees aghoras*

marmalade η μαρμελάδα πορτοκαλιού *ee marmeladha portokalyoo*

marriage certificate το πιστοποιητικό γάμου *to peestopyeeteeko ghamoo*

married παντρεμένος *pandremenos*

mass *(in church)* η Θεία Λειτουργία *ee theea leetooryeea*

match *(game)* ο αγώνας *o aghonas*

matches τα σπίρτα *ta speerta*

material το υλικό *to eeleeko*

matter: *it doesn't matter* δεν πειράζει *dhen peerazee*
what's the matter with you? τι έχεις; *tee ekhees*

mayonnaise η μαγιονέζα *ee mayoneza*

meal το γεύμα *to yevma*

to mean εννοώ *eno-o*

measles η ιλαρά *ee eelara*

meat το κρέας *to kreas*

mechanic ο μηχανικός *o meekhaneekos*

medicine *(drug)* το φάρμακο *to farmako*

Mediterranean η Μεσόγειος *ee mesoyeeos*

medium sweet *(wine)* μέτριο γλυκύ *metreeo ghleekee*
(steak, size) μέτριο *metreeo*

to meet συναντώ *seenando*

meeting η συνάντηση *ee seenandeesee*

melon το πεπόνι *to peponee*
(watermelon) το καρπούζι *to karpoozee*

member *(of club)* το μέλος *to melos*

men οι άντρες *ee andres*

menu ο κατάλογος *o kataloghos* // το μενού *to menoo*

message το μήνυμα *to meeneema*

metal το μέταλλο *to metalo*

meter ο μετρητής *o metreetees*

metre το μέτρο *to metro*

microwave *(oven)* ο φούρνος μικροκυμάτων *o foornos meekrokeematon*

midday το μεσημέρι *to meseemeree*

midnight τα μεσάνυχτα *ta mesaneekhta*

migraine η ημικρανία *ee eemeekraneea*

mile το μίλι *to meelee*

milk το γάλα *to ghala*

milkshake το μιλκσέικ *to meelkseyk*

millimetre το χιλιοστόμετρο *to kheelyostometro*

million το εκατομμύριο *to ekatomeereeo*

mince ο κιμάς *o keemas*

to mind: *do you mind if...?* σας ενοχλεί αν...; *sas enokhlee an...*

mineral water το επιτραπέζιο νερό *to epeetrapezeeo nero* *(sparkling)* το αεριούχο μεταλλικό νερό *to aeryookho metaleeko nero*

minimum ελάχιστος *elakheestos*

minor road ο δευτερεύων δρόμος *o dhefterevon dhromos*

mint *(herb)* ο δυόσμος *o dheeosmos*

minute το λεπτό *to lepto*

mirror ο καθρέφτης *o kathreftees*

to miss *(train, etc.)* χάνω *khano*

Miss η Δεσποινίς *ee dhespeenees*

missing χαμένος *khamenos* *he's missing* λείπει *leepee*

mistake το λάθος *to lathos*

misunderstanding η παρεξήγηση *ee parekseeyeesee*

mobile phone το κινητό (τηλέφωνο) *to keeneeto (teelefono)*

moisturizer η υδατική κρέμα *ee eedhateekee krema*

monastery το μοναστήρι *to monasteeree*

money τα χρήματα *ta khreemata* // τα λεφτά *ta lefta*

money order η ταχυδρομική επιταγή *ee takheedhromeekee epeetayee*

month ο μήνας *o meenas*

monument το μνημείο *to mneemeeo*

moon το φεγγάρι *to fengaree*

more περισσότερο *pereesotero*
more bread κι άλλο ψωμί *kee alo psomee*

morning το πρωί *to proee*

mosaic το μωσαϊκό *to mosaeeko*

mosque το τζαμί *to dzamee*

mosquito το κουνούπι *to koonoopee*

most το περισσότερο *to pereesotero*

moth η πεταλουδίτσα *ee petaloodheetsa*

mother η μητέρα *ee meetera*

mother-in-law η πεθερά *ee pethera*

motor η μηχανή *ee meekhanee*

motorbike η μοτοσικλέτα *ee motoseekleta*

motorboat το ταχύπλοο *to takheeplo-o*

motorway ο αυτοκινητόδρομος *o aftokeeneetodhromos*

mountain το βουνό *to voono*

mouse το ποντίκι *to pondeekee*

mousse το μους *to moos*

moustache το μουστάκι *to moostakee*

mouth το στόμα *to stoma*

to move κινούμαι *keenoome*

Mr Κύριος *keereeos*

Mrs Κυρία *keereea*

much πολύς *polees*
too much πάρα πολύ *para polee*
very much πάρα πολύ *para polee*

mumps οι μαγουλάδες *ee maghooladhes*

muscle ο μυς *o mees*

museum το μουσείο *to mooseeo*

mushroom το μανιτάρι *to maneetaree*

music η μουσική *ee mooseekee*

mussel το μύδι *to meedhee*

must: *I must go* πρέπει να πάω *prepee na pao*
you must go πρέπει να πας *prepee na pas*
he / she must go πρέπει να πάει *prepee na paee*
we must go πρέπει να πάμε *prepee na pame*

mustard η μουστάρδα *ee moostardha*

N

nail *(metal)* το καρφί *to karfee*
(on finger, toe) το νύχι *to neekhee*

nail polish το βερνίκι νυχιών *to verneekee neekhyon*

nail polish remover το ασετόν *to aseton*

nailbrush η βούρτσα των νυχιών *ee voortsa ton neekhyon*

naked γυμνός *yeemnos*

name το όνομα *to onoma*

napkin η πετσέτα *ee petseta*

nappy η πάνα *ee pana*

narrow στενός *stenos*

nationality η υπηκοότητα *ee eepeeko-oteeta*

navy blue μπλε μαρέν *ble maren*

near κοντά *konda*

necessary απαραίτητος *apareeteetos*

neck ο λαιμός *o lemos*

necklace το κολιέ *to kolye*

to need: *I need...* χρειάζομαι... *khreeazome...*

needle η βελόνα *ee velona*
a needle and thread βελόνα και κλωστή *velona ke klostee*

negative *(photography)* το αρνητικό *to arneeteeko*

neighbour ο γείτονας / η γειτόνισσα *o yeetonas / ee yeetoneesa*

nephew ο ανιψιός *o aneepsyos*

never ποτέ *pote*
I never go there δεν πηγαίνω ποτέ εκεί *dhen peeyeno pote ekee*

new καινούριος *kenooryos*

news *(TV, radio)* οι ειδήσεις *ee eedheesees*

newspaper η εφημερίδα *ee efeemereedha*

New Year: *happy New Year!* καλή χρονιά! *kalee khronya*

New Zealand η Νέα Ζηλανδία *ee nea zeelandheea*

next επόμενος *epomenos*

nice *(thing)* ωραίος *oreos*
(person) καλός *kalos*

niece η ανιψιά *ee aneepsya*

night η νύχτα *ee neekhta*

nightclub το νυχτερινό κέντρο *to neekhtereeno kendro*

nightdress το νυχτικό *to neekhteeko*

no όχι *okhee*

nobody κανένας *kanenas*

noise ο θόρυβος *o thoreevos*

non-alcoholic μη οινοπνευματώδης *mee eenopnevmatodhees*

none κανένα *kanena*

non-smoking μη καπνίζοντες *mee kapneezondes*

north ο βορράς *o voras*

Nothern Ireland η Βόρεια Ιρλανδία *ee voreea eerlandheea*

nose η μύτη *ee meetee*

not μη *mee* / δεν *dhen*
I am not δεν είμαι *dhen eeme*
don't stop μη σταματάς *mee stamatas*

note *(banknote)* το χαρτονόμισμα *to khartonomeesma*
(letter) το σημείωμα *to seemeeoma*

note pad το σημειωματάριο *to seemeeomatareeo*

nothing τίποτα *teepota*

now τώρα *tora*

nudist beach η παραλία γυμνιστών *ee paraleea yeemneeston*

number ο αριθμός *o areethmos*

number plate η πινακίδα κυκλοφορίας *ee peenakeedha keekloforeeas*

nurse η νοσοκόμα *ee nosokoma*

nut *(peanut)* το φιστίκι *to feesteekee*
(walnut) το καρύδι *to kareedhee*
(hazelnut) το φουντούκι *to foondookee*
(for bolt) το παξιμάδι *to pakseemadhee*

O

oar το κουπί *to koopee*

occasionally κάπου-κάπου *kapoo-kapoo*

octopus το χταπόδι *to khtapodhee*

odd number ο μονός αριθμός *o monos areethmos*

of: *of course* βέβαια *vevea*

off (light, machine, etc) σβυστός *sveestos*
it's off (rotten) είναι χαλασμένο *eene khalasmeno*

to offer προσφέρω *prosfero*

office το γραφείο *to ghrafeeo*

often συχνά *seekhna*

oil το λάδι *to ladhee*

oil filter το φίλτρο του λαδιού *to feeltro too ladhyoo*

ointment η αλοιφή *ee aleefee*

OK εντάξει *endaksee*

old (person) ηλικιωμένος *eeleekyomenos*
(thing) παλιός *palyos*
how old are you? πόσων χρονών είστε; *poson khronon eeste*

olive oil το ελαιόλαδο *to eleoladho*

olives οι ελιές *ee elyes*

omelette η ομελέτα *ee omeleta*

on πάνω *pano* (light, TV) ανοιχτός *aneekhtos*
on the table (πάνω) στο τραπέζι *(pano) sto trapezee*

once μία φορά *meea fora*

one ένας / μία / ένα *enas* (masculine) / *meea* (feminine) / *ena* (neuter)

one-way (street) ο μονόδρομος *o monodhromos*
(ticket) το απλό εισιτήριο *to aplo eeseeteereeo*

onion το κρεμμύδι *to kremeedhee*

only μόνο *mono*

to open ανοίγω *aneegho*

open adj ανοικτός *aneektos*

operator (telephone) η τηλεφωνήτρια *ee teelefoneetreea*

opposite απέναντι *apenandee*

or ή *ee*

orange (fruit) το πορτοκάλι *to portokalee*
(colour) πορτοκαλί *portokalee*

orange juice ο χυμός πορτοκαλιού *o kheemos portokalyoo*

orchard το περιβόλι *to pereevolee*

to order παραγγέλλω *parangelo*

organize οργανώνω *orghanono*

original αρχικός *arkheekos*

Orthodox (religion) ορθόδοξος *orthodhoksos*

other άλλος *alos*

out (light, etc.) σβησμένος *sveesmenos*
he's out λείπει / *eepee*

outdoors στην ύπαιθρο *steen eepethro*

outside έξω *ekso*

outskirts τα περίχωρα *ta pereekhora*

oven ο φούρνος *o foornos*

over πάνω από *pano apo*
over there εκεί πέρα *ekee pera*

to owe: *you owe me* μου χρωστάς *moo khrostas*

owner ο ιδιοκτήτης *o eedheeokteetees*

oxygen το οξυγόνο *to okseeghono*

oyster το στρείδι *to streedhee*

P

to pack πακετάρω *paketaro*

package το δέμα *to dhema*

package tour η οργανωμένη
εκδρομή *ee orghanomenee
ekdhromee*

packet το πακέτο *to paketo*

paddling pool η λιμνούλα για
παιδιά *ee leemnoola ya pedhya*

padlock το λουκέτο *to looketo*

paid πληρωμένος *pleeromenos*

pain ο πόνος *o ponos*

painful οδυνηρός *odheeneeros*
it's painful πονάει *ponaee*

painkiller το παυσίπονο *to
pafseepono*

painting ο πίνακας *o peenakas*

pair το ζευγάρι *to zevgharee*

palace το παλάτι *to palatee*

pale χλομός *khlomos*

pan η κατσαρόλα *ee katsarola*

pancake η κρέπα *ee krepa*

panties η κυλότα *ee keelota*

pants (men's underpants) το σλιπ *to
sleep*

panties (women's) η κυλότα *ee
keelota*

paper το χαρτί *to khartee*

parcel το δέμα *to dhema*

pardon παρακαλώ *parakalo*
I beg your pardon με συγχωρείτε
me seenkhoreete

parents οι γονείς *o ghonees*

park n το πάρκο *to parko*

to park (in car) παρκάρω *parkaro*

parsley ο μαϊντανός *o maeendanos*

part το μέρος *to meros*

party (group) η ομάδα *ee omadha*
(celebration) το πάρτυ *to party*

passenger ο επιβάτης *o
epeevatees*

passport το διαβατήριο *to
dheeavateereeo*

passport control ο έλεγχος
διαβατηρίων *o elengkhos
dheeavateereeon*

pasta τα ζυμαρικά *ta zeemareeka*

pastry η ζύμη *ee zeemee*
(cake) το γλύκισμα *to
ghleekeesma*

path το μονοπάτι *to monopatee*

pavement το πεζοδρόμιο *to
pezodhromeeo*

to pay πληρώνω *pleerono*

payment η πληρωμή *ee
pleeromee*

peach το ροδάκινο *to rodhakeeno*

peak hour η ώρα αιχμής *ee ora
ekhmees*

peanut το φιστίκι *to feesteekee*

pear το αχλάδι *to akhladhee*

peas ο αρακάς *o arakas*

pebble το πετραδάκι *to
petradhakee*

pedestrian (person) ο πεζός *o
pezos*

pedestrian crossing η
διασταύρωση πεζών *ee
dheeastavrosee pezon*

to peel ξεφλουδίζω *ksefloodheezo*

peg (for tent) ο πάσσαλος *o pasalos*
(for clothes) το μανταλάκι *to
mandalakee*

pen το στύλο *to steelo*

pencil το μολύβι *to moleevee*

penicillin η πενικιλλίνη *ee
peneekeeleenee*

penknife ο σουγιάς *o sooyas*

pensioner ο / η συνταξιούχος *o / ee seendaksyookhos*

pepper *(spice)* το πιπέρι *to peeperee*
(vegetable) η πιπεριά *ee peeperya*

per: *per hour* την ώρα *teen ora*

perfect τέλειος *teleeos*

performance η παράσταση *ee parastasee*

perfume το άρωμα *to aroma*

perhaps ίσως *eesos*

period *(menstruation)* η περίοδος *ee pereeodhos*

perm η περμανάντ *ee permanand*

permit άδεια *adheea*

person το πρόσωπο *to prosopo*

personal stereo το προσωπικό στερεοφωνικό *to prosopeeko stereofoneeko*

pet το κατοικίδιο ζώο *to kateekeedhyo zo-o*

petrol η βενζίνη *ee venzeenee*

petrol station το βενζινάδικο *to venzeenadheeko //* το πρατήριο βενζίνης *to prateereeo venzeenees*

phone *see* **telephone**

phonecard η τηλεκάρτα *ee teelekarta*

photocopy η φωτοτυπία *ee fototeepeea*

photograph η φωτογραφία *ee fotoghrafeea*

phrase book το βιβλιαράκι φράσεων *to veevleearakee fraseon*

picture η εικόνα *ee eekona*

pie η πίτα *ee peeta*

piece το κομμάτι *to komatee*

pier η αποβάθρα *ee apovathra*

pill το χάπι *to khapee*

pillow το μαξιλάρι *to makseelaree*

pillowcase η μαξιλαροθήκη *ee makseelarotheekee*

pin η καρφίτσα *ee karfeetsa*

pine το πεύκο *to pefko*

pineapple ο ανανάς *o ananas*

pink ροζ *roz*

pipe η πίπα *ee peepa*

pistachio nut το φυστίκι Αιγίνης *to feesteekee eyeenees*

plaster *(for broken limb)* ο γύψος *o yeepsos*

plastic πλαστικός *plasteekos*

plate το πιάτο *to pyato*

platform η αποβάθρα *ee apovathra*

to play παίζω *pezo*

playroom το δωμάτιο των παιδιών *to dhomateeo ton pedhyon*

please παρακαλώ *parakalo*

pleased ευχαριστημένος *efkhareesteemenos*

pliers η πένσα *ee pensa*

plug *(electric)* η πρίζα *ee preeza*

plum το δαμάσκηνο *to damaskeeno*

plumber ο υδραυλικός *o eedhravleekos*

poisonous δηλητηριώδης *dheeleeteereeodhees*

police η αστυνομία *ee asteenomeea*

policeman ο αστυνόμος *o asteenomos*

police station το αστυνομικό τμήμα *to asteenomeeko tmeema*

polish *(for shoes)* το βερνίκι *to verneekee*

131

polluted μολυσμένος *moleesmenos*

pollution η ρύπανση *ee reepansee*

pony trekking η ιππασία *ee eepaseea*

pool (for swimming) η πισίνα *ee peeseena*

popular δημοφιλής *dheemofeelees*
(fashionable) κοσμικός *kosmeekos*

pork το χοιρινό *to kheereeno*

port (harbour) το λιμάνι *to leemanee*

porter ο αχθοφόρος *o akhthoforos*

possible δυνατός *dheenatos*

to post (letter) ταχυδρομώ *takheedhromo*

postbox το ταχυδρομικό κουτί *to takheedhromeeko kootee*

postcard η καρτποστάλ *ee kartpostal*

postcode ο κωδικός *o kodheekos*

post office το ταχυδρομείο *to takheedhromeeo*

pot η κατσαρόλα *ee katsarola*

potato η πατάτα *ee patata*

pottery τα κεραμικά *to kerameeka*

pound (money) η λίρα *ee leera*

powdered milk το γάλα σε σκόνη *to ghala se skonee*

pram το καροτσάκι *to karotsakee*

prawn η γαρίδα *ee ghareedha*

to prefer προτιμώ *proteemo*

pregnant έγγυος *engeeos*

to prepare ετοιμάζω *eteemazo*

prescription η συνταγή *ee seendayee*

present (gift) το δώρο *to dhoro*

pretty ωραίος *oreos*

price η τιμή *ee teemee*

price list ο τιμοκατάλογος *o teemokataloghos*

priest ο παπάς *o papas*

private ιδιωτικός *eedheeoteekos*

prize το βραβείο *to vraveeo*

probably πιθανώς *peethanos*

problem το πρόβλημα *to provleema*

programme το πρόγραμμα *to proghrama*

prohibited απαγορευμένος *apaghorevmenos*

to pronounce προφέρω *profero*
how do you pronounce this? πώς το προφέρετε; *pos to proferete*

Protestant διαμαρτυρόμενος *dheeamarteeromenos*

prune το δαμάσκηνο ξερό *to dhamaskeeno ksero*

public δημόσιος *dheemoseeos*

public holiday η γιορτή *ee yortee*

to pull τραβώ *travo*

pullover το πουλόβερ *to poolover*

puncture το τρύπημα *to treepeema*

purple πορφυρός *porfeeros*

purse το πορτοφόλι *to portofolee*

to push σπρώχνω *sprokhno*

push chair το καροτσάκι (μωρού) *to karotsakee (moroo)*

to put βάζω *vazo*
to put down βάζω κάτω *vazo kato*

pyjamas οι πιζάμες *ee peezames*

Q

quality η ποιότητα *ee peeoteeta*

quay η προκυμαία *ee prokeemea*

queen η βασίλισσα *ee vaseeleesa*

question η ερώτηση *ee eroteesee*

queue η ουρά *ee oora*

quick γρήγορος *ghreeghoros*

quickly γρήγορα *ghreeghora*

quiet ήσυχος *eeseekhos*

quilt (duvet) το πάπλωμα *to paploma*

R

rabbit το κουνέλι *to koonelee*

rabies η λύσσα *ee leesa*

racket η ρακέτα *ee raketa*

radiator (car) το ψυγείο *to pseeyeeo*

radio το ραδιόφωνο *to radheeofono*

radish το ραπανάκι *to rapanakee*

railway station ο σιδηροδρομικός σταθμός *o seedheerodhromeekos stathmos*

rain η βροχή *ee vrokhee*

raincoat το αδιάβροχο *to adheeavrokho*

raining: *it's raining* βρέχει *vrekhee*

raisin η σταφίδα *ee stafeedha*

rare σπάνιος *spanyos* *(steak)* μισοψημένος *meesopseemenos*

rash (skin) το εξάνθημα *to eksantheema*

raspberries τα βατόμουρα *ta vatomoora*

rat ο αρουραίος *o arooreos*

rate ο ρυθμός *o reethmos* *rate of exchange* η ισοτιμία *ee eesoteemeea*

raw ωμός *omos*

razor το ξυράφι *to kseerafee*

razor blade το ξυραφάκι *to kseerafakee*

to read διαβάζω *dheeavazo*

ready έτοιμος *eteemos*

real πραγματικός *praghmateekos*

reason ο λόγος *o loghos*

receipt η απόδειξη *ee apodheeksee*

recently τελευταία *teleftea*

reception (desk) η ρεσεψιόν *ee resepsyon*

recipe η συνταγή *ee seendayee*

to recommend συνιστώ *seeneesto*

record (music, etc.) ο δίσκος *o dheeskos*

red κόκκινος *kokeenos*

reduction η έκπτωση *ee ekptosee*

refill το ανταλλακτικό *to andalakteeko*

refund η επιστροφή χρημάτων *ee epeestrofee khreematon*

registered (letter) συστημένο *seesteemeno*

regulations οι κανονισμοί *ee kanoneesmee*

to reimburse αποζημιώνω *apozeemeeono*

relations (family) οι συγγενείς *ee seengenees*

to relax ξεκουράζομαι *ksekoorazome*

reliable (person) αξιόπιστος *akseeopeestos* *(car, method)* δοκιμασμένος *dhokeemasmenos*

to remain απομένω *apomeno*

to remember θυμάμαι *theemame*

to rent νοικιάζω *neekyazo*

rental το νοίκι *to neekee*

to repair επιδιορθώνω
epeedheeorthono

to repeat επαναλαμβάνω
epanalamvano

reservation η κράτηση ee
krateesee

to reserve κρατώ krato

reserved κρατημένος krateemenos

rest ξεκούραση ksekoorasee
the rest οι υπόλοιποι ee
eepoleepee

to rest ξεκουράζομαι
ksekoorazome

restaurant το εστιατόριο to
esteeatoreeo

restaurant car το βαγόνι
ρεστωράν to vaghonee restoran

to retire βγαίνω στη σύνταξη
vyeno stee seendaksee

retired συνταξιούχος
seendaksyookhos

to return (go back, give back)
επιστρέφω epeestrefo

return ticket το εισιτήριο με
επιστροφή to eeseeteereeo me
epeestrofee

reverse-charge call κλήση
πληρωτέα από τον παραλήπτη
kleesee pleerotea apo ton
paraleeptee

rheumatism οι ρευματισμοί ee
revmateesmee

rice το ρύζι to reezee

rich (person, food) πλούσιος
plooseeos

riding (equestrian) η ιππασία ee
eepaseea

right (correct, accurate) σωστός
sostos
(on/to the) right δεξιά dheksya

ring το δαχτυλίδι to
dhakhteeleedhee

ripe ώριμος oreemos

river το ποτάμι to potamee

road ο δρόμος o dhromos

road map ο οδικός χάρτης o
odheekos khartees

roast το ψητό to pseeto

to rob ληστεύω leestevo

roll (of bread) το ψωμάκι to
psomakee

roof η στέγη ee steyee

roof rack η σχάρα ee skhara

room (in house, etc.) το δωμάτιο to
dhomateeo
(space) ο χώρος o khoros

room service η υπηρεσία
δωματίου ee eepereseea
dhomateeoo

rope το σχοινί to skheenee

rosé ροζέ roze

rotten (fruit) χαλασμένος
khalasmenos

rough (sea) τρικυμισμένη
treekeemeesmenee

round (shape) στρογγυλός
strongeelos
round Greece γύρω στην Ελλάδα
yeero steen eladha

route ο δρόμος o dhromos

to row (boat) κάνω κουπί kano
koopee

rowing boat η βάρκα με κουπιά
ee varka me koopya

royal βασιλικός vaseeleekos

rubber (substance) το καουτσούκ
to ka-ootsook
(eraser) η γόμα ee goma

rubber band το λαστιχάκι to
lasteekhakee

rubbish τα σκουπίδια ta skoopeedhya

rucksack ο σάκκος o sakos

ruins τα ερείπια ta ereepya

rum το ρούμι to roomee

to run τρέχω trekho

rush hour η ώρα αιχμής ee ora ekhmees

rusty σκουριασμένος skooryasmenos

S

sad λυπημένος leepeemenos

safe adj (harmless) αβλαβής avlavees
(not dangerous) ακίνδυνος akeendheenos
(secure, sure) ασφαλής asfalees

safe n το χρηματοκιβώτιο to khreematokeevotyo

safety pin η παραμάνα ee paramana

sailing η ιστιοπλοΐα ee eesteeoploeea

salad η σαλάτα ee salata

salad dressing το λαδολέμονο to ladholemono

sale (in shop) το ξεπούλημα to ksepooleema

salmon ο σολομός o solomos

salt το αλάτι to alatee

same ίδιος eedheeos

sand η άμμος ee amos

sandals τα πέδιλα ta pedheela

sandwich το σάντουϊτς to sandwich

sanitary towel η σερβιέτα ee servyeta

sardine η σαρδέλα ee sardhela

sauce η σάλτσα ee saltsa

saucepan η κατσαρόλα ee katsarola

saucer το πιατάκι to pyatakee

sausage το λουκάνικο to lookaneeko

savoury πικάντικος peekandeekos

to say λέω leo

scarf (long) το κασκόλ to kaskol
(square) το μαντήλι to mandeelee

school το σχολείο to skholeeo
(for 12- to 15-year-olds) το γυμνάσιο to yeemnaseeo
(for 15- to 18-year-olds) το λύκειο to leekeeo

scissors το ψαλίδι to psaleedhee

Scotland η Σκωτία ee skoteea

Scottish (person) ο Σκωτσέζος / η Σκωτσέζα o skotsezos / ee skotseza

screw η βίδα ee veedha

screwdriver το κατσαβίδι to katsaveedhee

sculpture το γλυπτό to ghleepto

sea η θάλασσα ee thalasa

seafood τα θαλασσινά ta thalaseena

seasickness η ναυτία ee nafteea

seaside (beach, seafront) η παραλία ee paraleea

seat (in theatre) η θέση ee thesee
(in car, etc.) το κάθισμα to katheesma

second δεύτερος dhefteros

second class (ticket, etc.) δεύτερη θέση dhefteree thesee

second-hand μεταχειρισμένος metakheereesmenos

to see βλέπω vlepo

self-service το σελφ σέρβις to self service

to sell πουλώ poolo

Sellotape ® το σελοτέιπ to seloteyp

send στέλνω stelno

separate χωριστός khoreestos

serious σοβαρός sovaros

to serve σερβίρω serveero

service (in restaurant, etc.) η εξυπηρέτηση ee ekseepeereteesee

service charge το ποσοστό υπηρεσίας to pososto eepeereseeas

set menu το καθορισμένο μενού to kathoreesmeno menoo

several διάφοροι dheeaforee

to sew ράβω ravo

shade η σκιά ee skeea

shallow ρηχός reekhos

shampoo το σαμπουάν to sambooan

shampoo and set λούσιμο και στέγνωμα looseemo ke steghnoma

to share μοιράζω meerazo

to shave ξυρίζομαι kseereezome

shaving cream η κρέμα ξυρίσματος ee krema kseereesmatos

she αυτή aftee

sheep το πρόβατο to provato

sheet το σεντόνι to sendonee

shellfish τα όστρακα ta ostraka

ship το πλοίο to pleeo

shirt το πουκάμισο to pookameeso

shock absorber το αμορτισέρ to amorteeser

shoe το παπούτσι to papootsee

to shop ψωνίζω psoneezo

shop το μαγαζί to maghazee

shop assistant (woman) η πωλήτρια ee poleetreea (man) ο πωλητής o poleetees

short κοντός kondos

short cut ο συντομότερος δρόμος o seendomoteros dhromos

shorts το σορτς to shorts

show n (in theatre, etc.) η παράσταση ee parastasee

to show δείχνω dheekhno

shower (in bath) το ντους to doos (rain) η μπόρα ee bora

shrimp η γαρίδα ee ghareedha

shut (closed) κλειστός kleestos

to shut κλείνω kleeno

shutters τα παντζούρια ta pantzooreea

sick (ill) άρρωστος arostos to be sick (vomit) κάνω εμετό kano emeto

sightseeing: to go sightseeing επισκέπτομαι τα αξιοθέατα epeeskeptome ta akseeotheata

sign (roadsign, notice, etc.) η πινακίδα ee peenakeedha

signature η υπογραφή ee eepoghrafee

silk το μετάξι to metaksee

silver ασημένιος aseemeneeos

similar παρόμοιος paromeeos

simple απλός aplos

to sing τραγουδώ traghoodho

single (not married) ελεύθερος eleftheros (not double) μονός monos

single bed το μονό κρεββάτι to mono krevatee

single room το μονόκλινο δωμάτιο to monokleeno dhomateeo

sink ο νεροχύτης o nerokheetees

sister η αδελφή ee adhelfee

to sit (down) κάθομαι kathome

size (of clothes, shoes) το νούμερο to noomero

ski το σκι to skee

to ski κάνω σκι kano skee

ski jacket το μπουφάν του σκι to boofan too skee

ski pants το παντελόνι του σκι to pandelonee too skee

ski pole το ραβδί του σκι to ravdhee too skee

ski run η διαδρομή του σκι ee dheeadhromee too skee

ski suit τα ρούχα του σκι ta rookha too skee

skimmed milk το αποβουτυρωμένο γάλα to apovooteeromeno ghala

skin το δέρμα to dherma

skin diving το υποβρύχιο κολύμπι to eepovreekheeo koleembee

skirt η φούστα ee foosta

sky ο ουρανός o ooranos

to sleep κοιμούμαι keemoome

sleeper το βαγκόν-λι to vagon-lee

sleeping bag το υπνόσακος o eepnosakos

sleeping pill το υπνωτικό χάπι to eepnoteeko khapee

slice η φέτα ee feta

slide (photography) το σλάιντ to slide

slippery γλιστερός ghleesteros

slow σιγά seegha

small μικρός meekros

smaller (than) μικρότερος (από) meekroteros (apo)

smell η μυρωδιά ee meerodhya

smile το χαμόγελο to khamoyelo

to smile χαμογελώ khamoyelo

smoke ο καπνός o kapnos

to smoke καπνίζω kapneezo

smoked καπνιστός kapneestos

snack bar το σνακ μπαρ to snack bar

snake το φίδι to feedhee

snorkel ο αναπνευστήρας o anapnevsteeras

snow το χιόνι to khyonee

snowed up αποκλεισμένος από το χιόνι apokleesmenos apo to khyonee

snowing: it's snowing χιονίζει khyoneezee

so (that's why) γι' αυτό yee afto
so much τόσο πολύ toso polee
so pretty τόσο ωραίος toso oreos
so that (in order to) για να ya na

soap το σαπούνι to sapoonee

soap powder το απορρυπαντικό to aporeepandeeko

sober ξεμέθυστος ksemetheestos

sock η κάλτσα ee kaltsa

socket (electrical) η πρίζα ee preeza

soda (water) η σόδα ee sodha

soft μαλακός malakos

soft drink το αναψυκτικό to anapseekteeko

some μερικοί mereekee

someone κάποιος kapyos

something κάτι katee

sometimes κάποτε kapote

son ο γιος o yos

song το τραγούδι to traghoodhee

soon σύντομα seendoma
as soon as possible το συντομότερο to seendomotero
sooner νωρίτερα noreetera

sore: it's sore πονάει ponaee

sorry: I'm sorry (apology) συγγνώμη seeghnomee
(regret) λυπούμαι leepoome

sort το είδος to eedhos

soup η σούπα ee soopa

south ο νότος o notos

souvenir το σουβενίρ to sooveneer

space (room) ο χώρος o khoros

spanner το κλειδί to kleedhee

spare wheel η ρεζέρβα ee rezerva

spark plug το μπουζί to boozee

sparkling (wine) αφρώδης afrodhees

to speak μιλώ meelo

special ειδικός eedheekos

speciality (in restaurant) η σπεσιαλιτέ ee spesyaleete

speed η ταχύτητα ee takheeteeta

speed limit το όριο ταχύτητας to oreeo takheeteetas

spell (to write) γράφω ghrafo
how do you spell it? πώς γράφεται; pos ghrafete

spicy πικάντικος peekandeekos

spinach το σπανάκι to spanakee

spirits τα οινοπνευματώδη ποτά ta eenopnevmatodhee pota

sponge το σφουγγάρι to sfoongaree

spoon το κουτάλι to kootalee

sport το σπορ to spor

spring (season) η άνοιξη ee aneeksee

square (in town) η πλατεία ee plateea

squash (sport) το σκουός to skoo-os
orange squash η πορτοκαλάδα ee portokaladha
lemon squash η λεμονάδα ee lemonadha

squid το καλαμάρι to kalamaree

stadium το στάδιο to stadheeo

stairs η σκάλα ee skala

stalls (in theatre) η πλατεία ee plateea

stamp το γραμματόσημο to ghramatoseemo

star (in sky) το άστρο to astro

to start αρχίζω arkheezo

starter (in meal) το ορεκτικό to orekteeko

station ο σταθμός o stathmos

stationer's το χαρτοπωλείο to khartopoleeo

to stay μένω meno

steak η μπριζόλα ee breezola

steep ανηφορικός aneeforeekos

sterling η αγγλική λίρα ee angleekee leera

steward (on a ship) ο καμαρότος o kamarotos
(on plane) ο αεροσυνοδός o aeroseenodhos

stewardess (on plane) η αεροσυνοδός ee aeroseenodhos

sticking plaster ο λευκοπλάστης o lefkoplastees

still (yet) ακόμα akoma
(immobile) ακίνητος akeeneetos
(water) μη αεριούχο mee aeryookho

sting το τσίμπημα to tseembeema

stomach το στομάχι *to stomakhee*

stomach upset η στομαχική διαταραχή *ee stomakheekee dheeatarakhee*

to stop σταματώ *stamato*

storm *(thunder)* η καταιγίδα *ee kateyeedha*

straight: straight on ευθεία *eftheea*

straw *(for drinking)* το καλαμάκι *to kalamakee*

strawberry η φράουλα *ee fraoola*

street ο δρόμος *o dhromos*

street plan ο οδικός χάρτης *o odheekos khartees*

string ο σπάγγος *o spangos*

striped ριγωτός *reeghotos*

strong δυνατός *dheenatos*

stuck *(jammed)* κολλημένος *koleemenos*

student ο φοιτητής / η φοιτήτρια *o feeteetees / ee feeteetreea*

stung: I've been stung by something κάτι με τσίμπησε *katee me tseembeese*

stupid ανόητος *anoeetos*

suddenly ξαφνικά *ksafneeka*

suede το καστόρι *to kastoree*

sugar η ζάχαρη *ee zakharee*

suit *(man's)* το κοστούμι *to kostoomee*
(woman's) το ταγιέρ *to ta-yer*

suitcase η βαλίτσα *ee valeetsa*

summer το καλοκαίρι *to kalokeree*

sun ο ήλιος *o eeleeos*

to sunbathe κάνω ηλιοθεραπεία *kano eeleeotherapeea*

sun block το αντιηλιακό *to andee-eelyako*

sunburn *(painful)* το κάψιμο από τον ήλιο *to kapseemo apo ton eeleeo*

sunglasses τα γυαλιά του ήλιου *ta yalya too eeleeoo*

sunny *(weather)* ηλιόλουστος *eelyoloostos*

sunrise η ανατολή *ee anatolee*

sunset το ηλιοβασίλεμα *to eeleeovaseelema*

sunshade η ομπρέλα *ee ombrela*

sunstroke η ηλίαση *ee eeleeasee*

suntan lotion το λάδι για τον ήλιο *to ladhee ya ton eeleeo*

supermarket το σούπερμάρκετ *to supermarket*

supper το δείπνο *to dheepno*

supplement το συμπλήρωμα *to seembleeroma*

surcharge η επιβάρυνση *ee epeevareensee*

surfboard η σανίδα σέρφινγκ *ee saneedha surfing*

surfing το σέρφινγκ *to surfing*

surname το επώνυμο *to eponeemo*

surrounded by τριγυρισμένος από *treeyeereesmenos apo*

suspension η ανάρτηση *ee anarteesee*

to sweat ιδρώνω *eedhrono*

sweater το πουλόβερ *to poolover*

sweet *adj (taste)* γλυκός *ghleekos*

sweet *n* το γλυκό *to ghleeko*

sweets οι καραμέλες *ee karameles*

sweetener η ζαχαρίνη *ee zakhareenee*

to swim κολυμπώ *koleembo*

swimming pool η πισίνα *ee peeseena*

swimsuit το μαγιό *to ma-yo*

swing *(for children)* η κούνια *ee koonya*

switch ο διακόπτης *o dheeakoptees*

to switch on ανάβω *anavo*

to switch off σβήνω *sveeno*

swollen *(ankle, etc.)* πρησμένος *preesmenos*

synagogue η συναγωγή *ee seenayoyee*

T

table το τραπέζι *to trapezee*

tablecloth το τραπεζομάντηλο *to trapezomandeelo*

tablespoon το κουτάλι *to kootalee*

tablet το χάπι *to khapee*

table tennis το πινγκ πονγκ *to ping pong*

to take παίρνω *perno*

to take out βγάζω *vghazo* *(from bank account)* αποσύρω *aposeero*

to talk μιλώ *meelo*

tall ψηλός *pseelos*

tame *(animal)* ήμερος *eemeros*

tampons τα ταμπόν *ta tambon*

tap η βρύση *ee vreesee*

tape recorder το μαγνητόφωνο *to maghneetofono* *(cassette player)* το κασετόφωνο *to kasetofono*

to taste δοκιμάζω *dhokeemazo*

taste *n* η γεύση *ee yefsee*

tax ο φόρος *o foros*

taxi το ταξί *to taksee*

taxi rank η πιάτσα για ταξί *ee pyatsa ya taksee*

tea το τσάι *to tsaee*

tea bag το φακελλάκι τσαγιού *to fakelakee tsa-yoo*

to teach διδάσκω *dheedhasko*

teacher ο δάσκαλος / η δασκάλα *o dhaskalos / ee dhaskala*

teapot η τσαγιέρα *ee tsa-yera*

tear *(in eye)* το δάκρυ *to dhakree* *(in material)* το σχίσιμο *to skheeseemo*

teaspoon το κουταλάκι *to kootalakee*

teat η ρώγα *ee rogha*

teeth τα δόντια *ta dhondeea*

telegram το τηλεγράφημα *to teeleghrafeema*

telephone το τηλέφωνο *to teelefono*

telephone box ο τηλεφωνικός θάλαμος *o teelefoneekos thalamos*

telephone call το τηλεφώνημα *to teelefoneema*

telephone directory ο τηλεφωνικός κατάλογος *o teelefoneekos kataloghos*

television η τηλεόραση *ee teeleorasee*

telex το τέλεξ *to telex*

to tell λέγω *legho* *(story)* διηγούμαι *dhee-eeghoome*

temperature η θερμοκρασία *ee thermokraseea*
to have a temperature έχω πυρετό *ekho peereto*

temple ο ναός *o naos*

temporary προσωρινός
prosoreenos

tennis το τένις to tenees

tennis ball η μπάλα του τένις ee bala too tennis

tennis court το γήπεδο του τένις to yeepedho too tenees

tennis racket η ρακέτα του τένις ee raketa too tenees

tent η σκηνή ee skeenee

tent peg ο πάσσαλος της σκηνής o pasalos tees skeenees

terminus το τέρμα to terma

terrace η ταράτσα ee taratsa

thank you ευχαριστώ efkhareesto

that εκείνος ekeenos
that book εκείνο το βιβλίο ekeeno to veevleeo
that one εκείνο ekeeno

theatre το θέατρο to theatro

then τότε tote

there εκεί ekee
there is υπάρχει eeparkhee
there are υπάρχουν eeparkhoon

thermometer το θερμόμετρο to thermometro

these αυτοί / αυτές / αυτά aftee (masculine) / aftes (feminine) / afta (neuter)
these books αυτά τα βιβλία afta ta veevleea

they αυτοί aftee see GRAMMAR

thick χοντρός khontros

thief ο κλέφτης o kleftees

thin λεπτός leptos

thing το πράγμα to praghma

third τρίτος treetos

thirsty: I'm thirsty διψάω dheepsao

this αυτός / αυτή / αυτό aftos (masculine) / aftee (feminine) / afto (neuter)
this book αυτό το βιβλίο afto to veevleeo
this one αυτό afto

those εκείνοι ekeenee
those books εκείνα τα βιβλία ekeena ta veevleea

thread η κλωστή ee klostee

throat ο λαιμός o lemos

throat lozenges οι παστίλιες για το λαιμό ee pasteelyes ya to lemo

through διαμέσου dheeamesoo

thunder ο κεραυνός o keravnos

thunderstorm η θύελλα ee theeela

ticket το εισιτήριο to eeseeteereeo

ticket collector ο ελεγκτής o elengtees

ticket office η θυρίδα ee theereedha

tie η γραβάτα ee ghravata

tight σφιχτός sfeekhtos

tights το καλσόν to kalson

till (cash) το ταμείο to tameeo

till (until) μέχρι mekhree

time (by the clock) η ώρα ee ora
what time is it? τι ώρα είναι; tee ora eene

timetable (buses, trains, etc) το δρομολόγιο to dromoloyeeo
(school, shop opening hours etc) το ωράριο to orareeo

tin η κονσέρβα ee konserva

tinfoil το αλουμινόχαρτο to aloomeenokharto

tin-opener το ανοιχτήρι για κονσέρβες to aneekhteeree ya konserves

tip (to waiter, etc.) το πουρμπουάρ to poorbooar

tipped (cigarettes) με φίλτρο me feeltro

tired κουρασμένος koorasmenos

tissue το χαρτομάντηλο to khartomandeelo

to σε se
  to the στο / στη / στο
  sto (masculine)
  stee (feminine)
  sto (neuter)
  to Greece στην Ελλάδα steen eladha

toast η φρυγανιά ee freeghanya

tobacco ο καπνός o kapnos

tobacconists το καπνοπωλείο to kapnopoleeo

today σήμερα seemera

together μαζί mazee

toilet η τουαλέτα ee tooaleta

toilet paper το χαρτί υγείας to khartee eeyeeas

toll τα διόδια ta dheeodheea

tomato η ντομάτα ee domata

tomato juice ο χυμός ντομάτας o kheemos domatas

tomorrow αύριο avreeo

tongue η γλώσσα ee ghlosa

tonic water το τόνικ to toneek

tonight απόψε apopse

too (also) επίσης epeesees
  (too much) πάρα πολύ para polee

tooth το δόντι to dhondee

toothache ο πονόδοντος o ponodhondos

toothbrush η οδοντόβουρτσα ee odhontovoortsa

toothpaste η οδοντόκρεμα ee odhondokrema

top το πάνω μέρος to pano meros (of mountain) η κορυφή ee koreefee

torch ο φακός o fakos

torn σχισμένος skheesmenos

total το σύνολο to seenolo

tough (of meat) σκληρός skleeros

tour η εκδρομή ee ekdhromee

tourist ο τουρίστας / η τουρίστρια o tooreestas / ee tooreestreea

tourist office το τουριστικό γραφείο to tooreesteeko ghrafeeo

tourist ticket το τουριστικό εισιτήριο to tooreesteeko eeseeteereeo

to tow ρυμουλκώ reemoolko

towel η πετσέτα ee petseta

tower ο πύργος o peerghos

town η πόλη ee polee

town centre το κέντρο της πόλης to kendro tees polees

town hall το δημαρχείο to dheemarkheeo

town plan ο χάρτης της πόλης o khartees tees polees

towrope το σχοινί ρυμούλκησης to skheenee reemoolkeesees

toy το παιχνίδι to pekhneedhee

traditional παραδοσιακός paradhosyakos

traffic η κυκλοφορία ee keekloforeea

traffic lights τα φανάρια (της τροχαίας) ta fanareea (tees trokheas)

trailer το τρέιλερ to trailer

train το τρένο to treno

training shoes τα αθλητικά παπούτσια ta athleeteeka papootsya

tram το τραμ *to tram*

to translate μεταφράζω *metafrazo*

translation η μετάφραση *ee metafrasee*

to travel ταξιδεύω *takseedhevo*

travel agent ο ταξιδιωτικός πράκτορας *o takseedhyoteekos praktoras*

travellers' cheques τα ταξιδιωτικά τσεκ *ta takseedhyoteeka tsek*

tray ο δίσκος *o dheeskos*

tree το δέντρο *to dhendro*

trim *n (hair)* το κόψιμο *to kopseemo*

trip η εκδρομή *ee ekdhromee*

trolley bus το τρόλεϊ *to troley*

trouble ο μπελάς *o belas*

trousers το παντελόνι *to pandelonee*

trout η πέστροφα *ee pestrofa*

true αληθινός *aleetheenos*

trunk το μπαούλο *to baoolo*

trunks το μαγιό *to ma-yo*

to try προσπαθώ *prospatho*

to try on δοκιμάζω *dhokeemazo*

T-shirt το μπλουζάκι *to bloozakee*

tuna ο τόνος *o tonos*

tunnel η σήραγγα *ee seeranga*

turkey η γαλοπούλα *ee ghalopoola*

to turn στρίβω *streevo*

turnip η ρέβα *ee reva*

to turn off *(on a journey)* στρίβω *streevo*
(radio, etc.) κλείνω *kleeno*
(engine, light) σβήνω *sveeno*

to turn on *(radio, TV)* ανοίγω *aneegho*
(engine, light) ανάβω *anavo*

TV η τηλεόραση *ee teeleorasee*

tweezers το τσιμπίδι *to tseembeedhee*

twice δύο φορές *dheeo fores*

twin ο δίδυμος *o dheedheemos*

twin-bedded το δίκλινο δωμάτιο *to dheekleeno dhomateeo*

to type δακτυλογραφώ *dhakteeloghrafo*

typical τυπικός *teepeekos*

tyre το λάστιχο *to lasteekho*

tyre pressure η πίεση στα λάστιχα *ee peeyesee sta lasteekha*

U

ugly άσχημος *askheemos*

umbrella η ομπρέλα *ee ombrela*

uncle ο θείος *o theeos*

uncomfortable άβολος *avolos*

unconscious αναίσθητος *anestheetos*

under κάτω από *kato apo*

underground *(railway)* το μετρό *to metro*

underpants see pants

underpass η υπόγεια διάβαση *ee eepoyeea dheeavasee*

to understand καταλαβαίνω *katalaveno*

underwear τα εσώρουχα *ta esorookha*

unemployed άνεργος *anerghos*

unfasten λύνω *leeno*

United States οι Ηνωμένες Πολιτείες *ee eenomenes poleeteeyees*

university το πανεπιστήμιο *to panepeesteemeeo*

unleaded petrol η αμόλυβδη βενζίνη *ee amoleevdhee venzeenee*

to unpack *(case)* αδειάζω *adheeazo*

up *(out of bed)* ξύπνιος *kseepneeos*
to go up ανεβαίνω *aneveno*

upstairs πάνω *pano*

urgently επειγόντως *epeeghondos*

urine τα ούρα *ta oora*

urn ο αμφορέας *o amforeas*

to use χρησιμοποιώ *khreeseemopyo*

useful χρήσιμος *khreeseemos*

usual συνηθισμένος *seeneetheesmenos*

usually συνήθως *seeneethos*

V

vacancy *(room)* το διαθέσιμο δωμάτιο *to dheeatheseemo dhomateeo*

vacuum cleaner η ηλεκτρική σκούπα *ee eelektreekee skoopa*

valid έγκυρος *engkeeros*

valley η κοιλάδα *ee keeladha*

valuable πολύτιμος *poleeteemos*

valuables τα πολύτιμα αντικείμενα *ta poleeteema andeekeemena*

value η αξία *ee akseea*

van το φορτηγάκι *to forteeghakee*

vase το βάζο *to vazo*

VAT ο ΦΠΑ *o fee pee a*

veal το μοσχάρι *to moskharee*

vegetables τα λαχανικά *ta lakhaneeka*

vegetarian ο χορτοφάγος *o khortofaghos*

vein η φλέβα *ee fleva*

velvet το βελούδο *to veloodho*

ventilator ο εξαεριστήρας *o eksaereesteeras*

very πολύ *polee*

vest η φανέλα *ee fanela*

via μέσω *meso*

video το βίντεο *to veedeo*

video camera η βιντεοκάμερα *ee veedeokamera*

video recorder το βίντεο *to veedeeo*

view η θέα *ee thea*

villa η βίλλα *ee veela*

village το χωριό *to khoryo*

vine leaves τα κληματόφυλλα *ta kleematofeela*

vinegar το ξύδι *to kseedhee*

visa η βίζα *ee veesa*

to visit επισκέπτομαι *epeeskeptome*

visit επίσκεψη *ee epeeskepsee*

vitamin η βιταμίνη *ee veetameenee*

vodka η βότκα *ee votka*

voice η φωνή *ee fonee*

volleyball το βόλεϊ *to volay*

voltage η τάση *ee tasee*

W

wage ο μισθός *o meesthos*

waist η μέση *ee mesee*

to wait for περιμένω *pereemeno*

waiter το γκαρσόνι *to garsonee*

waiting room η αίθουσα αναμονής *ee ethoosa anamonees*

waitress η σερβιτόρα *ee serveetora*

Wales η Ουαλία *ee ooaleea*

walk ο περίπατος *o pereepatos*

to walk περπατώ *perpato*

walking stick το μπαστούνι *to bastoonee*

wall ο τοίχος *o teekhos*

wallet το πορτοφόλι *to portofolee*

walnut το καρύδι *to kareedhee*

to want θέλω *thelo*

war ο πόλεμος *o polemos*

wardrobe η γκαρνταρόμπα *ee gardaroba*

warm ζεστός *zestos*

warning triangle το τρίγωνο αυτοκινήτου *to treeghono aftokeeneetoo*

to wash (clothes) πλένω *pleno* (oneself) πλένομαι *plenome*

washbasin ο νιπτήρας *o neepteeras*

washing machine το πλυντήριο *to pleendeereeo*

washing powder το απορρυπαντικό *to aporeepandeeko*

washing-up liquid το υγρό για τα πιάτα *to eeghro ya ta pyata*

wasp η σφήκα *ee sfeeka*

waste bin το καλάθι των αχρήστων *to kalathee ton akhreeston*

watch n το ρολόι *to roloee*

to watch (TV) βλέπω *vlepo* (someone's luggage) προσέχω *prosekho*

watchstrap το λουρί του ρολογιού *to looree too roloyoo*

water το νερό *to nero*
   fresh water το γλυκό νερό *to ghleeko nero*

salt water το αλμυρό νερό *to almeero nero*

waterfall ο καταρράκτης *o kataraktees*

water heater ο θερμοσίφωνας *o thermoseefonas*

water-skiing το θαλάσσιο σκι *to thalaseeo skee*

watermelon το καρπούζι *to karpoozee*

waterproof αδιάβροχος *adheeavrokhos*

wave (on sea) το κύμα *to keema*

wax το κερί *to keree*

way (method) ο τρόπος *o tropos*
   this way από 'δω *apodho*
   that way από 'κει *apokee*

we εμείς *emees*

weak αδύνατος *adheenatos*

to wear φορώ *foro*

weather ο καιρός *o keros*

wedding ο γάμος *o ghamos*

week η εβδομάδα *ee evdhomadha*

weekday η καθημερινή *ee katheemereenee*

weekend το σαββατοκύριακο *to savatokeereeako*

weekly (rate, etc.) εβδομαδιαίος *evdhomadhyeos*

weight το βάρος *to varos*

welcome καλώς ήλθατε *kalos eelthate*

well (healthy) υγιής *eeyee-ees*

well done (steak) καλοψημένος *kalopseemenos*

Welsh (person) ο Ουαλός / η Ουαλή *o ooalos / ee ooalee*

west η δύση *ee dheesee*

wet (damp) βρεγμένος vreghmenos
 (weather) βροχερός vrokheros

wetsuit η στολή για υποβρύχιο
 ψάρεμα ee stolee ya
 eepovreekheeo psarema

what τι tee
 what is it? τι είναι; tee eene

wheel ο τροχός o trokhos

wheelchair η αναπηρική καρέκλα
 ee anapeereekee karekla

when? πότε; pote

where? πού; poo

which? ποιος; pyos (masculine)
 ποια; pya (feminine)
 ποιο; pyo (neuter)
 which is it? ποιο είναι; pyo eene

while ενώ eno

whipped cream η σαντιγύ ee
 sandeeyee

whisky το ουίσκυ to whisky

white άσπρος aspros

who? ποιος; pyos

whole όλος olos

wholemeal bread ψωμί ολικής
 αλέσεως psomee oleekees aleseos

whose: *whose is it?* ποιου είναι;
 pyoo eene

why? γιατί; yatee

wide πλατύς platees

wife η σύζυγος ee seezeghos

wind ο αέρας o aeras

window το παράθυρο to paratheero

windmill ο ανεμόμυλος o
 anemomeelos

windscreen το παρμπρίζ to
 parbreez

windsurfing το γουιντσέρφινγκ to
 windsurfing

wine το κρασί to krasee

wine list ο κατάλογος των
 κρασιών o kataloghos ton krasyon

wine shop η κάβα ee kava

winter ο χειμώνας o kheemonas

with με me

without χωρίς khorees

woman η γυναίκα ee yeeneka

wood το ξύλο to kseelo

wool το μαλλί to malee

word η λέξη ee leksee

work η δουλειά ee dhoolya

to work (person) δουλεύω dhoolevo
 (machine) λειτουργεί leetooryee

worried ανήσυχος aneeseekhos

worse χειρότερος kheeroteros

worth: *2000 drachmas worth of
 petrol* 2000 δραχμές βενζίνη
 dheeo kheelyadhes dhrakhmes
 venzeenee
 it's worth 2000 drachmas αξίζει
 2000 δραχμές akseezee dheeo
 kheelyadhes dhrakhmes

to wrap (up) τυλίγω teeleegho

wrapping paper το χαρτί
 περιτυλίγματος to khartee
 pereeteeleeghmatos

to write γράφω ghrafo

writing paper το χαρτί
 αλληλογραφίας to khartee
 aleeloghrafeeas

wrong λάθος lathos
 you're wrong κάνετε λάθος
 kanete lathos

Y

yacht το γιοτ to yacht

year ο χρόνος o khronos

yellow κίτρινος keetreenos

yes ναι ne

yesterday χτες *khtes*

yet ακόμα *akoma*
  not yet όχι ακόμα *okhee akoma*

yoghurt το γιαούρτι *to yaoortee*

you *(singular/plural)* εσύ / εσείς *esee / esees*

young νέος *neos*

youth hostel ο ξενώνας νεότητος
  o ksenonas neoteetos

Z

zero το μηδέν *to meedhen*

zip το φερμουάρ *to fermooar*

zone η ζώνη *ee zonee*

zoo ο ζωολογικός κήπος *o zo-oloyeekos keepos*

Greek alphabet

*Greek is spelt exactly as it sounds. The only difficulty may occur with letters which have the same sound, eg. υ, η, ι, ει and οι are all pronounced **ee**. Also, see below for double consonants.*

			SOUND
α, Α	άλφα	**a**lfa	a
β, Β	βήτα	v**ee**ta	v
γ, Γ	γάμα	gh**a**ma	gh
δ, Δ	δέλτα	dh**e**lta	dh
ε, Ε	έψιλον	**e**pseelon	e
ζ, Ζ	ζήτα	**zee**ta	z
η, Η	ήτα	**ee**ta	ee
θ, Θ	θήτα	th**ee**ta	th
ι, Ι	γιώτα	y**o**ta	ee
κ, Κ	κάπα	k**a**pa	k
λ, Λ	λάμδα	l**a**mdha	l
μ, Μ	μι	mee	m
ν, Ν	νι	nee	n
ξ, Ξ	ξι	ksee	ks
ο, Ο	όμικρον	**o**meekron	o
π, Π	πι	pee	p
ρ, Ρ	ρο	ro	r
σ, ς, Σ	σίγμα	s**ee**ghma	s
τ, Τ	ταυ	taf	t
υ, Υ	ύψιλον	**ee**pseelon	ee
φ, Φ	φι	fee	f
χ, Χ	χι	khee	kh
ψ, Ψ	ψι	psee	ps
ω, Ω	ωμέγα	om**e**gha	o

Double consonants:

μπ, ΜΠ	=	b
ντ, ΝΤ	=	d
τζ, ΤΖ	=	j
γγ, ΓΓ	=	ng

Also beware!

αυ, ΑΥ	=	af, av
ευ, ΕΥ	=	ef, ev

α A

αβγό (το) *avgho* **egg**
  αβγά ημέρας *avgha eemeras*
  newly-laid eggs
άγαλμα (το) *aghalma* **statue**
αγάπη (η) *aghapee* **love**
αγαπώ *aghapo* **to love**
αγγελία (η) *angeleea*
  announcement
άγγελος (ο) *angelos* **angel**
Αγγλία (η) *angleea* **England**
αγγλικός/ή/ό *angleekos/ee/o*
  English *(thing)*
Άγγλος/Αγγλίδα (ο/η)
  anglos/angleedha **Englishman/-**
  woman
αγγούρι (το) *angooree* **cucumber**
άγιος/α/ο *agheeos/a/o* **holy ; saint**
  Άγιον Όρος (το) *agheeon oros*
  Mount Athos *(literally holy*
  mountain)
αγκινάρα (η) *angeenara* **artichoke**
άγκυρα (η) *angeera* **anchor**
αγορά (η) *aghora* **agora ; market**
αγοράζω *aghorazo* **to buy**
αγοραστής (ο) *aghorastees* **buyer**
αγόρι (το) *aghoree* **young boy**
άδεια (η) *adheea* **permit ; licence**
  άδεια οδήγησης *adheea*
  odheegheesees **driving licence**
άδειος/α/ο *adheeos/a/o* **empty**
αδελφή (η) *adhelfee* **sister**
αδελφός (ο) *adhelfos* **brother**
αδιάβροχο (το) *adheeavrokho*
  raincoat
αδιέξοδο (το) *adhee-eksodho*
  cul-de-sac ; no through road
αδίκημα (το) *adheekeema* **offence**

αέρας (ο) *a-eras* **wind**
αερογραμμές (οι) *a-eroghrames*
  airways
  Βρετανικές Αερογραμμές
  vretaneekes a-eroghrames
  British Airways
  Κυπριακές Αερογραμμές
  keepreeakes a-eroghrames
  Cyprus Airways
αεροδρόμιο (το) *a-erodhromeeo*
  airport
αεροπλάνο (το) *a-eroplano*
  aeroplane
αεροπορία (η) *aeroporeea* **air**
  force ; aviation
  Ολυμπιακή Αεροπορία
  oleempeeakee aeroporeea
  Olympic Airways
αεροπορικό εισιτήριο (το)
  a-eroporeeko eeseeteereeo
  air ticket
αεροπορικώς *a-eroporeekos* **by air**
αζήτητος/η/ο *azeeteetos/ee/o*
  unclaimed
Αθήνα (η) *atheena* **Athens**
αθλητικό κέντρο (το) *athleeteeko*
  kendro **sports centre**
αθλητισμός (ο) *athleeteesmos*
  sports
Αιγαίο (το) *egheo* **the Aegean**
  Sea
αίθουσα (η) *ethoosa* **room**
  αίθουσα αναμονής *ethoosa*
  anamonees **waiting room**
  αίθουσα αναχωρήσεων *ethoosa*
  anakhoreeseon **departure lounge**
αιμορραγώ *emoragho* **to bleed**
αίμα (το) *ema* **blood**
αίτημα (το) *eteema* **demand**
αίτηση (η) *eteesee* **application**

α
A
Α
Β
γ
Γ
δ
Δ
ε
Ε
ζ
Ζ
η
Η
θ
Θ
ι
Ι
κ
Κ
λ
Λ
μ
Μ
ν
Ν
ξ
Ξ
ο
Ο
π
Π
ρ
Ρ
σ/ς
Σ
τ
Τ
υ
Υ
φ
Φ
χ
Χ
ψ
Ψ
ω
Ω

ακάθαρτος/η/ο akathartos/ee/o
dirty

-άκι -akee (as a suffix means little)
καφεδάκι kafedhakee little
coffee

ακουστικά (τα) akoosteeka
earphones

ακουστικό βαρυκοΐας
akoosteeko vareekoeeas hearing
aid

ακουστικό (το) akoosteeko
receiver (telephone)

ακούω akooo to hear

άκρη (η) akree edge

Ακρόπολη (η) akropolee the
Acropolis

ακτή (η) aktee beach ; shore

ακτινογραφία (η)
akteenoghrafeea X-ray

ακυρώνω akeerono to cancel

αλάτι (το) alatee salt

αλεύρι (το) alevree flour

αλλαγή (η) alaghee change

αλλάζω alazo to change
δεν αλλάζονται dhen alazonte
goods will not be exchanged

αλληλογραφία (η) aleelografeea
correspondence

αλληλογραφώ aleelografo
to correspond

αλλοδαπός/ή alodhapos/ee
foreign national
αστυνομία αλλοδαπών
asteenomeea alodhapon
immigration police

αλμυρός/ή/ό almeeros/ee/o salty

αλυσίδα (η) aleeseedha chain

αμάξι (το) amaxee car ; vehicle

αμερικάνικος/η/ο
amereekaneekos/ee/o American
(thing)

Αμερικανός/Αμερικανίδα
amereekanos/amereekaneedha
American (man/woman)

Αμερική (η) amereekee America

αμέσως amesos at once ;
immediately

αμήν ameen amen

άμμος (η) amos sand

αμμουδιά (η) amoodheea sandy
beach

αμοιβή (η) ameevee reward ;
fare ; salary ; payment

αμπέλι (το) ambelee vine

αμύγδαλο (το) ameeghdhalo
almond

αμφιθέατρο (το) amfeetheatro
amphitheatre

αμφορέας (ο) amforeas jar ;
amphora

αν an if

αναβολή (η) anavolee delay

ανάβω anavo to switch on

αναγγελία (η) anangeleea
announcement

αναζήτηση (η) anazeeteesee
search

ανάκριση (η) anakreesee
interrogation

ανάκτορα (τα) anaktora palace

αναμονή (η) anamonee waiting
αίθουσα αναμονής ethoosa
anamonees waiting room

ανανάς (ο) ananas pineapple

ανανεώνω ananeono to renew

ανάπηρος/η/ο anapeeros/ee/o
handicapped ; disabled

αναπτήρας (ο) anapteeras
cigarette lighter

ανασκαφή (η) anaskafee
excavation

ανατολή (η) anatolee **east ; sunrise**

ανατολικός/ή/ό anatoleekos/ee/o
eastern

ΑΝΑΧΩΡΗΣΕΙΣ anakhoreesees
DEPARTURES

αναψυκτικό (το) anapseekteeko
soft drink

αναψυχή (η) anapseekhee
recreation ; pleasure

άνδρας (ο) andhras **man ; male**

ΑΝΔΡΟΝ andhron
GENTS

ανδρική μόδα (η) andhreekee
modha **men's fashions**

ανεμιστήρας (ο) anemeesteeras
fan

άνθη (τα) anthee **flowers**
(only on signs)

ανθοπωλείο (το) anthopoleeo
florist's

άνθρωπος (ο) anthropos **man ;
person**

ανοίγω aneegho **to open**

ΑΝΟΙΚΤΟ aneekto OPEN

άνοιξη (η) aneeksee **spring** (season)

ανταλλαγή (η) andalaghee
exchange

ανταλλακτικά (τα) andalakteeka
spare parts

αντιβιοτικά (τα) andeeveeoteeka
antibiotics

αντίγραφο (το) andeeghrafo **copy ;
reproduction**

αντίκες (οι) aneekes **antiques**

αντικλεπτικά (τα)
andeeklepteeka **anti-theft
devices**

αντίο andeeo **goodbye**

αντιπηκτικό (το)
andeepeekteekho **antifreeze**

αντιπρόσωπος (ο) andeeprosopos
representative

αντλία (η) andleea **pump**
αντλία βενζίνης andleea
venzeenes **petrol pump**

ανώμαλος/η/ο anomalos/ee/o
uneven ; rough

αξεσουάρ (τα) aksesooar
accessories
αξεσουάρ αυτοκινήτου
aksesooar aftokeeneetoo **car
accessories**

αξία (η) akseea **value**
αξία διαδρομής akseea
dheeadhromees **fare**

αξιοθέατα (τα) akseeotheata
the sights

απαγορεύω apaghorevo **to forbid ;
no...**
απαγορεύεται η αναμονή
apaghorevete ee anamonee
no waiting
απαγορεύεται η διάβαση
apaghorevete ee dheeavasee
keep off
απαγορεύεται η είσοδος
apaghorevete ee eesodhos
no entry
απαγορεύεται το κάπνισμα
apaghorevete to kapneesma
no smoking
απαγορεύεται η στάθμευση
apaghorevete ee stathmefsee
no parking

151

α
Α
β
Β
γ
Γ
δ
Δ
ε
Ε
ζ
Ζ
η
Η
θ
Θ
ι
Ι
κ
Κ
λ
Λ
μ
Μ
ν
Ν
ξ
Ξ
ο
Ο
π
Π
ρ
Ρ
σ/ς
Σ
τ
Τ
υ
Υ
φ
Φ
χ
Χ
ψ
Ψ
ω
Ω

απαγορεύονται τα σκυλιά
apaghorevonte ta skeeleea **no dogs**
απαγορεύεται η φωτογράφηση
apaghorevete ee fotoghrafeesee
no photography
απαγορεύεται το κολύμπι
apaghorevete to koleembee
no swimming
απαγορεύεται η κατασκήνωση
apaghorevete ee kataskeenosee
no camping
απαίτηση (η) *apeteesee* **claim**
απάντηση (η) *apanteesee* **answer**
απέναντι *apenandee* **opposite**
απεργία (η) *apergheea* **strike**
απογείωση (η) *apogheeosee*
takeoff
απόγευμα (το) *apoyevma*
afternoon
απόδειξη (η) *apodheeksee*
receipt
αποθήκη (η) *apotheekee*
warehouse ; store-room
αποκλειστικός/ή/ό
apokleesteekos/ee/o **exclusive**
απόκριες (οι) *apokree-es* **carnival**
αποσκευές (οι) *aposkeves*
luggage
αναζήτηση αποσκευών
anazeeteesee aposkevon **left-
luggage** (office)
απόψε *apopse* **tonight**

ΑΠΡΙΛΙΟΣ *apreeleeos*
APRIL

αργότερα *arghotera* **later**
αρέσω *areso* **to please**
μου αρέσει *moo aresee* **I like**
δεν μου αρέσει *dhen moo aresee*
I don't like

σου αρέσει *soo aresee* **you like**
δεν σου αρέσει *dhen soo aresee*
you don't like
αριθμός (ο) *areethmos* **number**
αριθμός διαβατηρίου *areethmos
dheevateereeoo* **passport
number**
αριθμός πτήσεως *areethmos
pteeseos* **flight number**
αριθμός τηλεφώνου *areethmos
teelefonoo* **telephone number**
αριστερά *areestera* **left** (opposite
of right)
αρνί (το) *arnee* **lamb**
αρρώστια (η) *arostea* **illness**
άρρωστος/η/ο *arostos/ee/o* **ill**
αρτοποιείο (η) *artopee-eeo*
bakery
αρχαιολογικός χώρος (ο)
arkheologheekos khoros
archaeological site
αρχαίος/α/ο *arkheos/a/o* **ancient**
αρχή (η) *arkhee* **start**
αρχίζω *arkheezo* **to begin ;
to start**
άρωμα (το) *aroma* **perfume**
ασανσέρ (το) *asanser* **lift ;
elevator**
ασθενής (ο/η) *asthenees* **patient**
άσθμα (το) *asthma* **asthma**
άσκοπος/η/ο *askopos/ee/o*
improper
άσκοπη χρήση *askopee khreesee*
improper use
ασπιρίνη (η) *aspeereenee* **aspirin**
άσπρος/η/ο *aspros/ee/o* **white**
αστακός (ο) *astakos* **lobster**
αστυνομία (η) *asteenomeea*
police

αστυνομία αλλοδαπών
asteenomeea alodhapon
immigration police
Ελληνική αστυνομία
eleeneekee **Greek police**

αστυνομική διάταξη (η)
asteenomeekee dheeatoxee **police
notice**

αστυνομικό τμήμα (το)
asteenomeeko tmeema **police
station**

αστυνομικός σταθμός (ο)
asteenomeekos stathmos **police
station**

αστυνόμος (ο) *asteenomos*
policeman

αστυφύλακας (ο) *asteefeelakas*
town policeman

ασφάλεια (η) *asfaleea* **insurance** ;
fuse
ασφάλεια έναντι κλοπής
asfaleea enandee klopees **theft
insurance**
ασφάλεια έναντι τρίτων
asfaleea enandee treeton **third-
party insurance**
ασφάλεια ζωής *asfaleea zoees*
life insurance

ασφάλιση (η) *asfaleesee* **insurance**
πλήρης ασφάλιση *pleerees
asfaleesee* **comprehensive
insurance**
ιατρική ασφάλιση *yatreekee
asfaleesee* **medical insurance**

ατομικός/ή/ό *atomeekos/ee/o*
personal

άτομο (το) *atomo* **person**
άτομο τρίτης ηλικίας *atomo
treetees eeleekeeas* **pensioner**

ατύχημα (το) *ateekheema*
accident

αυγή (η) *avghee* **dawn**
αυγό (το) *avgho* **egg**

ΑΥΓΟΥΣΤΟΣ *avgoostos*
AUGUST

αυτοκίνητο (το) *aftokeeneeto* **car**
ενοικιάσεις αυτοκινήτων
eneekeeasees aftokeeneeton
car hire
συνεργείο αυτοκινήτων
seenergheeon aftokeeneeton
car repairs

αυτοκινητόδρομος (ο)
aftokeeneetodhromos **motorway**

αυτόματος/η/ο *aftomatos/ee/o*
automatic

άφιξη (η) *afeeksee* **arrival**

ΑΦΙΞΕΙΣ *afeeksees*
ARRIVALS

αφορολόγητα (τα) *aforologheeta*
duty-free goods

Αφροδίτη *afrodheetee* **Aphrodite** ;
Venus

αχλάδι (το) *akhladhee* **pear**

άχρηστα (τα) *akhreesta* **waste**

αψίδα (η) *apseedha* **arch**

β Β

βαγόνι (το) *vaghonee* **carriage**
(train)

βάζω *vazo* **to put**

βαλβίδα (η) *valveedha* **valve**

βαλίτσα (η) *valeetsa* **suitcase**

βαμβακερός/ή/ό *vamvakeros/ee/o*
(made of) **cotton**

βαρέλι (το) *varelee* **barrel**
μπίρα από βαρέλι *beera apo
varelee* **draught beer**

βαρελίσιο κρασί (το) *vareleeseeo krasee* house wine

βάρκα (η) *varka* boat

βάρος (το) *varos* weight

βαφή (η) *vafee* paint ; dye ; painting ; dyeing

βάφω *vafo* to paint

βγάζω *vghazo* to take off

βγαίνω *vgheno* to go out

βελόνα (η) *velona* needle

βενζίνη (η) *venzeenee* petrol ; gasoline

βήχας (ο) *veekhas* cough

βιβλίο (το) *veevleeo* book

βιβλιοθήκη (η) *veevleeotheekee* bookcase ; library

Δημοτική Βιβλιοθήκη *dheemoteekee veevleeotheekee* Public Library

Κεντρική Βιβλιοθήκη *khendreekee veevleeotheekee* Central Library

βιβλιοπωλείο (το) *veevleeopoleeo* bookshop

Βίβλος (η) *veevlos* the Bible

βιταμίνη (η) *veetameenee* vitamin

βιτρίνα (η) *veetreena* shop window

βλέπω *vlepo* to see

βοήθεια (η) *voeethea* help
οδική βοήθεια *odheekee voeethea* breakdown service
πρώτες βοήθειες *protes voeethee-es* casualty (hospital)

βόμβα (η) *vomva* bomb

βόρειος/α/ο *voreeos/a/o* northern

βορράς (ο) *voras* north

βουλή (η) *voolee* parliament

βουνό (το) *voono* mountain

βούρτσα (η) *voortsa* brush

βούτυρο (το) *vooteero* butter

βράδυ (το) *vradhee* evening

βραδινό (το) *vradheeno* evening meal

βράζω *vrazo* to boil

βραστός/ή/ό *vrastos/ee/o* boiled

Βρετανία (η) *vretaneea* Britain

βρετανικός/ή/ό *vretaneekos/ee/o* British *(thing)*

Βρετανός/Βρετανίδα (ο/η) *vretanos/vretaneedha* British *(man/woman)*

βρέχει *vrekhee* it is raining

βρίσκω *vreesko* to find

βροχή (η) *vrokhee* rain

γ Γ

γαϊδούρι *ghaeedhooree* donkey

γάλα (το) *ghala* milk

γαλάζιος/α/ο *ghalazeeos/a/o* blue ; light blue

γαλακτοπωλείο (το) *ghalaktopoleeo* dairy shop

Γαλλία (η) *ghaleea* France

γαλλικός/ή/ό *ghaleekos/ee/o* French *(thing)*

Γάλλος/Γαλλίδα (ο/η) *ghalos/ghaleedha* French *(man/woman)*

γαλοπούλα (η) *ghalopoola* turkey

γάμος (ο) *ghamos* wedding ; marriage

γαμήλια δεξίωση *ghameelya dhekseeosee* wedding reception

γαρίδα (η) *ghareedha* shrimp ; prawn

γειά σας *ya sas* **hello ; goodbye** *(formal)*

γειά σου *ya soo* **hello ; goodbye** *(informal)*

γεμάτος/η/ο *yematos/ee/o* **full**

γενέθλια (τα) *yenethleea* **birthday**

γενικός/ή/ό *yeneekos/ee/o* **general**
Γενικό Νοσοκομείο *yeneeko nosokomeeo* **General Hospital**

γέννηση (η) *yeneesee* **birth**

Γερμανία (η) *yermaneea* **Germany**

γερμανικός/ή/ό *yermaneekos/ee/o* **German** *(thing)*

Γερμανός/Γερμανίδα (ο/η) *yermanos/yermaneedha* **German** *(man/woman)*

γεμιστός/ή/ό *yemeestos/ee/o* **stuffed**

γεύμα (το) *yevma* **meal**

γέφυρα (η) *yefeera* **bridge**

για *ya* **for**

γιαγιά (η) *yaya* **grandmother**

γιαούρτι (το) *yaoortee* **yoghurt**

γιασεμί (το) *yasemee* **jasmine**

γιατί; *yatee* **why?**

γιατρός (ο/η) *yatros* **doctor**

γίνομαι *yeenome* **to become**
γίνονται δεκτές πιστωτικές κάρτες *yeenonte dhektes peestoteekes kartes* **we accept credit cards**

γιορτή (η) *yortee* **festival ; celebration ; name day**

γιος (ο) *yos* **son**

γιοτ (το) *yot* **yacht**

γκάζι (το) *gazee* **accelerator** *(car)* ; **gas**

γκαλερί *galeree* **art gallery ; art sales**

γκαράζ (το) *garaz* **garage**

γκαρσόν (το)/γκαρσόνι (το) *garson/garsonee* **waiter**

γλυκός/ιά/ό *ghleekos/eea/o* **sweet**
γλυκό (το)/γλυκά (τα) *ghleeko/ghleeka* **cakes and pastries ; desserts**
γλυκό ταψιού *ghleeko tapseeoo* **traditional pastries with syrup**

γλύπτης/γλύπτρια (ο/η) *ghleeptees/ghleeptreea* **sculptor**

γλυπτική (η) *ghleepteekee* **sculpture**

γλώσσα (η) *ghlosa* **tongue ; language ; sole** *(fish)*

γονείς (οι) *ghonees* **parents**

γουιντσέρφινγκ (το) *weendserfeeng* **windsurfing**

γράμμα (το) *ghrama* **letter**
γράμμα κατεπείγον *ghrama katepeeghon* **express letter**
γράμμα συστημένο *ghrama seesteemeno* **recorded delivery**

γραμμάριο (το) *ghramareeo* **gram**

γραμματοκιβώτιο (το) *ghramatokeevoteeo* **letter box**

γραμματόσημο (το) *ghramatoseemo* **stamp**

γραφείο (το) *ghrafeeo* **office ; desk**
Γραφείο Τουρισμού *ghrafeeo tooreesmoo* **Tourist Office**

γράφω *ghrafo* **to write**

γρήγορα *ghreegora* **quickly**

γρίπη (η) *ghreepee* **influenza**

γυαλί (το) *yalee* **glass**
γυαλιά (τα) *yalya* **glasses**
γυαλιά ηλίου *yalya eeleeoo* **sunglasses**

γυαλικός/ή/ό yaleekos/ee/o
made of glass

γυναίκα (η) yeeneka **woman**

ΓΥΝΑΙΚΩΝ yeenekon
LADIES

γύρω yeero **round ; about**

γωνία (η) ghoneea **corner**

δ Δ

δακτυλίδι (το) dakteeleedee
ring (for finger)

δαμάσκηνο (το) dhamaskeeno
plum

δαντέλα (η) dhandela **lace**

δασκάλα (η) dhaskala **teacher**
(female)

δάσκαλος (ο) dhaskalos **teacher**
(male)

δάσος (το) dhasos **forest**

δείπνο (το) dheepno **dinner**

δέκα dheka **ten**

ΔΕΚΕΜΒΡΙΟΣ dhekemvreeos
DECEMBER

δελτίο (το) dhelteeo **card ; coupon**
  δελτίο αφίξεως dhelteeo
  afeekseos **arrival card**

δελφίνι (το) dhelfeenee **dolphin**
  ιπτάμενο δελφίνι eeptameno
  dhelfeenee **hydrofoil**

Δελφοί (οι) dhelfee **Delphi**

Δεμέστιχα dhemesteekha **dry**
wine (white or red)

δεν dhen **not**
  δεν δίνεται ρέστα dhen dheenete
  resta **no change given**

ΔΕΝ ΛΕΙΤΟΥΡΓΕΙ
dhen leetoorghee
OUT OF ORDER

δεξιά dhekseea **right** (opposite of
left)

δέρμα (το) dherma **skin ; leather**

δεσποινίς/δεσποινίδα (η)
  dhespeenees/dhespeeneedha **Miss**

ΔΕΥΤΕΡΑ dheftera
MONDAY

δεύτερος/η/ο dhefteros/ee/o
second

δηλητήριο (το) dheeleeteereeo
poison

δήλωση (η) dheelosee
announcement
  δήλωση συναλλάγματος
  dheelosee seenalaghmatos
  currency declaration
  είδη προς δήλωση eedhee pros
  seenalaghmatos **goods to declare**
  ουδέν προς δήλωση oodhen
  pros seenalaghmatos **nothing to
  declare**

δημαρχείο (το) dheemarkheeo
town hall

δημόσιος/α/ο dheemoseeos
public/state
  δημόσια έργα dheemoseea ergha
  road works
  δημόσιος κήπος dheemoseeos
  keepos **public gardens**

δημοτικός/ή/ό deemoteekos
public/municipal
  Δημοτική Αγορά dheemoteekee
  aghora **public market**
  Δημοτική Βιβλιοθήκη
  dheemoteekee veevleeotheekee
  Public Library

διάβαση (η) *dheeavasee* **crossing**
διάβαση πεζών *dheeavasee pezon* **pedestrian crossing**
υπόγεια διάβαση πεζών *eepoya dheeavasee pezon* **pedestrian subway**

διαβατήριο (το) *dheeavateereeo* **passport**
αριθμός διαβατηρίου *areethmos dheeavateereeoo* **passport number**
έλεγχος διαβατηρίων *elenghos dheeavateereeon* **passport control**

διαβήτης (ο) *dheeaveetees* **diabetes**

διαδρομή (η) *dheeadhromee* **route**

δίαιτα (η) *dheeeta* **diet**

διακεκριμένος/η/ο *dheeakekreemenos* **distinguished**
διακεκριμένη θέση *dheeakekreemenee thesee* **business class**

διακοπές (οι) *dheeakopes* **holidays**

διάλειμμα (το) *dheealeema* **interval ; break**

διαμέρισμα (το) *dheeamereesma* **flat ; apartment**

διανυχτερεύει *dheeaneekhterevee* **open all night**

διασκέδαση (η) *dheeaskedhasee* **entertainment**
κέντρο διασκεδάσεως *kendro dheeaskedaseos* **nightclub**

διασταύρωση (η) *dheeastavrosee* **crossroads ; junction**

διεθνής/ής/ές *dhee-ethnees/ees/es* **international**

διερμηνέας (ο/η) *dhee-ermeeneas* **interpreter**

διεύθυνση (η) *dheeeftheensee* **address**

διευθυντής (ο) *dhee-eftheentees* **manager**

δικαστήριο (το) *dheekasteereeo* **court**

δικηγόρος (ο/η) *dheekeeghoros* **lawyer**

δίνω *dheeno* **to give**

δίπλα *dheepla* **next to**

διπλός/ή/ό *dheeplos/ee/o* **double**
διπλό δωμάτιο *dheeplo domateeo* **double room**
διπλό κρεββάτι *dheeplo krevatee* **double bed**

δισκοθήκη (η) *dheeskotheekee* **disco** *(Cyprus)* ; **music collection**

δίχτυ (το) *dheekhtee* **net**

διψώ *dheepso* **to be thirsty**

δολάριο (το) *dholareeo* **dollar**

δόντι (το) *dhondee* **tooth**

δράμα (το) *dhrama* **drama** ; **play**

δραχμή (η) *dhrakhmee* **drachma**

δρομολόγιο (το) *dhromologheeo* **timetable ; route**
δρομολόγια εξωτερικού *dhromologhea eksotereekoo* **international routes**
δρομολόγια εσωτερικού *dhromologhea esotereekoo* **domestic routes**

δρόμος (ο) *dhromos* **street ; way**

δύση (η) *dheesee* **west ; sunset**

δυσκοιλιότητα (η) *dheeskeeleeoteeta* **constipation**

δύσκολος/η/ο *dheeskolos/ee/o* **difficult**

δυστύχημα (το) *dheesteekheema* **accident ; mishap**

δυτικός/ή/ό *dheeteekos/ee/o* **western**

Δωδεκάνησα (τα) *dhodhekaneesa* **the Dodecanese**

δωμάτιο (το) *dhomateeo* **room**

δωρεάν *dhorean* **free of charge**

δώρο (το) *dhoro* **present ; gift**

ε E

εβδομάδα (η) *evdhomadha* **week**

εγγραφή (η) *engrafee* **registration**

εγγύηση (η) *engeeyeesee* **guarantee**

έγχρωμος/η/ο *enkhromos/ee/o* **coloured**

έγχρωμες φωτογραφίες *enkhromes fotohrafeees* **colour photographs**

εδώ *edho* **here**

ΕΕ *epseelon epseelon* **EU**

εθνικός/ή/ό *ethneekos/ee/o* **national**

Εθνικό Θέατρο *ethneeko theatro* **National Theatre**

εθνική οδός *ethneekee odhos* **motorway**

Εθνικός Κήπος *ethneekos keepos* **National Garden** *(in Athens)*

εθνικός ύμνος *ethneekos eemnos* **national anthem**

έθνος (το) *ethnos* **nation**

εθνικότητα *ethneekoteeta* **nationality**

ειδικός/ή/ό *eedheekos/ee/o* **special ; specialist**

είδος (το) *eedhos* **kind ; sort**
είδη *eedhee* **goods**
είδη κήπου *eedhee keepoo* **garden centre**

είμαι *eeme* **to be**

εισιτήριο (το) *eeseeteereeo* **ticket**
απλό εισιτήριο *aplo eeseeteereeo* **single ticket**
εισιτήριο με επιστροφή *eeseeteereeo me epeestrofee* **return ticket**
ατμοπλοϊκό εισιτήριο *atmoploeeko epeestrofee* **boat ticket**
σιδηροδρομικό εισιτήριο *seedheerodromeeko epeestrofee* **rail ticket**
φοιτητικό εισιτήριο *feeteeteeko epeestrofee* **student ticket**

ΕΙΣΟΔΟΣ *eesodhos* **ENTRANCE**

εκδόσεις εισιτηρίων *ekdhosees eeseeteereeon* **ticket office**

εκδοτήρια (τα) *ekdhoteereea* **ticket machines**

εκεί *ekee* **there**

έκθεση (η) *ekthesee* **exhibition**

εκθεσιακό κέντρο *ektheseeako kendro* **exhibition centre**

εκκλησία (η) *ekleeseea* **church ; chapel**

έκπτωση (η) *ekptosee* **discount**

ΕΚΠΤΩΣΕΙΣ *ekptosees* **SALE**

εκτελούνται έργα *ekteloonde ergha* **road works**

εκτός *ektos* **except ; unless**
εκτός λειτουργίας *ektos leetoorgheeas* **out of order**

έλα! *ela* **come on!** *(singular)*

ελάτε! *elate* **come on!** *(plural)*

ελαιόλαδο (το) *eleoladho* **olive oil**

ελαστικό (το) *elasteeko* **tyre**
σέρβις ελαστικών *servees elasteekon* **tyre service**

ελαττώνω *elatono* **to reduce ; to decrease**
ελαττώσατε ταχύτητα *elatosate takheeteeta* **reduce speed**

έλεγχος (ο) *elenkhos* **control**
έλεγχος διαβατηρίων *elenkhos dheeavateereeon* **passport control**
έλεγχος εισιτηρίων *elenkhos eeseeteereeon* **check-in**
έλεγχος ελαστικών *elenkhos elasteekon* **tyre check**

ελεύθερος/η/ο *eleftheros/ee/o* **single** (unmarried) (lit. = free)

ΕΛΕΥΘΕΡΟ *eleEfthero* **FREE**

ελιά (η) *elya* **olive ; olive tree**
έλκος (το) *elkos* **ulcer**
Ελλάδα (η) *eladha* **Greece**
Έλληνας/Ελληνίδα (ο/η) *eleenas/eleeneedha* **Greek** (man/woman)
ελληνικά (τα) *eleeneeka* **Greek** (language)
ελληνικός/ή/ό *eleeneekos/ee/o* **Greek** (thing)
Ελληνικά Ταχυδρομεία *eleeneeka takheedhromeea* **Greek Post Office (ELTA)**
Ελληνική Δημοκρατία *eleeneekee dheemokrateea* **Republic of Greece**
Ελληνικής κατασκευής *eleeneekees kataskevees* **Made in Greece**
Ελληνικός Οργανισμός Τουρισμού *eleeneekos orghaneesmos tooreesmoo* **Greek Tourist Organisation (EOT)**

Ελληνικό προϊόν *eleeneeko proeeon* **product of Greece**

ΕΛΞΑΤΕ *elksate* (written only) **PULL**

εμπρός *embros* **forward ; in front ; 'hello!'** (on phone)

εμφανίζω *emfaneezo* **to develop** (film)

εμφάνιση (η) *emfaneesee* **film developing**

εναντίον *enandeeon* **against**

έναρξη (η) *enarksee* **opening ; beginning**

ένας/μία/ένα *enas/meea/ena* **one**

ένεση (η) *enesee* **injection**

ενήλικος (ο) *eneeleekos* **adult**

εννέα/εννιά *enea/enya* **nine**

ενοικιάζω *eneekeeazo* **to rent ; to hire**
ενοικιάζεται *eneekeeazete* **to let**
ενοικιάσεις *eneekeeasees* **for hire**

ενοίκιο (το) *eneekeeo* **rent**

ενορία (η) *enoreea* **parish**

εντάξει *endaksee* **all right ; OK**

εντομοκτόνο (το) *endomoktono* **insecticide**

έντυπο (το) *endeepo* **form** (to fill in)

έξι *eksee* **six**

ΕΞΟΔΟΣ *eksodhos* **EXIT**

εξοχή (η) *eksokhee* **countryside**

εξυπηρέτηση (η) *ekseepeereteesee* **service**

εξυπηρετώ *ekseepeereto* **to serve**

έξω *ekso* **out ; outside**

εξώστης (ο) *eksostees* **circle ; balcony** (theatre)

εξωτερικός/ή/ό *eksotereekos/ee/o* **external**

το εξωτερικό *to eksotereeko* **abroad**

εξωτερικού *eksotereekoo* **letters abroad** *(on postbox)*

πτήσεις εξωτερικού *pteesees eksotereekoo* **international flights**

ΕΟΚ *e-ok* **EEC (EC)**

ΕΟΤ *e-ot* **Greek/Hellenic Tourist Organization**

επάγγελμα (το) *epangelma* **occupation ; profession**

επείγον/επείγουσα *epeeghon/epeeghoosa* **urgent ; express**

επείγοντα περιστατικά *epeeghonta pereestateeka* **casualty department**

επιβάτης/τρια (ο/η) *epeevatees/treea* **passenger**

διερχόμενοι επιβάτες *dhee-erkhomenee epeevates* **passengers in transit**

επιβεβαιώνω *epeeveveono* **to confirm**

επιβίβαση (η) *epeeveevasee* **boarding**

κάρτα επιβιβάσεως *karta epeeveevaseos* **boarding card**

επιδόρπιο (το) *epeedhorpeeo* **dessert**

επικίνδυνος/η/ο *epeekeendeenos/ee/o* **dangerous**

επίσης *epeesees* **also ; the same to you**

επισκεπτήριο (το) *epeeskepteereeo* **visiting hours**

επισκέπτης (ο) *epeeskeptees* **visitor**

επισκευή (η) *epeeskevee* **repair**

επισκευές *epeeskeves* **repairs**

επίσκεψη (η) *epeeskepsee* **visit**

ώρες επισκέψεων *ores epeeskepseon* **visiting hours**

επιστροφή (η) *epeestrofee* **return ; return ticket**

επιστροφή νομισμάτων *epeestrofee nomeesmaton* **returned coins**

επιστροφές *epeestrofes* **returned goods ; refunds**

επιταγή (η) *epeetaghee* **cheque ; invoice**

ταχυδρομική επιταγή *takheedhromeekee epeetaghee* **postal order**

επόμενος/η/ο *epomenos/ee/o* **next**

εποχή (η) *epokhee* **season**

επτά/εφτά *epta/efta* **seven**

Επτάνησα (τα) *eptaneesa* **Ionian Islands**

επώνυμο (το) *eponeemo* **surname ; last name**

έργα (τα) *ergha* **works**

εργαλείο (το) *erghaleeo* **tool**

έργο *ergo* **film ; play ; TV program**

εργοστάσιο (το) *erghostaseeo* **factory**

έργο τέχνης (το) *ergho tekhnees* **artwork**

έρχομαι *erkhome* **to come**

ερώτηση (η) *eroteesee* **question**

εστιατόριο (το) *esteeatoreeo* **restaurant**

εσώρουχα (τα) *esorookha* **underwear ; lingerie**

εσωτερικός/ή/ό *esotereekos/ee/o* **internal**

εσωτερικού *esotereekoo* inland (on post boxes) ; **domestic**
πτήσεις εσωτερικού *pteesees esotereekoo* **domestic flights**
εταιρ(ε)ία (η) *etereea* **company ; firm**
έτος (το) *etos* **year**
έτσι *etsee* **so ; like this**
ευθεία (η) *eftheea* **straight line**
κατ᾽ ευθείαν *kat᾽ eftheean* **straight on**
ευθύνη (η) *eftheenee* **responsibility**
ευκαιρία (η) *efkereea* **opportunity ; bargain**
ευκολία (η) *efkoleea* **ease ; convenience**
ευκολίες πληρωμής *efkolees* **credit terms**
εύκολος/η/ο *efkolos/ee/o* **easy**
ευρωπαϊκός/ή/ό *evropaeekos/ee/o* **European**
Ευρώπη (η) *evropee* **Europe**
ευχαριστώ *efkhareesto* **thank you**
εφημερίδα (η) *efeemereedha* **newspaper**
έχω *ekho* **to have**

ζ Ζ

ζάλη (η) *zalee* **dizziness**
ζαμπόν (το) *zambon* **ham**
ζάχαρη (η) *zakharee* **sugar**
ζαχαροπλαστείο (το) *zakharoplasteeo* **patisserie**
ζέστη (η) *zestee* **heat**
κάνει ζέστη *kanee zestee* **it's hot**
ζευγάρι (το) *zevgharee* **couple**
ζημιά (η) *zeemya* **damage**
πάσα ζημιά τιμωρείται *pasa zeemya teemoreete* **anyone causing damage will be prosecuted**

ζητώ *zeeto* **to ask ; to seek**
ζυγαριά (η) *zeeghareea* **scales** (for weighing)
ζυμαρικά (τα) *zeemareekha* **pasta products**
ζωγραφική (η) *zoghrafeekee* **painting** (art)
ζώνη (η) *zonee* **belt**
ζώνη ασφαλείας *zonee asfaleeas* **safety belt ; seat belt**
ζώο (το) *zo-o* **animal**
ζωολογικός κήπος (ο) *zo-ologheekos keepos* **zoo**

η Η

η *ee* **the** (with feminine nouns)
ή *ee* **or**
ηλεκτρικός/ή/ό *eelektreekos/ee/o* **electrical**
ηλεκτρισμός (ο) *eelektreesmos* **electricity**
ηλεκτρονικός/ή/ό *eelektroneekos/ee/o* **electronic**
ηλιακός/ή/ό *eeleeakos/ee/o* **solar**
ηλίαση (η) *eeleeasee* **sunstroke**
ηλικία (η) *eeleekeea* **age**
ηλιοβασίλεμα (το) *eeleeovaseelema* **sunset**
ηλιοθεραπεία (η) *eeleeotherapeea* **sunbathing**
ήλιος (ο) *eeleeos* **sun**
Ήλιος *eeleeos* **a dry white wine from Rhodes**
ημέρα (η) *eemera* **day**
ημερήσιος/α/ο *eemereeseeos/a/o* **daily**

161

ημερομηνία αναχωρήσεως
eemeromeeneea anakhoreeseos
date of departure

ημερομηνία αφίξεως
eemeromeeneea afeekseos **date of
arrival**

ημερομηνία γεννήσεως
eemeromeeneea yeneeseos **date
of birth**

ημερομηνία λήξης
eemeromeeneea leeksees **expiry
date**

ημιδιατροφή (η)
eemeedheeatrofee **half board**

Ηνωμένο Βασίλειο (το)
eenomeno vaseeleeo **United
Kingdom (UK)**

ΗΠΑ **USA**

Ηνωμένες Πολιτείες της
Αμερικής *eenomenes poleeteees
tees amereekees* **United States
of America**

ησυχία (η) *eesekheea* **calm ;
quiet**

ήσυχος/η/ο *eeseekhos* **calm ;
quiet**

θ Θ

θάλασσα (η) *thalasa* **sea**

θαλάσσιος/α/ο *thalaseeos/a/o*
of the sea
θαλάσσιο αλεξίπτωτο *thalaseeo
alekseeptoto* **paragliding**
θαλάσσιο σκι *thalaseeo skee*
water-skiing

θέατρο (το) *theatro* **theatre**

θέλω *thelo* **to want ; to need**

Θεός (ο) *theos* **God**

θεός/θεά (ο/η) *theos/theo* **god ;
goddess**

θεραπεία (η) *therapeea* **treatment**

θέρμανση (η) *thermansee* **heating**

θερμίδα (η) *thermeedha* **calorie**

θερμοστάτης (ο) *thermostatees*
thermostat

θέση (η) *thesee* **place ; seat**
διακεκριμένη θέση
dheeakekreemenee thesee
business class
κράτηση θέσης *krateesee
thesees* **seat reservation**
οικονομική θέση *eekonomeekee
thesee* **economy class**
πρώτη θέση *protee* **first class**

Θεσσαλονίκη (η) *thesaloneekee*
Salonica/Thessaloniki

θύελλα (η) *theeela* **storm**

θύρα (η) *theera* **gate** *(airport)*

θυρίδα (η) *theereedha* **ticket
window**

ι Ι

ΙΑΝΟΥΑΡΙΟΣ *eeanooareeos*
JANUARY

ιατρική περίθαλψη (η) *yatreekee
pereethalpsee* **medical treatment**

ιατρός (ο/η) *yatros* **doctor**

ιδιοκτήτης/τρια (ο/η)
eedheeokteetees/treea **owner**

ΙΔΙΩΤΙΚΟΣ ΧΩΡΟΣ
eedheeoteekos khoros **PRIVATE**

Ιόνιο Πέλαγος (το) *eeoneeo
pelaghos* **Ionian sea**

ΙΟΥΛΙΟΣ *eeooleeos* **JULY**

ΙΟΥΝΙΟΣ *eeooneeos* JUNE

ιππασία (η) *eepaseea* horse riding

ιπποδρομίες (οι) *eepodhromeees* horse racing

ιππόκαμπος (ο) *eepokampos* sea-horse

ιπτάμενο δελφίνι *eeptameno dhelfeenee* hydrofoil (flying dolphin)

Ισθμός της Κορίνθου *eesthmos tees koreenthoo* Corinth canal

ΙΣΟΓΕΙΟ *eesoyeeo* GROUND FLOOR

ισοτιμία (η) *eesoteemeea* exchange rate

Ισπανία (η) *eespaneea* Spain

ισπανικός/ή/ό *eespaneekos/ee/o* Spanish *(thing)*

Ισπανός/ίδα (ο/η) *eespanos/eedha* Spaniard *(man/woman)*

ιστιοπλοΐα (η) *eesteeoploeea* sailing

Ιταλία (η) *eetaleea* Italy

ιταλικός/ή/ό *eetaleekos/ee/o* Italian *(thing)*

Ιταλός/ίδα (ο/η) *eetalos/eedha* Italian *(man/woman)*

ιχθυοπωλείο (το) *eekhtheeopoleeo* fishmonger's

κ Κ

κάβα (η) *kava* wine merchant; off-licence

κάβουρας (ο) *kavooras* crab

καζίνο (το) *kazeeno* casino

καθαριστήριο (το) *kathareesteereeo* dry-cleaner's

καθαρίστρια (η) *kathareestreea* cleaner

καθαρός/ή/ό *katharos/ee/o* clean

κάθε *kathe* every ; each
κάθε μέρα *kathe mera* every day

καθεδρικός ναός (ο) *kathedhreekos naos* cathedral

καθημερινός/ή/ό *katheemereenos/ee/o* daily
καθημερινά δρομολόγια *katheemereena dhromologheea* daily departures

κάθισμα (το) *katheesma* seat

καθολικός/ή/ό *katholeekos/ee/o* Catholic ; total

καθυστέρηση (η) *katheestereesee* delay

και *ke* and

καιρός (ο) *keros* weather ; time

κακάο (το) *kakao* cocoa ; chocolate flavour

κακοκαιρία (η) *kakokereea* bad weather

καλά *kalathee* well ; all right

καλάθι (το) *kalathee* basket

καλαμάρι (το) *kalamaree* squid ; calamari

καλημέρα *kaleemera* good morning

καληνύχτα *kaleeneekhta* good night

καλησπέρα *kaleespera* good evening

καλοκαίρι (το) *kalokeree* summer

καλοριφέρ (το) *kaloreefer* central heating ; radiator

καλοψημένο *kalopseemeno* well done *(meat)*

α
A
β
B
γ
Γ
δ
Δ
ε
E
ζ
Z
η
H
θ
Θ
ι
I
κ
K
λ
Λ
μ
M
ν
N
ξ
Ξ
ο
O
π
Π
ρ
P
σ/ς
Σ
τ
T
υ
Y
φ
Φ
χ
X
ψ
Ψ
ω
Ω

καλσόν (το) kalson **tights**

κάλτσα (η) kaltsa **sock ; stocking**

καμαριέρα (η) kamareeera **chambermaid**

κάμερα (η) kamera **camcorder**

καμπίνα (η) kambeena **cabin**

κανάλι (το) kanalee **canal ; channel** (TV)

κανέλα (η) kanela **cinnamon**

κανένας kanenas **noone**

κάνω kano **to do**

καπέλο (το) kapelo **hat**

καπετάνιος (ο) kapetaneeos **captain** (of ship)

καπνίζω kapneezo **to smoke**
μην καπνίζετε meen kapneezete **no smoking**

καπνιστός/ή/ό kapneestos/ee/o **smoked**
καπνιστός σολομός kapneestos solomos **smoked salmon**
καπνιστό χοιρινό kapneesto kheereeno **smoked ham**
καπνιστό ψάρι kapneesto psaree **smoked fish**
καπνιστό τυρί kapneesto teeree **smoked cheese**

κάπνισμα (το) kapneesma **smoking**
απαγορεύεται το κάπνισμα apaghorevete to kapneesma **no smoking**

καπνιστής (ο) kapneestees **smoker**

καπνοπωλείο (το) kapnopoleeo **tobacconist**

καπνός (ο) kapnos **smoke**

κάποτε kapote **sometimes ; one time**

καράβι (το) karavee **boat ; ship**

καραμέλα (η) karamela **sweet**

κάρβουνο (το) karvoono **coal ; charcoal**

στα κάρβουνα sta karvoona **charcoal-grilled**

καρδιά (η) kardheea **heart**

καρναβάλι (το) karnavalee **carnival**

καροτσάκι (το) karotsakee **pushchair**
καροτσάκι αναπηρικό karotsakee anapeereeko **wheelchair**

καρπούζι (το) karpoozee **watermelon**

κάρτα (η) karta **card ; postcard**
κάρτα απεριόριστων διαδρομών karta apereeoreeston dheeadhromon **rail card for unlimited monthly travel**
κάρτα επιβιβάσεως karta epeeveevaseos **boarding card**
επαγγελματική κάρτα epangelmateekee karta **business card**
μόνο με κάρτα mono me karta **cardholders only**
πιστωτική κάρτα peestoteekee karta **credit card**
κάρτα αναλήψεως karta analeepseos **ATM card ; cash card**

καρτοτηλέφωνο (το) kartoteelefono **card phone**

καρτποστάλ (το) kartpostal **postcard**

καρύδα (η) kareedha **coconut**

καρύδι (το) kareedhee **walnut**

καρχαρίας (ο) karkhareeas **shark**

κασέτα (η) kaseta **tape ; cassette** (for recording)
CD (το) seedee **CD**

κασετόφωνο (το) kasetofono **tape recorder**

κάστανο (το) kastano **chestnut**

κάστρο (το) kastro **castle ; fortress**

κατάθεση (η) katathesee deposit ; statement to police

καταιγίδα (η) kategheedha storm

καταλαβαίνω katalaveno to understand
καταλαβαίνεις; katalavenees do you understand? (familiar form)
καταλαβαίνετε; katalavenete do you understand? (polite form)

κατάλογος (ο) kataloghos list ; menu ; directory
τηλεφωνικός κατάλογος teelefoneekos kataloghos telephone directory

καταπραϋντικό (το) katapraeenteeko tranquillizer

κατασκήνωση (η) kataskeenosee camping

κατάσταση (η) katastasee condition ; situation

κατάστημα (το) katasteema shop

κατάστρωμα (το) katastroma deck

κατεπείγον/κατεπείγουσα katepeeghon/katepeeghoosa urgent ; express

κατεψυγμένος/η/ο katepseeghmenos/ee/o frozen

κατηγορία (η) kateghoreea class (of hotel)

κατσαρόλα (η) katsarola saucepan ; pot

κατσίκα (η) katseeka goat

κατσικάκι (το) katseekakee kid (young goat)

κάτω kato under ; lower ; down

καύσιμα (τα) kafseema fuel

καφέ kafe brown

καφενείο (το) kafeneeo coffee house

καφές (ο) kafes coffee (usually Greek)
καφές γλυκός kafes ghleekos sweet coffee
καφές μέτριος kafes metreeos medium sweet coffee
καφές σκέτος kafes sketos strong black coffee
καφές στιγμιαίος kafes steeghmee-eos instant coffee (Nescafé)
καφές φραπέ kapes frape iced coffee (Nescafé)

καφετερία (η) kafetereea cafeteria

καφετιέρα (η) kafetee-era coffee maker

κέικ (το) ke-eek cake

κεντρικός/ή/ό kendreekos/ee/o central

κέντρο (το) kendro centre
κέντρο αλλοδαπών kendro allodhapon immigration office
κέντρο διασκεδάσεως kendro dheeaskedhaseos nightclub
κέντρο εκδώσεως kendro ekdhoseos ticket office
κέντρο υγείας kendro eegheeas health centre
αθλητικό κέντρο athleeteeko kendro sports centre
τηλεφωνικό κέντρο teelefoneeko kendro telephone exchange

κεράσι (το) kerasee cherry

Κέρκυρα (η) kerkeera Corfu

κέρμα (το) kerma coin

κερνώ kerno to buy a drink
να κεράσω na keraso can I buy (you) a drink... ?

κεφάλι (το) kefalee head

κεφτέδες (οι) keftedhes meatballs

κήπος (ο) keepos **garden**
δημόσιος κήπος dheemoseeos keepos **public garden**
ζωολογικός κήπος zo-ologheekos keepos **zoo**

κιβώτιο (το) keevoteeo **large box**
κιβώτιο ταχυτήτων keevoteeo takheeteeton **gearbox**

κιλό (το) keelo **kilo**

κίνδυνος (ο) keendheenos **danger**
κίνδυνος θανάτου keendheenos thanatoo **extreme danger**

κινητό (το) keeneeto **mobile phone**

κίτρινος/η/ο keetreenos/ee/o **yellow**

κλαμπ (το) klab **club**

κλειδί (το) kleedhee **key ; spanner**

κλείνω kleeno **to close**

ΚΛΕΙΣΤΟ kleesto **CLOSED**

κλέφτης (ο) kleftees **thief**

κλέφτικο (το) klefteeko **lamb dish**

κλήση (η) kleesee **summons**
κλήση τροχαίας (η) kleesee trokheas **traffic ticket**

κλίμα (το) kleema **climate**

κλινική (η) kleeneekee **clinic ; hospital ; ward**

κοιμάμαι keemame **to sleep**

κοινωνικός/ή/ό keenoneekos/ee/o **social**
κοινωνικές ασφαλίσεις keenoneekes asfaleesees **national insurance**

κόκκινος/η/ο kokeenos/ee/o **red**

κολοκυθάκι (το) kolokeethakee **courgette**

κολοκύθι (το) kolokeethee **marrow**

κόλπος (ο) kolpos **gulf ; vagina**

κολύμπι (το) koleembee **swimming**

κολυμπώ koleembo **to swim**

κολώνα (η) kolona **pillar ; column**

κομμωτήριο (το) komoteereeo **hairdresser's**

κομμωτής/μώτρια (ο/η) komotees/komotreea **hairstylist**

κονιάκ (το) konyak **cognac ; brandy**

κονσέρβα (η) konserva **tinned food**

κονσέρτο (το) konserto **concert**

κοντά konda **near**

κόρη (η) koree **daughter**

κορίτσι (το) koreetsee **young girl**

κόρνα (η) korna **horn** (in car)

κοσμήματα (τα) kosmeemata **jewellery**

κοσμηματαπωλείο (το) kosmeematapoleeo **jewellery shop**

κοστούμι (το) kostoomee **man's suit**

κότα (η) kota **hen**

κοτολέτα (η) kotoleta **chop**

κοτόπουλο (το) kotopoolo **chicken**

κουβέρτα (η) kooverta **blanket**

κουζίνα (η) koozeena **kitchen ; cuisine**
ελληνική κουζίνα eleeneekee koozeena **Greek cuisine**

κουμπί (το) koombee **button**

κουνέλι (το) koonelee **rabbit**

κουνούπι (το) koonoopee **mosquito**

κουνουπίδι (το) koonoopeedhee **cauliflower**

κουπί (το) koopee **oar**

κουρείο (το) kooreeo **barber's shop**

κουταλάκι (το) kootalakee **teaspoon**

κουτάλι (το) kootalee **tablespoon**

κουτί (το) kootee **box**

κραγιόν (το) kra-yon **lipstick**

κρασί (το) krasee **wine**
κρασί γλυκό krasee ghleeko **sweet wine**
κρασί ξηρό krasee kseero **dry wine**
κρασί κόκκινο krasee kokeeno **red wine**
κρασί λευκό krasee lefko **white wine**
κρασί ροζέ krasee roze **rosé wine**

κρατήσεις (οι) krateesees **bookings ; reservations**
κρατήσεις ξενοδοχείων krateesees ksenodhokheeon **hotel bookings**

κράτηση (η) krateesee **reservation**
κράτηση θέσης krateesee thesees **seat reservation**

κρέας (το) kreas **meat**
κρέας αρνίσιο kreas arneeseeo **lamb**
κρέας μοσχαρίσιο kreas moskhareeseeo **beef**
κρέας χοιρινό kreas kheereeno **pork**

κρεββάτι (το) krevatee **bed**

κρεββατοκάμαρα (η) krevatokamara **bedroom**

κρέμα (η) krema **cream**

κρεμμύδι (το) kremeedhee **onion**

κρεοπωλείο (το) kreopoleeo **butcher's shop**

Κρήτη (η) kreetee **Crete**

κρουαζιέρα (η) krooazyera **cruise**

κρύος/α/ο kreeos/a/o **cold**

κτηνιατρείο (το) kteenyatreeo **veterinary surgery**

κωμωδία (η) komodeea **comedy**

κυβέρνηση (η) keeverneesee **government**

κυβερνήτης (ο) keeverneetees **captain** (of aircraft)

Κυκλάδες (οι) keekladhes **Cyclades** (islands)

κύκλος (ο) keeklos **circle**

κυκλοφορία (η) keekloforeea **traffic ; circulation**

κυλικείο (το) keeleekeeo **canteen ; cafeteria**

Κύπρος (η) keepros **Cyprus**

Κύπριος/Κυπρία (ο/η) keepreeos/keepreea **from Cyprus ; Cypriot** (man/woman)

κυρία (η) keereea **Mrs ; lady**

ΚΥΡΙΑΚΗ keereeakee SUNDAY

κύριος (ο) keereeos **Mr ; gentleman**

κωδικός (ο) kodheekos **code**
ταχυδρομικός κωδικός takheedhromeekos kodheekos **postcode**
τηλεφωνικός κωδικός teelefoneekos kodheekos **dialling code ; area code**

κωμωδία (η) komodheea **comedy**

λ Λ

λάδι (το) ladhee **oil**
λάδι ελιάς ladhee elyas **olive oil**

α
Α
β
Β
γ
Γ
δ
Δ
ε
Ε
ζ
Ζ
η
Η
θ
Θ
ι
Ι
κ
Κ
λ
Λ
μ
Μ
ν
Ν
ξ
Ξ
ο
Ο
π
Π
ρ
Ρ
σ/ς
Σ
τ
Τ
υ
Υ
φ
Φ
χ
Χ
ψ
Ψ
ω
Ω

λαϊκός/ή/ό *laeekos/ee/o* **popular ; folk**

λαϊκή αγορά *laeekee aghora* **market**

λαϊκή μουσική *laeekee mooseekee* **popular music**

λαϊκή τέχνη *laeekee tekhnee* **folk art**

λάστιχο (το) *lasteekho* **tyre ; rubber ; elastic**

λαχανικά (τα) *lakhaneeka* **vegetables**

λαχείο (το) *lakheeo* **lottery ticket**

λεμονάδα (η) *lemonadha* **lemonade**

λεμόνι (το) *lemonee* **lemon**

χυμός λεμονιού *kheemos lemoneeoo* **lemon juice**

λεξικό (το) *lekseeko* **dictionary**

λεπτό (το) *lepto* **minute**

λεπτός/ή/ό *leptos/ee/o* **thin ; slim**

λευκός/ή/ό *lefkos/ee/o* **white**

λεφτά (τα) *lefta* **money**

λέω *leo* **to say**

λεωφορείο (το) *leoforeeo* **bus**

λεωφόρος (η) *leoforos* **avenue**

λήξη (η) *leeksee* **expiry**

λιανικός/ή/ό *leeaneekos/ee/o* **retail**

λιανική πώληση *leeaneekee poleesee* **retail sale**

λίγος/η/ο *leeghos/ee/o* **a few ; a little**

λίγο ψημένο *leegho pseemeno* **rare** (meat)

λικέρ (το) *leeker* **liqueur**

λιμάνι (το) *leemanee* **port ; harbour**

Λιμενικό Σώμα (το) *leemeneeko soma* **coastguard ; Port Police**

λίμνη (η) *leemnee* **lake**

λίρα (η) *leera* **pound**

λίτρο (το) *leetro* **litre**

λογαριασμός (ο) *loghareeasmos* **bill**

λουκάνικο (το) *lookaneeko* **sausage**

λουκανικόπιτα (η) *lookaneekopeeta* **sausage pie**

λουκούμι (το) *lookoomee* **Turkish delight**

λουλούδι (το) *looloodhee* **flower**

λύσσα (η) *leesa* **rabies**

μ Μ

μαγαζί (το) *maghazee* **shop**

μαγειρεύω *magheerevo* **to cook**

μαγιό (το) *ma-yo* **swimsuit**

μαϊντανός (ο) *maeendanos* **parsley**

ΜΑΙΟΣ *maeeos* **MAY**

μακαρόνια (τα) *makaroneea* **macaroni ; spaghetti dishes**

μάλιστα *maleesta* **yes ; of course**

μαλλί (το) *malee* **wool**

μαλλιά (τα) *malya* **hair**

μάλλινος/η/ο *maleenos/ee/o* **woollen**

μαμά (η) *mama* **mum**

μανιτάρια (τα) *maneetareea* **mushrooms**

μανταρίνι (το) *mandareenee* **mandarin orange ; tangerine**

μαντήλι (το) *mandeelee* **handkerchief**

μαξιλάρι (το) *makseelaree* **pillow ; cushion**

μαργαρίνη (η) *marghareenee* **margarine**

μαργαριτάρι (το) marghareetaree pearl

μάρμαρο (το) marmaro marble

μαρμελάδα (η) marmeladha jam

μαρούλι (το) maroolee lettuce

ΜΑΡΤΙΟΣ marteeos MARCH

μαύρος/η/ο mavros/ee/o black

μαχαίρι (το) makheree knife

μαχαιροπήρουνα (τα) makheropeeroona cutlery

με me with

μεγάλος/η/ο meghalos large ; big

μέγαρο (το) megharo hall ; palace ; block of apartments
μέγαρο μουσικής megharo mooseekees concert hall

μέγεθος (το) meghethos size

μεζεδάκια (τα) mezedhakeea selection of appetizers and salads (like tapas)

μέλι (το) melee honey

μελιτζάνα (η) meleetzana aubergine ; eggplant

μέλος (το) melos member

μενού (το) menoo menu

μέρα (η) mera day

μερίδα (η) mereedha portion

μέσα mesa in ; inside

μεσάνυχτα (τα) mesaneekhta midnight

μεσημέρι (το) meseemeree midday

μεσημεριανό (το) meseemereeano midday meal

Μεσόγειος (η) mesoyeeos Mediterranean Sea

μέσω meso via

μετά meta after

μετάξι (το) metaksee silk

μεταξύ metaksee between ; among
εν τω μεταξύ en to metaksee meanwhile

μεταφράζω metafrazo to translate

μεταχειρισμένος/η/ο metakheereesmenos/ee/o used ; second-hand

μετεωρολογικό δελτίο (το) meteorologheeko dhelteeo weather forecast

μετρητά (τα) metreeta cash

μετρό (το) metro underground (railway)

μη... mee do not...
μην καπνίζετε mee kapneezete no smoking
μην κόπτετε άνθη meen koptete anthee do not pick flowers
μην πατάτε το πράσινο meen patate to praseeno keep off the grass
μη ρίπτετε σκουπίδια mee reeptete skoopeedheea no dumping (rubbish)
μη σταθμεύετε me stathmevete no parking

μηδέν meedhen zero

μήλο (το) meelo apple

μηλόπιτα (η) meelopeeta apple pie

μήνας (ο) meenas month
μήνας του μέλιτος meenas too meleetos honeymoon

μητέρα (η) meetera mother

μηχανάκι (το) meekhanakee moped ; motorbike

μηχανή (η) meekhanee machine ; engine

μηχάνημα (το) meekhaneema machine (general)

μηχανικός (ο) meekhaneekos mechanic ; engineer

μία meea a(n) ; one (with feminine nouns)

μικρός/ή/ό meekros/ee/o small

μιλάω/μιλω meelao/meelo to speak

μόδα (η) modha fashion

μολύβι (το) moleevee pencil

μόλυνση (η) moleensee infection ; pollution

μοναστήρι (το) monasteeree monastery

μονόδρομος (ο) monodhromos one-way street

μονοπάτι (το) monopatee path

μόνος/η/ο monos/ee/o alone ; only
μόνο είσοδος/έξοδος mono eesodhos/eksodhos entrance/exit only

μοσχάρι (το) moskharee calf ; beef

μοτοσυκλέτα (η) motoseekleta motorcycle

ΜΟΥΣΕΙΟ mooseeo MUSEUM

Αρχαιολογικό Μουσείο arkheologheeko mooseeo Archaeological Museum

Μουσείο Λαϊκής Τέχνης mooseeo laeekees tekhnees Folk Museum

μουσική (η) mooseekee music

μουστάρδα (η) moostardha mustard

μπακάλης (ο) bakalees grocer

μπαμπάς (ο) babas dad

μπανάνα (η) banana banana

μπάνιο (το) banyo bathroom ; bath

μπαρμπούνι (το) barboonee red mullet

μπαταρία (η) batareea battery

μπέικον (το) beeekon bacon

μπιζέλια (τα) beezelya peas

μπίρα (η) beera beer

μπισκότο (το) beeskoto biscuit

μπλε ble blue

μπλούζα (η) blooza blouse

μπογιά (η) bo-ya paint (for decorating houses)

μπουζούκι (το) boozookee bouzouki

μπουκάλι (το) bookalee bottle
μεγάλο μπουκάλι meghalo bookalee large bottle
μικρό μπουκάλι meekro bookalee half-bottle

μπουρνούζι (το) boornoozee bathrobe

μπριζόλα (η) breezola chop ; steak

μπύρα (η) beera beer

Μυκήναι meekeene Mycenae

Μυκηναϊκός πολιτισμός (ο) meekeenaeekos poleeteesmos Mycenean civilization

μύτη (η) meetee nose

μωρό (το) mora baby
για μωρά ya mora for babies

μωσαϊκό (το) mosaeeko mosaic

ν N

ναι ne yes

ναός (ο) naos temple ; church

νάιλον (το) *naeelon* **nylon**

ναυλωμένος/η/ο *navlomenos/ee/o* **chartered**
ναυλωμένη πτήση *navlomenee pteesee* **charter flight**

ναυτία (η) *nafteea* **travel sickness**

ναυτικός όμιλος (ο) *nafteekos omeelos* **sailing club**

νεκροταφείο (το) *nekrotafeeo* **cemetery**

νεοελληνικά (τα) *neoeleeneeka* **Modern Greek**

νερό (το) *nero* **water**
επιτραπέζιο νερό *epeetrapezeeo nero* **still mineral water**
μεταλλικό νερό *metaleeko nero* **mineral water**
πόσιμο νερό *poseemo nero* **drinking water**

νεφρός (ο) *nefros* **kidney**

νηπιαγωγείο (το) *neepeeaghogheeo* **nursery school**

νησί (το) *neesee* **island**

νησίδα (η) *neeseedha* **traffic island**

νίκη (η) *neekee* **victory**

ΝΟΕΜΒΡΙΟΣ *noemvreeos* **NOVEMBER**

νοίκι (το) *neekee* **rent**

νομίζω *nomeezo* **to think**

νόμισμα (το) *nomeesma* **coin ; currency**

νοσοκομείο (το) *nosokomeeo* **hospital**

νοσοκόμος/α (ο/η) *nosokomos/a* **nurse**

νότιος/α/ο *noteeos/a/o* **southern**

νότος (ο) *notos* **south**

νούμερο (το) *noomero* **number**

ντομάτα (η) *domata* **tomato**

ντουζίνα (η) *doozeena* **dozen**

ντους (το) *doos* **shower** *(in bath)*

νυκτερινός/ή/ό *neektereenos/ee/o* **all-night** *(chemists, etc)*

νύχτα (η) *neekhta* **night**

ξ Ξ

ξεκουράζω *ksekoorazo* **to have a rest ; to relax**

ξεναγός (ο/η) *ksenaghos* **guide**

ξενοδοχείο (το) *ksenodhokheeo* **hotel**
κρατήσεις ξενοδοχείων *krateeseees ksenodokheeon* **hotel reservations**

ξένος/η/ο *ksenos/ee/o* **foreign**
ξένος/η (ο/η) *ksenos/ee* **foreigner ; visitor**

ξενώνας (ο) *ksenonas* **guesthouse**

ξέρω *ksero* **to know**

ξεχνώ *ksekhno* **to forget**

ξηρός/ή/ό *kseeros/ee/o* **dry**
ξηροί καρποί *kseeree karpee* **dried fruit and nuts**

ξιφίας (ο) *kseefeeas* **swordfish**

ξύδι (το) *kseedhee* **vinegar**

ξύλο (το) *kseelo* **wood**

ξυριστική μηχανή (η) *kseereesteekee meekhanee* **safety razor**

ο Ο

οδηγία (η) *odheegheea* **instruction**
οδηγίες χρήσεως *odheegheees khreeseos* **instructions for use**

οδηγός (ο) *odheeghos* **driver ; guidebook**

οδηγώ *odheegho* **to drive**

οδική βοήθεια (η) *odheekee voeetheea* **breakdown service**

οδοντιατρείο (το) *odhondeeatreeo* **dental surgery**

οδοντίατρος (ο/η) *odhondeeatros* **dentist**

οδοντόβουρτσα (η) *odhondovoortsa* **toothbrush**

οδοντόκρεμα (η) *odhondokrema* **toothpaste**

οδοντοστοιχία (η) *odhondosteekheea* **denture(s)**

οδός (η) *odhos* **road ; street**

οικογένεια (η) *eekoyenya* **family**

οικονομική θέση (η) *eekonomeekee thesee* **economy class**

οινοπνευματώδη ποτά (τα) *eenopnevmatodhee pota* **spirits**

οκτώ/οχτώ *okto/okhto* **eight**

ΟΚΤΩΒΡΙΟΣ *oktovreeos*
OCTOBER

ολισθηρόν οδόστρωμα (το) *oleestheeron odhostroma* **slippery road surface**

όλος/η/ο *olos/ee/o* **all of**

Ολυμπία (η) *oleempeea* **Olympia**

ολυμπιακός/ή/ό *oleempeeakos/ee/o* **Olympic**

Ολυμπιακή Αεροπορία *oleempeeakee aeroporeea* **Olympic Airways**

Ολυμπιακό Στάδιο *oleempeeako stadheeo* **Olympic stadium**

Ολυμπιακοί Αγώνες *oleempeeakee aghones* **Olympic games**

Όλυμπος (ο) *oleempos* **Mount Olympus**

ομελέτα (η) *omeleta* **omelette**

όμιλος (ο) *omeelos* **club**
ναυτικός όμιλος *nafteekos omeelos* **sailing club**

ομπρέλα (η) *ombrela* **umbrella**

όνομα (το) *onoma* **name**

ονοματεπώνυμο (το) *onomateponeemo* **full name**

όπερα (η) *opera* **opera**

οπτικός (ο) *opteekos* **optician**

οργανισμός (ο) *orghaneesmos* **organization**

Οργανισμός Σιδηροδρόμων Ελλάδος (ΟΣΕ) *orghaneesmos seedheerodhromon eladhos (O.S.E.)* **Greek Railways**

οργανωμένος/η/ο *orghanomenos/ee/o* **organized**
οργανωμένα ταξίδια *orghanomena takseedheea* **organized tours**

ορειβασία (η) *oreevaseea* **mountaineering**

ορεκτικό (το) *orekteeko* **starter ; appetizer**

όρεξη (η) *oreksee* **appetite**
καλή όρεξη *kalee oreksee* **enjoy your meal!**

ορθόδοξος/η/ο *orthodhoksos/ee/o* **orthodox**

όρος (ο) *oros* **condition**
όροι ενοικιάσεως *oree eneekeeaseos* **conditions of hire**

όροφος (ο) *orofos* **floor ; storey**

ΟΣΕ *ose* **Greek Railways**

OTE *ote* Greek Telecom
ούζο (το) *oozo* ouzo
ουρά (η) *oora* tail ; queue
όχι *okhee* no

π Π

παγάκι (το) *paghakee* ice cube
παϊδάκι (το) *paeedhakee* lamb chop
πάγος (ο) *paghos* ice
παίρνω *perno* to take
παγωμένος/η/ο *paghomenos/ee/o* frozen
παγωτό (το) *paghoto* ice cream
παιδικός/ή/ό *pedheekos/ee/o* for children
παιδικά *pedeeka* children's wear
παιδικός σταθμός *pedheekos stathmos* crèche
πακέτο (το) *paketo* parcel ; packet
παλτό (το) *palto* coat
πάνα (η) *pana* nappy
Παναγία (η) *panagheea* the Virgin Mary
πανεπιστήμιο (το) *panepeesteemeeo* university
πανσιόν (η) *panseeon* guesthouse
πάντα/πάντοτε *panda/pandote* always
παντελόνι (το) *pandelonee* trousers
παντοπωλείο (το) *pandopoleeo* grocer's
παντρεμένος/η/ο *pantremenos/ee/o* married
παντρεύω *pantrevo* to marry

πάνω *pano* up ; on ; above
παπάς (ο) *papas* priest
πάπλωμα (το) *paploma* duvet
παππούς (ο) *papoos* grandfather
παπούτσι (το) *papootsee* shoe
παραγγελία (η) *parangheleea* order
παραγγέλνω *paranghelno* to order
παραγωγή (η) *paraghoghee* production
Ελληνικής παραγωγής *eleeneekees paraghoghees* produce of Greece
παράθυρο (το) *paratheero* window
παρακαλώ *parakalo* please
παρακαμπτήριος (ο) *parakampteereeos* by-pass
παραλία (η) *paraleea* seashore ; beach
παράξενος/η/ο *paraksenos/ee/o* strange

ΠΑΡΑΣΚΕΥΗ *paraskevee* FRIDAY

παράσταση (η) *parastasee* performance
παρέα (η) *parea* company ; group
Παρθενώνας (ο) *parthenonas* the Parthenon
πάρκο (το) *parko* park
παρμπρίζ (το) *parbreez* windscreen
πάστα (η) *pasta* pastry ; cake
παστέλι (το) *pastelee* honey and sesame seed bar
Πάσχα (το) *paskha* Easter

173

α
Α
β
Β
γ
Γ
δ
Δ
ε
Ε
ζ
Ζ
η
Η
θ
Θ
ι
Ι
κ
Κ
λ
Λ
μ
Μ
ν
Ν
ξ
Ξ
ο
Ο
π
Π
ρ
Ρ
σ/ς
Σ
τ
Τ
υ
Υ
φ
Φ
χ
Χ
ψ
Ψ
ω
Ω

πατάτα (η) *patata* **potato**
  πατάτες πουρέ *patates poore*
  creamed/mashed potatoes
  πατάτες τηγανητές *patates
  teeghaneetes* **chips**
  πατάτες φούρνου *patates
  foornoo* **roast potatoes**
πατέρας (ο) *pateras* **father**
παυσίπονο (το) *pafseepono*
  painkiller
πάω *pao* **to go**
πεζοδρόμιο (το) *pezodhromeeo*
  pavement

ΠΕΖΟΔΡΟΜΟΣ *pezodhromos*
PEDESTRIAN AREA

πεζός (ο) *pezos* **pedestrian**
πεθαμένος/η/ο *pethamenos/ee/o*
  dead
Πειραιάς (ο) *peereas* **Piraeus**
πελάτης/πελάτιοσα (ο/η)
  pelatees/pelateesa **customer**
Πελοπόννησος (η) *peloponeesos*
  Peloponnese

ΠΕΜΠΤΗ *pemptee* **THURSDAY**

πένα (η) *pena* **pen ; penny**
πεπόνι (το) *peponee* **melon**
περιοδικό (το) *pereeodheeko*
  magazine
περιοχή (η) *pereeokhee* **area**
περίπατος (ο) *pereepatos* **walk**
περίπτερο (το) *pereeptero* **kiosk**
περιστέρι (το) *pereesteree* **pigeon ;
  dove**
πέτρα (η) *petra* **stone**
πετρέλαιο (το) *petreleo* **diesel
  fuel**

πέτρινος/η/ο *petreenos/ee/o*
  made of stone
πετσέτα (η) *petseta* **towel**
πεύκο (το) *pefko* **pine tree**
πηγαίνω *peegheno* **to go**
πιάτο (το) *pyato* **plate ; dish**

ΠΙΕΣΑΤΕ *pyesate* **PUSH**

πίεση (η) *peeesee* **pressure**
  πίεση αίματος *peeesee ematos*
  blood pressure
πιλότος (ο) *peelotos* **pilot**
πινακίδα (η) *peenakeedha* **sign ;
  number plate**
  πινακίδα κυκλοφορίας
  peenakeedha keekloforeeas
  number plate
πινακοθήκη (η) *peenakotheekee*
  **art gallery ; collection of
  paintings**
πίνω *peeno* **to drink**
πίπα (η) *peepa* **pipe** *(for smoking)*
πιπέρι (το) *peeperee* **ground
  pepper**
  πιπεριά (η) *peeperya* **pepper**
  πιπεριές γεμιστές *peeperyes
  yemeestes* **stuffed peppers**
πισίνα (η) *peeseena* **swimming
  pool**
πιστοποιητικό (το)
  peestopyeeteeko **certificate**
πιστωτική κάρτα (η)
  peestoteekee karta **credit card**
πίσω *peeso* **behind ; back**
πίτα (η) *peeta* **pie**
πιζάμα (η) *peezama* **pyjamas**
πίτσα (η) *peetsa* **pizza**
πιτσαρία (η) *peetsareea* **pizzeria**
πλαζ (η) *plaz* **beach**

πλάι _plaee_ **next to**

πλατεία (η) _plateea_ **square**

πλατίνες (οι) _plateenes_ **points (in car)**

πλεκτά (τα) _plekta_ **knitwear**

ΠΛΗΡΟΦΟΡΙΕΣ _pleeroforeeyes_ **INFORMATION**

πληροφορίες δρομολογίων _pleeroforeeyes dhromologheeon_ **travel information**

πλήρωμα (το) _pleeroma_ **crew** τα μέλη του πληρώματος _ta melee too pleeromatos_ **crew members**

πληρωμή (η) _pleeromee_ **payment** ευκολίες πληρωμής _efkoleeyes pleeromees_ **credit facilities** προς πληρωμή _pros pleeromee_ **insert money**

πληρώνω _pleerono_ **to pay**

πλοίο (το) _pleeo_ **ship**

πλυντήριο (το) _pleenteereeo_ **washing machine** πλυντήριο αυτοκινήτων _pleenteereeo aftokeeneeton_ **car wash** πλυντήριο πιάτων _pleenteereeo pyaton_ **dish washer**

ποδηλάτης (ο) _podheelatees_ **cyclist**

ποδήλατο (το) _podheelato_ **bicycle** ποδήλατο της θάλασσας _podheelato tees thalasas_ **pedalo**

πόδι (το) _podhee_ **foot ; leg**

ποδόσφαιρο (το) _podhosfero_ **football**

ποιος/ποια/ποιο _pyos/pya/pyo_ **who ; which**

ποιότητα (η) _peeoteeta_ **quality**

πόλη (η) _polee_ **town ; city**

πολίτης (ο) _poleetees_ **citizen**

πολιτική (η) _poleeteekee_ **politics**

πολυκατάστημα (το) _poleekatasteema_ **department store**

πολυκατοικία (η) _poleekateekeea_ **block of flats**

πολύς/πολλή/πολύ _polees/polee/polee_ **much ; many**

πονόδοντος (ο) _ponodhontos_ **toothache**

πονοκέφαλος (ο) _ponokefalos_ **headache**

πονόλαιμος (ο) _ponolemos_ **sore throat**

πόνος (ο) _ponos_ **pain**

πόρτα (η) _porta_ **door**

πορτοκαλάδα (η) _portokaladha_ **orangeade**

πορτοκάλι (το) _portokalee_ **orange** χυμός πορτοκαλιού _kheemos portokalyoo_ **orange juice**

πορτοφόλι (το) _portofolee_ **wallet**

πόσα; _posa_ **how many?**

πόσο; _poso_ **how much?** πόσο κάνει; _poso kanee_ **how much is it?** πόσο κοστίζει; _poso kosteezee_ **how much does it cost?**

ποσοστό (το) _pososto_ **rate ; percentage** ποσοστό υπηρεσίας _pososto eepeereseeas_ **service charge** συμπεριλαμβανομένου ποσοστού υπηρεσίας _seempereelamvanomenoo posostoo eepeereseeas_ **service included**

ποσότητα (η) _posoteeta_ **quantity**

ποτάμι (το) _potamee_ **river**

πότε; *pote* when?

ποτέ *pote* never

ποτήρι (το) *poteeree* glass
(for drinking)

ποτό (το) *poto* drink

πού; *poo* where?

πουκάμισο (το) *pookameeso* shirt

πούλμαν (το) *poolman* coach

πουλώ *poolo* to sell

πουρμπουάρ (το) *poorbwar* tip
(to waiter, etc)

πούρο (το) *pooro* cigar

πράκτορας (ο) *praktoras* agent

πρακτορείο (το) *praktoreeo* agency

πράσινος/η/ο *praseenos/ee/o*
green

πρατήριο (το) *prateereeo*
specialist shop
πρατήριο βενζίνης *prateereeo*
venzeenees petrol station
πρατήριο άρτου *prateereeo artoo*
baker's

πρεσβεία (η) *presveea* embassy

πρίζα (η) *preeza* socket

πριν *preen* before

πρόγραμμα (το) *proghrama*
programme

πρόεδρος (ο) *proedhros* president
προεδρικό μέγαρο *proedhreeko*
megharo presidential palace

προειδοποίηση (η) *proeedhopee-*
eesee warning

προϊόν (το) *proeeon* product
Ελληνικό προϊόν *eleeneeko*
proeeon product of Greece

προκαταβολή (η) *prokatavolee*
deposit

προκρατήσεις (οι) *prokrateesees*
advance bookings

προορισμός (ο) *pro-oreesmos*
destination

προπληρώνω *propleerono* to pay
in advance

Προ-πο (το) *propo* Greek
football pools

προσγείωση (η) *prosgheeosee*
landing

προσδεθείτε *prosdhetheete* fasten
safety belts

πρόσκληση (η) *proskleesee*
invitation

προσοχή (η) *prosokhee* attention

προτεστάντης (ο) *protestantees*
protestant

πρόστιμο (το) *prosteemo* fine

πρόχειρος/η/ο *prokheeros/ee/o*
impromptu ; rough
πρόχειρο φαγητό *prokheero*
fayeeto snack

πρωί (το) *proee* morning

πρωινός/ή/ό *proeenos/ee/o*
morning

πρωινό (το) *proeeno* breakfast

πρωτεύουσα (η) *protevoosa*
capital city

πρωτομαγιά (η) *protoma-ya*
May Day

πρώτος/η/ο *protos* first
πρώτες βοήθειες *protes*
voeethee-es first aid
πρώτη θέση *protee thesee*
first class

πρωτοχρονιά (η) *protokhronya*
New Years Day

πτήση (η) *pteesee* flight
πτήσεις εξωτερικού *pteesees*
eksotereekoo international
flights

176

πτήσεις εσωτερικού pteesees esotereekoo domestic flights
αριθμός πτήσης areethmos pteesees flight number
τακτικές πτήσεις takteekes pteesees scheduled flights

πυροσβεστήρας (ο) peerosvesteeras fire extinguisher

πυροσβέστης (ο) peerosvestees fireman

πυροσβεστική (η) peerosvesteekee fire brigade
πυροσβεστική υπηρεσία peerosvesteekee eepeereseea fire brigade
πυροσβεστικός σταθμός peerosvesteekos stathmos fire station

πώληση (η) poleesee sale
λιανική πώληση leeaneekee poleesee retail sale
χονδρική πώληση khondhreekee poleesee wholesale

πωλητής/ήτρια(ο/η) poleetees/eetreea sales assistant

ΠΩΛΕΙΤΑΙ poleete FOR SALE

πώς; pos how?

ρ Ρ

ρεζέρβα (η) rezerva spare wheel

ρεσεψιόν (η) resepsyon reception (desk)

ρέστα (τα) resta change (money)

ρετσίνα (η) retseena retsina

ρεύμα (το) revma current ; electricity

ρόδα (η) rodha wheel

ροδάκινο (το) rodhakeeno peach

ρόδι (το) rodhee pomegranate

Ρόδος (η) rodhos Rhodes (island)

ρολόι (το) roloee watch ; clock

ρούμι (το) roomee rum

ρούχα (τα) rookha clothes

ρύζι (το) reezee rice

ρυμουλκώ reemoolko to tow

σς Σ

ΣΑΒΒΑΤΟ savato SATURDAY

Σαββατοκύριακο (το) savatokeereeako weekend

σακάκι (το) sakakee jacket (menswear)

σαλάμι (το) salamee salami

σαλάτα (η) salata salad

σαλιγκάρι (το) saleengkaree snail

σάλτσα (η) saltsa sauce

σαμπάνια (η) sambanya champagne

σαμπουάν (το) sambooan shampoo

σάντουιτς (το) sandwich sandwich

σαπούνι (το) sapoonee soap

σβήνω sveeno to extinguish ; to rub out
σβήσατε τα τσιγάρα σας sveesate ta tseeghara sas extinguish cigarettes

ΣΕΠΤΕΜΒΡΙΟΣ septemvreeos SEPTEMBER

σέρβις (το) servees service (of car etc)

σεφ (ο) sef chef

σήμα (το) *seema* sign ; signal
σήμα κατατεθέν *seema katatethen* trademark
σήμα κινδύνου *seema keendheenoo* emergency signal
σήμερα *seemera* today
σιγά *seegha* slowly
σιδηρόδρομος (ο) *seedheerodhromos* railway
σιδηροδρομικός σταθμός *seedheerodhromeekos stathmos* railway station
σιδηροδρομικώς *seedheerodhromeekos* by rail
σινεμά (το) *seenema* cinema
σκάλα (η) *skala* ladder ; staircase
σκαλί (το) *skalee* step
σκέτος/η/ο *sketos* plain
καφές σκέτος *kafes sketos* black coffee
σκηνή (η) *skeenee* tent ; stage
σκι (το) *skee* ski
θαλάσσιο σκι *thalaseeo skee* water-skiing
σκοινί (το) *skeenee* rope
σκορδαλιά (η) *skordhalya* garlic and potato mash
σκόρδο (ο) *skordho* garlic
σκουπίδια (τα) *skoopeedheea* rubbish ; refuse
σκυλί (το) *skeelee* dog
Σκωτία (η) *skoteea* Scotland
σκωτσέζικος/η/ο (η) *skotsezeekos/ee/o* Scottish (thing)
Σκωτσέζος/Σκωτσέζα (ο/η) *skotsezos/skotseza* Scotsman/Scotswoman
σόδα (η) *sodha* soda
σοκολάτα (η) *sokolata* chocolate

σολομός (ο) *solomos* salmon
σόμπα (η) *soba* stove ; heater
σούβλα (η) *soovla* skewer
σουβλάκι (το) *soovlakee* meat cooked on skewer
σούπα (η) *soopa* soup
σοφέρ(ο) *sofer(o)* chauffeur
σπανάκι (το) *spanakee* spinach
σπανακόπιτα (η) *spanakopeeta* spinach pie
σπαράγγι (το) *sparangee* asparagus
σπεσιαλιτέ της κουζίνας *speseealeete tees koozeenas* todays special dish
σπίρτο (το) *speerto* match
σπίτι (το) *speetee* house ; home
σπιτικός/ή/ο *speeteekos/ee/o* homemade
σπορ (τα) *spor* sports
Σποράδες (οι) *sporadhes* the Sporades
στάδιο (το) *stadheeo* stadium ; stage
σταθμεύω *stathmevo* to park
απαγορεύεται η στάθμευση *apaghorevete ee stathmevsee* no parking
μη σταθμεύετε *stathmevete* no parking
χώρος σταθμεύσεως *khoros stathmevseos* parking area
σταθμός (ο) *stathmos* station
πυροσβεστικός σταθμός *peerosvesteekos stathmos* fire station
σιδηροδρομικός σταθμός *seedheerodhromeekos stathmos* railway station

σταθμός υπεραστικών λεωφορείων *stathmos eeperasteekon leoforeeon* **bus station** *(intercity)*

σταμάτα! *stamata* **stop!**

στάση (η) *stasee* **stop**
στάση εργασίας *stasee ergaseeas* **strike**
στάσις ΗΛΠΑΠ *stasees eelpap* **trolley bus stop**
στάση λεωφορείου *stasee leoforeeoo* **bus stop**

σταυροδρόμι (το) *stavrodhromee* **crossroads**

σταφίδα (η) *stafeedha* **raisin**

σταφύλι (το) *stafeelee* **grape**

στεγνοκαθαριστήριο (το) *steghnokathareesteereeo* **dry-cleaner's**

στιγμή (η) *steeghmee* **moment**

στοά (η) *stoa* **arcade**

στροφή (η) *strofee* **turn ; bend**

στρώμα (το) *stroma* **mattress**

στυλό (η) *steelo* **pen**

συγγνώμη *seeghnomee* **sorry ; excuse me**

συγχαρητήρια *seenkhareeteereea* **congratulations**

συγχωρώ:με συγχωρείτε *seenkhoro : me seenkhoreete* **excuse me**

σύζυγος (ο/η) *seezeeghos* **husband/wife**

σύκο (το) *seeko* **fig**

συκώτι (το) *seekotee* **liver**

συλλυπητήρια (τα) *seeleepeeteereea* **condolences**

συμπεριλαμβάνω *seempereelamvano* **to include**

συμπλέκτης (ο) *seemplektees* **clutch** *(of car)*

συμπληρώνω *seempleerono* **to fill in**

σύμπτωμα (το) *seemptoma* **symptom**

συμφωνία (η) *seemfoneea* **agreement**

συμφωνώ *seemfono* **to agree**

συνάλλαγμα (το) *seenalaghma* **foreign exchange**
δήλωση συναλλάγματος *dheelosee seenalaghmatos* **currency declaration**
η τιμή του συναλλάγματος *ee teemee too seenalaghmatos* **exchange rate**

συνάντηση (η) *seenandeesee* **meeting**

συναντώ *seenando* **to meet**

συναυλία (η) *seenavleea* **concert**

συνεργείο (το) *seenergheeo* **workshop ; garage for car repairs**
συνεργείο αυτοκινήτων *seenergheeo aftokeeneeton* **car repairs**

σύνθεση (η) *seenthesee* **ingredients ; flower arrangement**

σύνολο (το) *seenolo* **total**

σύνορα (τα) *seenora* **border ; frontier**

συνταγή (η) *seendayee* **prescription ; recipe**

ΣΥΡΑΤΕ *seerate* **PULL**

σύστημα κλιματισμού (το) *seesteema kleemateesmoo* **air conditioning**

συστημένη επιστολή (η) *seesteemenee epeestolee* **recorded delivery**

συχνά *seekhna* **often**

σφράγισμα (το) *sfragheesma* **filling** (in tooth)

σχηματίζω *skheemateezo* **to form**
σχηματίστε τον αριθμό *skheemateeste ton areethmo* **dial the number**

σχολείο (το) *skholeeo* **school**

σχολή (η) *skholee* **school**
σχολή οδηγών *skholee odheeghon* **driving school**
σχολή σκι *skholee skee* **ski school**

σώζω *sozo* **to save ; to rescue**

σώμα (το) *soma* **body**

σωσίβιο (το) *soseeveeo* **life jacket**

τ T

ταβέρνα (η) *taverna* **tavern with traditional food and wine**

ταινία (η) *teneea* **film ; strip ; tape**

TAMEIO *tameeo* **CASH DESK**

ταμίας (ο/η) *tameeas* **cashier**

ταμιευτήριο (το) *tamee-efteereeo* **savings bank**

ταξί (το) *taksee* **taxi**
αγοραίο ταξί *aghoreo taksee* **minicab** (no meter)
γραφείο ταξί *grafeeo taksee* **taxi office**
ραδιοταξί *radheeotaksee* **radio taxi**

ταξίδι (το) *takseedhee* **journey ; tour**
καλό ταξίδι *kalo takseedhee* **have a good trip**
ταξιδιωτικό γραφείο *takseedheeoteeko ghrafeeo* **travel agent**

οργανωμένα ταξίδια *orghanomena takseedeea* **organized tours**

ταραμοσαλάτα (η) *taramosalata* **taramosalata**

ταυτότητα (η) *taftoteeta* **identity ; identity card**

ταχεία (η) *takheea* **express train**

ταχυδρομείο (το) *takheedhromeeo* **post office**
Ελληνικά Ταχυδρομεία (ΕΛΤΑ) *eleeneeka takheedhromeea* **Greek Post Office**

ταχυδρομικά τέλη *takheedhromeeka telee* **postage**
ταχυδρομικές επιταγές *takheedhromeekes epeetaghes* **postal orders**
ταχυδρομικός κώδικας *takheedhromeekos kodheekas* **postcode**
ταχυδρομικώς *takheedhromeekos* **by post**

ταχύμετρο (το) *takheemetro* **speedometer**

ταχύτητα/ταχύτης (η) *takheeteeta/takheetees* **speed**
κιβώτιο ταχυτήτων *keevoteeo takheeteeton* **gearbox**

τελευταίος/α/ο *telefteos* **last**

τέλος (το) *telos* **end ; tax ; duty**
οδικά τέλη *odheeka telee* **road tax**
τέλος πάντων *telos pandon* **well ; anyway** (to start sentence)

τελωνείο (το) *teloneeo* **customs**

τένις (το) *tenees* **tennis**

τέντα (η) *tenda* **awning**

τέρμα (το) *terma* **terminus ; end of route**

180

ΤΕΤΑΡΤΗ tetartee WEDNESDAY

τέχνη (η) tekhnee art
λαϊκή τέχνη laeekee tekhnee
folk art

τζαμί (το) dzamee mosque

τζάμι (το) dzamee glass (of window)

τζατζίκι (το) tzatzeekee tsatsiki (yoghurt, cucumber and garlic)

τηγανίτα (η) teeghaneeta pancake

τηλεκάρτα (η) teelekarta phonecard

τηλεόραση (η) teeleorasee television

τηλεπικοινωνίες (οι) teelepeekeenonees telecommunications

τηλεφώνημα (το) teelefoneema telephone call

ΤΗΛΕΦΩΝΟ teelefono TELEPHONE

τηλεφωνικός θάλαμος teelefoneekos thalamos phone box
τηλεφωνικός κατάλογος teelefoneekos kataloghos telephone directory
τηλεφωνικός κωδικός teelefoneekos kodheekos dialling code ; area code

τι; tee what?
τι είναι; tee eenee what is it?

τιμή (η) teemee price ; honour
τιμή εισιτηρίου teemee eeseeteereeoo price of ticket ; fare

τιμοκατάλογος (ο) teemokataloghos price list

τιμολόγιο (το) teemologheeo invoice

τιμόνι (το) teemonee steering wheel

τιμωρώ teemoro to punish

τίποτα teepota nothing
έχετε τίποτα να δηλώσετε ekhete teepota na dheelosete have you anything to declare

τμήμα (το) tmeema department ; police station

το to it ; the (with neuter nouns)

τοιχοκόλληση (η) teekhokoleesee bill posting

τόκος (ο) tokos interest (bank)

τόνος (ο) tonos ton ; tuna fish

τοστ (το) tost toasted sandwich

ΤΟΥΑΛΕΤΕΣ tooaletes TOILETS

τουρισμός (ο) tooreesmos tourism

τουρίσταςlστρια (ο/η) tooreestas/streea tourist

τουριστικός/ή/ό tooreesteekos/ee/o tourist
τουριστικά είδη tooreesteeka eedhee souvenirs
τουριστική αστυνομία tooreesteekee asteenomeea Tourist Police

Τουρκία (η) toorkeea Turkey

τραγούδι (το) traghoodhee song

τραγωδία (η) traghodheea tragedy

τράπεζα (η) trapeza bank

τραπεζαρία (η) trapezareea dining room

τραπέζι (το) *trapezee* **table**
τρένο (το) *treno* **train**

ΤΡΙΤΗ *treetee* **TUESDAY**

τρόλεϋ (το) *troley* **trolley bus**
τροχαία (η) *trokhea* **traffic police**
τροχός (ο) *trokhos* **wheel**
τροχόσπιτο (το) *trokhospeeto* **caravan ; mobile home**
τρώγω/τρώω *trogho/troo* **to eat**
τσάι (το) *tsaee* **tea**
τσάντα (η) *tsanda* **bag**
τσάρτερ (το) *tsarter* **charter flight**
τσιγάρο (το) *tseegharo* **cigarette**
τυρί (το) *teeree* **cheese**
τυρόπιτα (η) *teeropeeta* **cheese pie**
τυφλός/ή/ό *teeflos/ee/o* **blind**
τώρα *tora* **now**

υ Υ

υγεία (η) *eeyeea* **health**
στην υγειά σας *steen eeyeea sas* **your health ; cheers**
υγειονομικός έλεγχος (ο) *eeyeeonomeekos elenkhos* **health inspection**
Ύδρα (η) *eedhra* **Hydra (island)**
Υμηττός (ο) *eemeetos* **Mount Hymettos**
υπεραγορά (η) *eeperaghora* **supermarket**
υπεραστικό λεωφορείο (το) *eeperasteeko leoforeeo* **long-distance coach**
υπερωκεάνιο (το) *eeperokeaneeo* **liner**

υπηρεσία (η) *eepereseea* **service**
ποσοστό υπηρεσίας *pososto eepereseeas* **service charge**
υπηρέτης (ο) *eepeeretees* **servant**
υπηρέτρια (η) *eepeeretreea* **maid**
υπόγειος/α/ο *eepoyeeos/a/o* **underground**
υπόγεια διάβαση πεζών *eepoyeea dheeavasee pezon* **pedestrian subway**
υπόγειος σιδηρόδρομος *eepoyeeos seedheerodhromos* **underground** *(railway)*
υπολογιστής (ο) *eepologheestees* **computer**
υπουργείο (το) *eepoorgheeo* **ministry**
υψηλός/ή/ό *eepseelos/ee/o* **high**
υψηλή τάση *eepseelee tasee* **high voltage**
ύφασμα (το) *eefasma* **fabric ; cloth**
υφάσματα *eefasmata* **textiles**
υφάσματα επιπλώσεων *eefasmata epeeploseon* **upholstery fabrics**
ύψος (το) *eepsos* **height**
ύψος περιορισμένο *eepsos pereeoreesmeno* **height limit**

φ Φ

φαγητό (το) *fa-yeeto* **food ; meal**
φαΐ (το) *fay-ee* **food**
φακός (ο) *fakos* **lens ; torch**
φακοί επαφής *fakee epafees* **contact lenses**
φακές (οι) *fakes* **lentils**
φανάρι (το) *fanaree* **traffic light ; lantern**
φαξ (το) *faks* **fax**

φαρμακείο (το) *farmakeeo* chemist's

φάρμακο (το) *farmako* medicine

φάρος (ο) *faros* lighthouse

φασολάκι (το) *fasolakee* green bean

φασόλι (το) *fasolee* haricot bean

φάω *fao* to eat

ΦΕΒΡΟΥΑΡΙΟΣ *fevrooareeos* FEBRUARY

φεριμπότ (το) *fereebot* ferry boat

φέτα (η) *feta* feta cheese ; slice

φιλενάδα (η) *feelenadha* girlfriend

φιλέτο (το) *feeleto* fillet of meat

φιλμ (το) *feelm* film
εμφανίσεις φιλμ *emfaneesees feelm* film developing

φίλος/η (ο/η) *feelos/ee* friend

φίλτρο (το) *feeltro* filter
φίλτρο αέρος *feeltro aeros* air filter
φίλτρο λαδιού *feeltro ladheeoo* oil filter
καφές φίλτρου *kafes feeltroo* filter coffee

φις (το) *fees* plug (electric)

φλας (το) *flas* flash (camera) ; indicators (on car)

φοιτητής/φοιτήτρια (ο/η) *feeteetees/feeteetreea* student

φοιτητικό εισιτήριο (το) *feeteeteeko eeseeteereeo* student fare

φόρεμα (το) *forema* dress

φόρος (ο) *foros* tax

φουντούκι (το) *foondookee* hazelnut

φούρνος (ο) *foornos* oven ; bakery

φουσκωτά σκάφη (τα) *fooskota skafee* inflatable boats

ΦΠΑ (ο) *feepeea* VAT

φράουλα (η) *fraoola* strawberry

φρένο (το) *freno* brake (in car)

φρέσκος/ια/ο *freskos/eea/o* fresh

φρούτο (το) *frooto* fruit

φρουτοσαλάτα (η) *frootosalata* fruit salad

φύλακας (ο) *feelakas* guard

φύλαξη αποσκευών (η) *feelaksee aposkevon* left-luggage office

φυστίκι (το) *feesteekee* peanut
φυστίκια Αιγίνης *feesteekeea eyeenees* pistachio nuts

φυτό (το) *feeto* plant

φως (το) *fos* light

φωτιά (η) *fotya* fire

φωτογραφία (η) *fotoghrafeea* photograph
έγχρωμες φωτογραφίες *enkhromes fotoghrafees* colour photographs

φωτογραφίζω *fotoghrafeezo* to take photographs
μη φωτογραφίζετε *me fotoghrafeezete* no photographs

φωτογραφική μηχανή (η) *fotoghrafeekee meekhanee* camera

φωτοτυπία (η) *fototeepeea* photocopy

χ Χ

χαίρετε *kherete* hello (polite)

χάπι (το) *khapee* pill

χάρτης (ο) *khartees* map
οδικός χάρτης *odheekos khartees* road map

α **α**
Α
β **β**
Β
γ **γ**
Γ
δ **δ**
Δ
ε **ε**
Ε
ζ **ζ**
Ζ
η **η**
Η
θ **θ**
Θ
ι **ι**
Ι
κ **κ**
Κ
λ **λ**
Λ
μ **μ**
Μ
ν **ν**
Ν
ξ **ξ**
Ξ
ο **ο**
Ο
π **π**
Π
ρ **ρ**
Ρ
σ/ς **σ/ς**
Σ
τ **τ**
Τ
υ **υ**
Υ
φ **φ**
Φ
χ **χ**
Χ
ψ **ψ**
Ψ
ω **ω**
Ω

χαρτί (το) *khartee* **paper**
χαρτί κουζίνας *khartee koozeenas* **kitchen paper**

χαρτικά (τα) *kharteeka* **stationery**

χαρτομάντηλο (το) *khartomandeelo* **tissue**

χαρτονόμισμα (το) *khartonomeesma* **banknote**

χαρτοπωλείο (το) *khartopoleeo* **stationer's shop**

χειροποίητος/η/ο *kheeropeeeetos/ee/o* **handmade**

χειροτεχνία (η) *kheerotekhneea* **handicraft**

χειρούργος (ο) *kheeroorghos* **surgeon**

χειρόφρενο (το) *kheerofreno* **handbrake**

χέρι (το) *kheree* **hand**

χιλιόμετρο (το) *kheeleeometro* **kilometre**

χιόνι (το) *kheeonee* **snow**

χοιρινό (το) *kheereeno* **pork**

χορός (ο) *khoros* **dance**

χορτοφάγος (ο/η) *hortofaghos* **vegetarian**

χορωδία (η) *khorodheea* **choir**

χουρμάς (ο) *khoormas* **date** (fruit)

χρειάζομαι *khreeazome* **to need**

χρήματα (τα) *khreemata* **money**

χρηματοκιβώτιο (το) *khreematokeevoteeo* **safe** (for valuables)

χρήση (η) *khreesee* **use**
οδηγίες χρήσεως *odheegheees khreeseos* **instructions for use**

χρήσιμος/η/ο *khreeseemos/ee/o* **useful**

χρησιμοποιώ *khreeseemopyo* **to use**

χριστιανός/ή *khreesteeanos/ee* **Christian**

Χριστούγεννα (τα) *khreestooyena* **Christmas**
Καλά Χριστούγεννα *kala khreestooyena* **Merry Christmas**

χρόνος (ο) *khronos* **time ; year**

χρυσός/ή/ό *khreesos/ee/o* **(made of) gold**
Χρυσός Οδηγός *khreesos odheeghos* **Yellow Pages**

χρώμα (το) *khroma* **colour ; paint**

χταπόδι (το) *khtapodhee* **octopus**

χτένα (η) *khtena* **comb**

χτες *khtes* **yesterday**

χυμός (ο) *kheemos* **juice**
χυμός λεμονιού *kheemos lemoneeoo* **lemon juice**
χυμός πορτοκαλιού *kheemos portokaleeoo* **orange juice**

χώρα (η) *khora* **country**

χωράφια (τα) *khorafeea* **fields**

χωριάτικο ψωμί (το) *khoreeateeko psomee* **bread** (round, flat loaf)

χωριό (το) *khoreeo* **village**

χωρίς *khorees* **without**

χώρος (ο) *khoros* **area ; site**
αρχαιολογικός χώρος *arkheologheekos khoros* **archaeological site**
ιδιωτικός χώρος *eedheeoteekos khoros* **private land**
χώρος σταθμεύσεως *khoros stathmefseos* **parking area**

ψ Ψ

ψάρεμα (το) *psarema* **fishing**

ψαρεύω *psarevo* **to fish**

ψάρι (το) *psaree* fish

ψαρόβαρκα (η) *psarovarka* fishing boat

ψαροταβέρνα (η) *psarotaverna* fish tavern

ψημένος/η/ο *pseemenos/ee/o* roasted ; grilled

ψητός/ή/ό *pseetos/ee/o* roasted ; grilled

ψυγείο (το) *pseegheeo* fridge ; radiator *(of car)*

ψύχω *pseekho* to cool

ψωμάς (ο) *psomas* baker

ψωμί (το) *psomee* bread

ω Ω

ΩΘΗΣΑΤΕ *otheesate* PUSH

ωτοστόπ (το) *otostop* hitchhiking

ώρα (η) *ora* time ; hour
ώρες επισκέψεως *ores epeeskepseos* visiting hours
ώρες λειτουργίας *ores leetoorgheeas* opening hours
ώρες συναλλαγής *ores seenalaghees* banking hours
της ώρας *tees oras* freshly cooked *(food)*

ωραίος/α/ο *oreos/a/o* beautiful

ωράριο (το) *orareeo* timetable

ως *os* as

ωστόσο *ostoso* however

Grammar

The following basic rules of Greek grammar will help you make full use of
the information in this book.

NOUNS

Greek nouns can be *masculine*, *feminine* or *neuter* and the words for **the**
and **a** (the articles) change according to the gender of the noun.

ένας *(enas)*	= **a** with *masculine* nouns
μία *(meea)*	= **a** with *feminine* nouns
ένα *(ena)*	= **a** with *neuter* nouns
ο *(o)*	= **the** with *masculine* nouns
η *(ee)*	= **the** with *feminine* nouns
το *(to)*	= **the** with *neuter* nouns

The article is the most reliable indication of the gender of a noun, i.e.
whether it is *masculine*, *feminine* or *neuter*.

In the dictionary sections you will come across examples like this: ο / η
γιατρός *(yatros)* **doctor**. This means that the same ending is used for men
as well as women doctors i.e. ο γιατρός is a male doctor, η γιατρός is a
female doctor.

You will also encounter entries like ο Άγγλος / η Αγγλίδα indicating that
an **Englishman** is referred to as ο Άγγλος *(anglos)* while an **Englishwoman**
is η Αγγλίδα *(angleedha)*.

The most common endings of *masculine* nouns are -ος *(os)*, -ας *(as)*, -ης
(ees), e.g.

ο καιρός *(keros)*	**the weather**
ο πατέρας *(pateras)*	**the father**
ο κυβερνήτης *(keeverneetees)*	**the captain** *(of aeroplane)*

The most common endings of *feminine* nouns are -α *(a)*, -η *(ee)*, e.g.

η μητέρα *(meetera)*	**the mother**
η Κρήτη *(kreetee)*	**Crete**

The most common *neuter* endings are: -ο *(o)*, -ι *(ee)*, e.g.

το κτίριο *(kteereeo)*	**the building**
το πορτοκάλι *(portokalee)*	**the orange** *(fruit)*

PLURALS

The article **the** changes in the plural. For *masculine* (o) and *feminine* (η) nouns it becomes οι *(ee)*. For *neuter* nouns (το) it becomes τα *(ta)*.

Nouns have different endings in the plural. *Masculine* nouns change from -ος to -οι and from -ας and -ης to -ες. *Feminine* nouns change from -α and -η to -ες. *Neuter* nouns have an -α ending in the plural.

Examples:

masculine	ο βράχος *(o vrakhos)*	**the rock**
	οι βράχοι *(ee vrakhee)*	**the rocks**
	ο άντρας *(o andhras)*	**the man**
	οι άντρες *(ee andhres)*	**the men**
feminine	η κυρία *(ee keereea)*	**the lady**
	οι κυρίες *(ee keeree-es)*	**the ladies**
	η αδελφή *(ee adhelfee)*	**the sister**
	οι αδελφές *(ee adelfes)*	**the sisters**
neuter	το κτίριο *(to kteereeo)*	**the building**
	τα κτίρια *(ta kteereea)*	**the buildings**
	το κλειδί *(to kleedhee)*	**the key**
	τα κλειδιά *(ta kleedheea)*	**the keys**

ADJECTIVES

Adjective endings must agree with the gender and number of the noun they describe, e.g.

ο καλός πατέρας *(kalos pateras)*	**the good father**
η καλή κυρία *(kalee keereea)*	**the good lady**
οι καλοί πατέρες *(kalee pateres)*	**the good fathers**
οι καλές κυρίες *(kales keeree-es)*	**the good ladies**

You will see that in the Greek-English dictionary section of this book, all adjectives are given with their endings clearly marked e.g.

κρύος/α/ο *(kree-os/a/o)*   **cold**

The most common adjectival endings are -ος *(os)* for *masculine*, -η *(ee)* for *feminine* and -o *(o)* for *neuter*.

In Greek, adjectives can come before or after the noun they describe.

POSSESSIVE ADJECTIVES

In Greek the possessive adjective: my, your, his, etc. follow the noun. And they don't change even if the noun is *masculine*, *feminine*, *singular* or *plural*. The article will still go in front of the noun.

my	μου	*moo*	**our**	μας	*mas*
your	σου	*soo*	**your**	σας	*sas**
his	του	*too*	**their**	τους	*toos*
her	της	*tees*			
its	του/της	*too/tees*			

*This is also the polite form

my key	το κλειδί μου	*to kleedhee moo*
your room	το δωμάτιό σας	*to dhomateeo sas*

VERBS

The most essential verbs in Greek are the verbs είμαι **I am** and έχω **I have**. Unlike verbs in English, Greek verbs have a different ending for each person and number.

I am

είμαι	**I am**	*eeme*
είσαι	**you are**	*eese*
είναι	**he/she/it is**	*eene*
είμαστε	**we are**	*eemaste*
είστε	**you are**	*eeste**
είναι	**they are**	*eene*

* This form is also used when addressing people that you do not know very well; it is generally referred to as the polite plural (like the French 'vous').

NOTE: While in English it is necessary to use the personal pronoun i.e. **we**, **you** etc, in order to distinguish between **we are**, **you are** etc, in Greek this function is carried out by the different endings of the verb itself. This way in Greek, **we are** and **they are** can be simply είμαστε *(eemaste)*, είναι *(eene)*.

I have

έχω	**I have**	*ekho*
έχεις	**you have**	*ekhees*
έχει	**he/she/it has**	*ekhee*
έχουμε	**we have**	*ekhoome*
έχετε	**you have**	*ekhete*
έχουν	**they have**	*ekhoon*

NOTE: As above, **I have** can be expressed in Greek with simply the verb έχω; each ending is particular to a specific person.

Verbs in Greek in the active voice, end in -ω *(o)* or -ώ *(o)*. This is the ending with which they generally appear in dictionaries. Please note that in everyday speech a more usual ending for -ώ *(o)* is -άω *(ao)*. If a verb does not have an active voice form, in a dictionary it will appear with the ending -μαι *(-me)*, e.g. λυπάμαι *(leepame)* **to be sad** or **sorry**, θυμάμαι *(theemame)* **to remember**.

The verb αγαπώ *aghapo* **to love** has typical endings for verbs ending in -ώ *(-o)* while those ending in -ω *(-o)* follow the pattern of έχω *(ekho)* above.

αγαπώ/άω *(aghapo/ao)*	**I love**
αγαπάς *(aghapas)*	**you love**
αγαπά *(aghapa)*	**he/she/it loves**
αγαπούμε *(aghapoome)*	**we love**
αγαπάτε *(aghapate)*	**you love**
αγαπούν *(aghapoon)*	**they love**

In Greek, there are two ways of addressing people, depending on their age, social or professional position, and how formal or informal the relationship is between two people. e.g. an older person will probably speak to a much younger one using the singular (informal way) but the younger person will use the plural (formal) unless well acquainted. Similarly two friends will speak to each other using the informal singular:

Yι κάνεις; *(tee kanees)*	**How are you?**
Λαλά, εσύ; *(kala esee)*	**Fine, and you?**

While two acquaintances will address each other in a more formal way using the second person plural, like this:

Yι κάνετε; *(tee kanete)*	**How are you?**
Λαλά, εσείς; *(kala esees)*	**Fine, and you?**

PERSONAL PRONOUNS

There are times when the pronoun needs to be used as e.g. in conjunction with the verb in order to establish the sex of the person involved, i.e. **he** or **she**, or indeed **it**.

εγώ	I	egho
εσύ	you	esee
αυτός	he	aftos
αυτή	she	aftee
αυτό	it	afto
εμείς	we	emees
εσείς	you	esees
αυτοί	they (masc.)	aftee
αυτές	they (fem.)	aftes
αυτά	they (neut.)	afta

Thus: αυτός έχει (aftos ekhee)   **he has**

αυτή έχει (aftee ekhee)   **she has**